Cognitive A Supported Human-Robot Collaboration

Intelligent Data-Centric Systems

Cognitive Assistant Supported Human-Robot Collaboration

Cecilio Angulo
IDEAI-UPC, Automatic Control Dept.
Universitat Politècnica de Catalunya - UPC
Barcelona, Spain

Alejandro Chacón
Electrical, Electronic and Telecom Dept.
Universidad de las Fuerzas Armadas - ESPE
Quito, Ecuador

Pere Ponsa
EEBE School, Automatic Control Dept.
Universitat Politècnica de Catalunya - UPC
Barcelona, Spain

Series Editor Fatos Xhafa
Universitat Politècnica de Catalunya, Barcelona, Spain

ACADEMIC PRESS
An imprint of Elsevier

Academic Press is an imprint of Elsevier
125 London Wall, London EC2Y 5AS, United Kingdom
525 B Street, Suite 1650, San Diego, CA 92101, United States
50 Hampshire Street, 5th Floor, Cambridge, MA 02139, United States

Notices

Knowledge and best practice in this field are constantly changing. As new research and experience broaden our understanding, changes in research methods, professional practices, or medical treatment may become necessary.

Practitioners and researchers must always rely on their own experience and knowledge in evaluating and using any information, methods, compounds, or experiments described herein. In using such information or methods they should be mindful of their own safety and the safety of others, including parties for whom they have a professional responsibility.

To the fullest extent of the law, neither the Publisher nor the authors, contributors, or editors, assume any liability for any injury and/or damage to persons or property as a matter of products liability, negligence or otherwise, or from any use or operation of any methods, products, instructions, or ideas contained in the material herein.

ISBN: 978-0-443-22135-4

For information on all Academic Press publications
visit our website at https://www.elsevier.com/books-and-journals

Publisher: Mara Conner
Editorial Project Manager: Emily Thomson
Production Project Manager: Neena S. Maheen
Cover Designer: Mark Rogers

Typeset by VTeX

Working together
to grow libraries in
developing countries

www.elsevier.com • www.bookaid.org

To our beloved and patient families.

Contents

List of figures

Biography

Cecilio Angulo

Received the BSc and MSc degrees in Mathematics from the University of Barcelona, Spain, and the PhD in Sciences from the Universitat Politècnica de Catalunya (UPC), Spain in 2001. Founder of the Research Centre on Intelligent Data Science and Artificial Intelligence (IDEAI-UPC) in 2018. He is currently Full Professor of Artificial Intelligence and Robotics at UPC and President of the Catalan Association for Artificial Intelligence (ACIA). He has worked on applications on recommender systems, cognitive social robots and assistive technologies. He has authored books in machine learning and robots and published more than 275 papers in international and national journals and conferences. He has led and participated in 40 R&D competitive projects, 15 of them funded by the European Commission.

Alejandro Chacón

Received the MSc degree in automatic and robotic from the Universitat Politècnica Catalunya Barcelona Tech, Spain, in 2010, and the PhD degree in Automatic, Robotic, and Vision from Universitat Politècnica Catalunya Barcelona Tech, Spain, in 2022. He is currently Professor and Researcher of the University of the Armed Forces ESPE on Ecuador. He has published publications and book chapters. His research interests include cognitive assistants, industrial internet of things, artificial intelligence, human-centered design, and collaborative robotics.

Pere Ponsa

Received the BSc degree in Science from the Universitat Autònoma of Barcelona and the PhD degree from Universitat Politècnica Catalunya Barcelona Tech, Spain, in 2003. He is currently Assistant Professor of the Barcelona East School of Engineering and a member of the Automatic Control Department. He has published more than 150 refereed publications, including conferences, journals, book, and book chapters. His research interests include automation, smart control systems, human-centered design, and robotics. He is a member of the Smart Control Systems research group and a member of the Human–Computer Interaction Association (AIPO). He served as Conference Chair of Interacción'15 XVI International Conference on Human–Computer Interaction (Vilanova i la Geltrú, Spain, 2015).

Foreword

I am pleased to write this foreword for the book *Cognitive Assistant Supported Human–Robot Collaboration* by Prof. Angulo, Dr. Chacón, and Dr. Ponsa. The authors have outlined, analyzed, and discussed important research and development issues in the field of new generation of robotics, namely, as a multidisciplinary field to which converge robotics, Artificial Intelligence, Internet of Things, and Human Cyber-Physical Systems. The very fast development in the Cloud and IoT technologies, leading to the Cloud-to-thing Continuum Computing, has greatly impacted all fields of engineering. Robotics is not an exception as part of the current IoT Digital Transformation. Also coined as *IoRT – Internet of Robotic Things* – or Robotics with IoT, it is the field of research and development that combines the fields of Internet of Things and Robotics.

The authors have achieved an excellent narrative that shows how the *old* fields of Robotics and Artificial Intelligence are interlinked with the *new* fields of Cloud, Internet of Things, and human collaboration for the development of new generation of robotics and Industry 5.0. It is remarkable that this book places humans in the IoRT ecosystem through the paradigm of humans in the loop by giving humans a central role in the IoRT Human–Robot Collaboration, together with associating them with modeling, simulation, and experimentation studies. The exposition and discussion on human roles in a Human-centered Cyber-Physical System makes this book unique. The book has also practical importance for current and future Workspace Requirements and Design of modern augmented workspaces based on human–robot collaboration.

The great knowledge and expertise of the authors of the books on Robotics, Artificial Intelligence, Cognitive Sciences, and Internet of Things have made it possible for them to write an excellent book on the topics in these fields in a comprehensive way. Likewise, the authors of the book have priorly written and published scientific works on these and related topics, making their book content very well linked to current agenda of the research issues and challenges in the field.

Researchers, developers, and practitioners in the field will find in the book a thorough coverage of the topics of *IoRT* and the role of humans toward the development of new cognitive-based robotics systems in which human–robot collaboration is dwelled and envisaged as central to such systems.

Lastly, I would like to congratulate the authors of this book for the achievement and wish the readers enjoy the book!

Prof. Fatos Xhafa
Department of Computer Science,
Universitat Politècnica de Catalunya,
Barcelona, Spain

Preface

The purpose of writing this book is providing a comprehensive methodology from a sociotechnical approach for the development of cognitive assistants to operators working in human–robot teams in the Artificial Internet of Things domain.

This book covers design and development of cognitive assistants in the smart factory era, its application domains, current state of the art in assistance systems with collaborative robotics and IoT technologies, standards, platforms, and solutions. Furthermore, it provides a sociotechnical view of collaborative work in human–robot teams. In addition, it covers tools and techniques to analyze assistance systems. Finally, it highlights the main challenges in handling assistants in production systems.

Cecilio Angulo
Alejandro Chacón
Pere Ponsa

Introduction

Abstract

Internet of Things (IoT) systems are becoming increasingly complex due to the heterogeneity of the elements involved and the demand for real-time processing near to the devices. In this context, Artificial Intelligence (AI) technologies offer powerful capabilities to enhance IoT devices with intelligent services, resulting in the emerging field known as Artificial Internet of Things (AIoT). Operators find themselves at the center of this complexity, tasking with understanding the situation and making effective real-time decisions. Therefore human factors, especially cognitive aspects, become a significant concern.

The cognitive aspects of human involvement must be framed together with intelligent artefacts, a systematic approach being necessary within the domain of Joint Cognitive Systems (JCSs). New software development methods, in the form of assistants and wizards, are essential to assist operators in becoming context-aware and reducing their technical workload related to coding or computer-oriented skills. This shift allows them to focus more effectively on the tasks or services at hands.

Considering research experiences in the literature regarding the role of human workers in an AIoT environment, this book analyzes the described situation in terms of Human-Centered Cyber-Physical Systems (HCPSs) with the aim of proposing a conceptual framework for these assistance systems at the cognitive level. To validate this proposal in collaborative tasks, several illustrative examples will be presented.

This chapter serves as a general introduction, outlining the different topics shaping the basic aspects of the book. Initially, we delve into generic aspects of disruptive technologies within the context of Industry *4.0* or Society *5.0*. Following this, we emphasize the significance of the synergy between the Internet of Things and Artificial Intelligence. Moreover, we provide a clear definition of the concept of a cognitive assistant and elucidate its relationship with human–robot teams. Lastly, we offer a detailed overview of the book's objectives and its contents.

The expressions Internet of Things (IoT) and Cyber-Physical System (CPS) originate from different contexts but share overlapping definitions. They both refer to the trends involving the integration of digital capabilities, network connectivity, and computation with physical devices and systems. Examples of such integration can be found in several domains, ranging from intelligent vehicles to advanced manufacturing systems, and they are applied in sectors as diverse as energy, agriculture, or smart cities (Greer et al., 2019).

Internet of Things (IoT) systems are increasingly becoming complex. This complexity arises from several factors, including the heterogeneity of devices within the system in terms of hardware, software, computing capacity, and connectivity. Additionally, the high degree of decentralization and autonomy required in Industry *4.0* contributes significantly to this complexity (Estrada-Jimenez et al., 2021).

Another major source of complexity lies in the embedding of IoT systems into broader Cyber-Physical Systems (CPSs) or Digital Twins (DTs). These systems encompass devices capable not only of data collection but also of real-time data processing for decision-making (Tao et al., 2019). The presence of feedback loops, where physical processes influence cyber components and vice versa, empowers CPSs and DTs to enhance manufacturing systems with increased efficiency, resilience, and intelligence.

Moreover, in the context of these Cyber-Physical Systems (CPSs), it is essential to consider not only sensors but also actuators. This becomes particularly crucial in industrial domains, where collaborative robots, commonly referred to as *cobots*, play a significant role (Angulo, 2022). Cobots offer scalable functionality:

- In sensory integration, cobots are equipped with sensors such as cameras and vision-based subsystems, as well as force / torque sensors;
- In interaction with the operator, cobots showcase complex cooperation in tasks;
- In safety, for risk prevention or speed and force limitation control; and
- In programming, cobots scale from simple pick-and-place algorithms to programming using recursion and acceptance of orders from higher levels of management (Segura et al., 2021).

In the context of Cyber-Physical Systems, Artificial Intelligence (AI) technologies provide formidable capabilities to endow IoT devices with intelligent services, giving rise to the concept of Artificial Internet of Things (AIoT) (Marco, 2022), which represents an IoT-oriented version of CPS. Furthermore, the introduction of the human element into smart manufacturing envisions collaborative human-AI systems playing a pivotal role in the future of work as elements involved in Industry *4.0* / Society *5.0*. This transition toward more resilient, sustainable, and human-centered industries requires that models and governance structures be adjusted (Izsak et al., 2021).

The introduction of disruptive technologies in Industry *4.0* (Lasi et al., 2014), such as AIoT, integrated through Cyber-Physical Systems, introduces new challenges for operators (Weyer et al., 2015). The incoming generation of operators is characterized by smart and highly qualified operators who:

- Perform their work with the support of machines;
- Interact with collaborative robots and advanced systems; and
- Utilize enabling technologies such as wearable devices and augmented and virtual reality.

The correct interaction between the workforce and various enabling technologies of the *4.0 / 5.0* paradigm represents a key aspect of the success of the smart factory (Valentina et al., 2021). In this intricate landscape, the operator is in the middle of this complexity, tasking with comprehending the current situation and making effective real-time decisions to establish a human–automation symbiosis (Romero et al., 2016a). These challenges manifest in the increased demands placed on operator's physical, sensory, and cognitive skills (Rauch et al., 2020), including tasks such as identifying, judging, attending, perceiving, remembering, reasoning, deciding, problem-solving, and planning. Consequently, human factors, particularly the cognitive aspects, constitute a major concern to be addressed within the context of human-centric smart manufacturing (Neumann et al., 2021).

In the Industry *4.0* environment, cognitive skills of the operators are increasingly required over physical strength (Gualtieri et al., 2022). However, operators are generally not trained in the cognitive skills and abilities required for their workplace tasks, resulting in situations of increased mental load, reduced performance, and consequent declines in process efficiency and effectiveness (Wittenberg, 2016). To address these demands and render the complexity of processes manageable, it is necessary to support them (Angulo et al., 2023).

This support can be provided through digital assistance systems designed to aid operators in coping with a diversity of working systems (Bousdekis et al., 2022). Beyond the concept of a mere software tool, these support systems may encompass a set of functions that augment human capabilities. Examples include exoskeletons (Bances et al., 2020) and collaborative robots to enhance physical capabilities and virtual (Wolfartsberger et al., 2020) as well as augmented reality (Eswaran and Bahubalendruni, 2022; Chu and Liu, 2023) to bolster sensory capabilities. The effectiveness of these digital assistance systems (Prinz et al., 2017) would be adequate as long as there is a good knowledge of human teams and human–technology interactions.

In alignment with our prior work in Angulo et al. (2023), this book advocates for the need of engineering cognitive assistants to support human operators in factory workplaces, with a particular focus on the examination of human–robot collaboration in manufacturing. The conventional automation perspective alone proves insufficient in addressing the cognitive dimension. An additional viewpoint, therefore, is indispensable, one that accommodates the human element.

A sociotechnical system perspective is presented, rooted in the cognitive systems engineering domain, offering a suitable framework for the comprehensive study of human–machine interaction as the meaningful behavior of a unified system (Sony and Naik, 2020). Joint Cognitive Systems (JCSs) (Hollnagel and Woods, 2005) are introduced providing a principled methodology for studying collaborative human work with complex technology.

Within this context, cognitive assistants are examined through the lens of AIoT embedded in a human-centered CPS. The analysis will be illustrated sketching several examples from existing research in the literature. As a conclusion of this analysis, we propose a conceptual framework inspired by human–robot interaction for the design of cognitive assistants (Chacón et al., 2020a).

1.1 From Industry *4.0* to Society *5.0*

Smart manufacturing is currently being shaped through two primary paradigms: Industry *4.0*, which advocates the transition to digitalization and automation of processes, and the emerging Industry *5.0*, which places a significant emphasis on human centricity (Golovianko et al., 2023). Furthermore, the concept of Society *5.0* extends this latter vision from the factory environment to the society (Banholzer, 2022). As pointed out by Carayannis and Morawska-Jancelewicz (2022), the concepts of Society *5.0* and Industry *5.0* are not a simple chronological continuation or an alternative to Industry *4.0* paradigm.

Industry *4.0*, translated from *Industrie 4.0* as in German, is a term introduced in 2011 at the Hannover Fair originated from a project within the high-tech strategy of the German government (Xu et al., 2021). *SmartFactory* (Weyer et al., 2015), as a *factory of things*, is one of its key associated initiatives (Zuehlke, 2010). In the Industry *4.0* era, production systems can make intelligent decisions through real-time communication and collaboration among *manufacturing things* (Lu et al., 2020). This enables us the flexible production of high-quality personalized products at mass efficiency. In short, Industry *4.0* refers to a paradigm shift in the manufacturing model (Vaidya et al., 2018), departing from the previous Computer-Integrated Manufacturing (CIM) approach, which primarily envisioned fully automated factories operating with minimal human intervention (Osterrieder et al., 2020). Elements driving this evolution are digital transformation, connected enterprise, the increasing complexity of the relationship between emerging technologies, and the management of data from diverse sources. This is also sometimes referred as *lean automation* (Kolberg and Zühlke, 2015).

Many countries have introduced similar strategic initiatives to advance their manufacturing sectors. For instance, the Industrial Internet Consortium, which was rebranded as the Industry IoT Consortium (Ebraheem and Ivanov, 2022) in August 2021, in the USA, has been at the forefront. Sweden launched the Produktion 2030 initiative (Warrol and Stahre, 2015), whereas Japan has embraced the concept of Society *5.0* (Deguchi et al., 2020), to name a few (Sung, 2018; Ebraheem and Ivanov, 2022). In the context of Chinese industry, they have favored the *Made in China 2025* approach (Li, 2018), and more recently, they have adopted the broader concept of *5.0*.

Society *5.0* (Narvaez Rojas et al., 2021), as proposed in the Japanese *5th Science and Technology Basic Plan*, represents a vision of the future society that Japan should aspire to. It follows a historical progression from the hunting society (Society 1.0), agricultural society (Society 2.0), and industrial society (Society 3.0) to the information society (Society 4.0). It is defined as a human-centered society that balances economic advancement with the resolution of social problems. It does so through a highly integrated system that bridges cyberspace and physical space (Holroyd, 2022).

In 2021, the European Commission formally called for the Fifth Industrial Revolution (Industry *5.0*) (Maddikunta et al., 2022) by the formal release of the document entitled "Industry *5.0*: Towards a Sustainable, Human-centric, and Resilient European Industry" on 4 January 2021 (European Commission et al., 2021). This move bears a resemblance to the introduction of Industry *4.0* in 2011 by the German government (Kagermann et al., 2013), devising a top-down initiative in response to the changing societal and geopolitical landscape. It aims to place human well-being at the core of manufacturing systems, thereby striving to achieve social objectives that extend beyond employment and growth to provide prosperity robustly for the sustainable development of all humanity (Leng et al., 2022).

Just as Industry *4.0* carries out the digital transformation across industrial perspectives, Society *5.0* encourages everyday life to leap toward a digital revamp expanding across different tiers of the community (Nair et al., 2021). This human-centered perspective is the rationale behind our preference for the term Society *5.0* over Industry *5.0* (Longo et al., 2020), as proposed by the European Commission. However, it is important to note that the book primarily focuses on Human–Robot Collaboration (HRC) (Demir et al., 2019), wherein robots are seamlessly integrated with the human work, serving as collaborators rather than competitors (Nahavandi, 2019). In this context of human-centric smart manufacturing (Wang et al., 2023), all the three definitions – Industry *4.0*, Society *5.0*, and Industry *5.0* – will be accepted and utilized during this transition (Mourtzis et al., 2022).

In broad terms, Industry *4.0* is often regarded as technology-driven, whereas Industry *5.0* is value-driven, and Society *5.0* is society-driven (Enang et al., 2023). Human centricity is a significant element in both Industry *5.0* and Society *5.0*. An illustrative example to distinguish these human-centered approaches is provided by Huang et al. (2022): in Industry *5.0*, manufacturing systems and production processes are customized to accommodate the unique characteristics of individual workers and augment human ability by utilizing advanced technologies. For instance, robots and collaborative robots (cobots) are designed to adapt their interaction strategies when different workers join the production collaboration. Augmented Reality (AR), Virtual Reality (VR), and Mixed Reality (MR) technologies can provide custom-tailored contents to train engineers and workforce, among other applications. In contrast, Society *5.0* envisions human-centric services extending to every member of society, profoundly impacting the daily lives of individuals. For instance, individuals may have the convenience of purchasing custom-tailored food, clothes, and other items. In essence, the impact extends beyond the factory environment permeating the society daily life. Society *5.0*, also referred to as the *superintelligent society*, intends to use advanced technologies of Industry *4.0* to enhance the enjoyment of humankind, to promote an interconnection between people and systems in cyberspace with optimization of results by artificial intelligence. The challenge lies in governing this evolutionary process and purposely guiding the integration of individuals within CPSs to move toward the desired scenario (Fantini et al., 2020).

1.2 **Disruptive technologies in smart manufacturing**

The march of industrial progress is characterized by the emergence of disruptive technologies that trigger revolutions with profound social and economic implications (Coelho et al., 2023). Disruptive technology is a term encompassing changes that exert a significant influence on production processes, markets, product design, and services. Moreover, work skills and education are compromised (Bakir and Dahlan, 2023), leading to the development of strategies such as lifelong learning and transdisciplinary education (Gürdür Broo et al., 2022).

In the present day, a process of cross-fertilization involving a wide range of concepts is taking place, commonly referred to as digital transformation. However, there is no consensus about which enabling technologies should be considered in this group of disruptive technologies in Industry *4.0*. Drawing upon our experience and an extensive literature review, a list of disruptive technologies in Industry *4.0* is proposed in Table 1.1. Notably, we have highlighted four technologies within this list that exhibit strong connections with Artificial Internet of Things. It is worth noting that several of the technologies mentioned in this list already existed before the emergence of Industry *4.0*. However, the paradigm shift has accentuated their progress an enhanced their innovative potential (Choi et al., 2022).

Table 1.1 Disruptive technologies in Industry *4.0*.

Disruptive technology
Internet of Things (IoT)
Cloud Computing
Artificial Intelligence and Machine Learning
Edge Computing
Cyber-Security
Digital Twin
Additive Manufacturing
Augmented Reality
Autonomous Robots
Big Data and Analytics

In a similar line, a study conducted by the Boston Consulting Group (BCG) in Rüßmann et al. (2015) categorizes nine technologies, collectively referred to as the nine pillars of Industry *4.0*. These pillars include the Industrial Internet of Things (IIoT) and Big Data and Analytics, with the latter category potentially including Artificial Intelligence and Machine Learning methods. Kasinathan et al. (2022) discuss the technological potential for attaining the Sustainable Development Goals through a list of ten disruptive technologies, including Artificial Intelligence, Big Data Analytics, Robotics, and the Internet of Things. This study proposes an integrated framework for including new age technologies to establish the concepts of Industry *5.0* and Society *5.0* integrated into smart cities and villages. Moreover, Frank et al. (2019) introduces a conceptual framework for these technologies, categorizing them into front-end and base technologies. The front-end technologies span four dimensions: Smart Manufacturing, Smart Products, Smart Supply Chain, and Smart Working. In contrast, the base technologies consider four elements: the Internet of Things, Cloud Services, Big Data, and Analytics. Finally, to provide only just a few examples, nine key technologies associated with Smart Manufacturing are enumerated by Phuyal et al. (2020), including Cyber-Physical System, Big Data Analytics, Artificial Intelligence, and the Internet of Things / Industrial Internet of Things.

Two of the most prominent technology drivers frequently named in the literature are the Internet of Things (IoT) and Artificial Intelligence (AI). The proliferation of interconnected devices (referred to as *things*) in smart manufacturing is experiencing an exponential surge. Concurrently, the integration of machine learning algorithms is becoming increasingly ubiquitous. This situation of higher technological complexity in human-centric smart manufacturing systems is steering the focus toward the *5.0* concept, wherein the information society created with the emerging disruptive technologies adopts a human-centric orientation, embodied by Industry *5.0* and Society *5.0*. To abound in this positive shift toward a *5.0* vision, a systematic literature review about AI as a disruptive technology was conducted by Păvăloaia and Necula (2023). Utilizing sentiment analysis of titles and abstracts, the findings reveal that a majority of recent publications exhibit a positive connotation regarding the disruptive impact of edge technologies. Notably, the two most prominent examples that emerge from this analysis are AI and IoT.

Furthermore, the disruptive technologies approached in this book align with the trends identified by prominent standards organizations such as the International Electrotechnical Commission (IEC), the International Organization for Standardization (ISO), and the International Telecommunication Union (ITU), which have revealed their projected trends until 2030. Firstly, during the World Standards Day in 2018, it was stressed that disruptive technologies such as AI, Robotics, and the IoT are the hallmarks of the Fourth Industrial Revolution. Subsequently, in 2019 the ISO elaborated on the four trends that make up the disruptive forces shaping the direction of standards organizations' future strategy in the period leading up to 2030. Among them is enlisted digital transformation, where AI (through ML) will enhance companies' productivity and efficiency while fostering innovation and competitive advantages.

1.2.1 Artificial Intelligence as a disruptive technology

Artificial Intelligence currently holds the distinction of being the most widely adopted and disruptive technology across all industries, with a particularly pronounced impact in the domains of Industry *4.0* / Industry *5.0* (Yu, 2022), as well as their subdomains like intelligent logistics robotics (Jia et al., 2022). In the context of manufacturing, Artificial Intelligence in the form of machine learning models contributes to human-centric smart manufacturing (Wang, 2019). Representative applications refer to scenarios around the concept of Human–Robot Collaboration (HRC). In such scenarios, data collected from sensors and field devices are transformed into actionable knowledge through the application of appropriate machine learning models. Consequently, human operators can collaborate with robots in a secure and immersive environment. Furthermore, robots can anticipate the actions of humans and provide real-time assistance as needed.

From maintenance to postproduction support, from customer service to product quality checks, the range of examples showcasing AI-driven applications in Industry 5.0 and, more precisely, in smart manufacturing, is vast (Sahoo and Lo, 2022). This extensive list of applications remarks the disruption potential of this technology, which has been comprehensively examined in the literature (Xu et al., 2022b; Jan et al., 2023; Shojaeinasab et al., 2022; Soori et al., 2023).

In addition to its impact on processes and systems, we would like to highlight the profound influence of AI on people and the labor market. Artificial Intelligence has opened up tremendous opportunities in the workplace, propelled by robotics innovation that encompass both Artificial Intelligence and the Internet of Things. It is warned by Oosthuizen (2022) that disruptive technologies such as AI will have a significant influence on the workplace by widening the work force skill gaps more quickly than educational systems can adjust. Consequently, employers are encouraged to invest in training courses and programs, cognitive assistants, and support systems aimed at raising awareness among their employees regarding disruptive technologies and their impacts on the workforce. As new job roles continue to emerge, it becomes necessary to cultivate the required skills and competences (Gladysz et al., 2023).

Numerous studies alert about the disruptive potential of technologies like Artificial Intelligence and Machine Learning in the context of job displacement. These studies often point toward the need for employee retraining and diversion to alternative roles. Interviewed talent management experts working in information technology, manufacturing, and administration have underscored these challenges (Murugesan et al., 2023). Furthermore, particular examples of real-life case studies examining the impact of digital technology implementation are actively being researched (Li et al., 2023b; Maretto et al., 2023). These studies demonstrate that to create and effectively use AI, specific technical expertise is needed. Hence the demand for technical roles is on the rise, but it represents a significant challenge in terms of skill acquisition.

1.2.2 Internet of Things as a disruptive technology

According to Gubbi et al. (2013), the term Internet of Things (IoT) was originally coined by Kevin Ashton, MIT's Executive Director of Auto-ID Labs, back in 1999 within the context of supply chain management (Granell et al., 2020), and officially gained prominence in 2009. Over the years, its definition has evolved to become more inclusive, covering a wide range of applications (Atzori et al., 2010). The continuous advancement of the features of these devices has enabled them to be adapted to various fields, including healthcare and smart city, as well as industries like manufacturing and waste management. According to the bibliometric work conducted by Sadeghi-Niaraki (2023), scientific publications on IoT spanning over a decade

(2010–2021) cover eight main categories: applications, security, technologies, types, data communications, networks, development, and protocol standards.

The emergence of the IoT concept has resulted in numerous definitions, with earlier references primarily emphasizing the technological aspects. An IoT device possesses two fundamental capabilities: data collection via sensors and data transmission via a communication system (Jesse, 2016). The methodological review in Sorri et al. (2022) gathers 122 definitions and consolidates them into a novel framework that unifies the traditional technology focus and integrates additional elements that are likely to increase the adoption of a comprehensive definition to support the development of future business applications: interaction, virtual thing, services, physical, standardized technologies, information, data, ubiquitous, user, and uniqueness. Internet of Things connects devices, humans, locations, and even abstract items like events. Its potential for connectivity, processing, and scalability, particularly coupled with Artificial Intelligence, positions the Internet of Things as one of the leading disruptive technologies (Sandner et al., 2020).

An application of significant relevance is the integration of the Internet of Things into the framework of manufacturing (Garg et al., 2022). IoT-enabled manufacturing is about creating an environment where all available information originating from the plant floor is captured in real time, rendered visible, and turned into actionable insights (Zhong and Ge, 2018). Hence the concept of the Industrial Internet of Things (IIoT) came into being in roughly 2010 as an extension of the IoT. IIoT employs actuators and smart sensors, which are networked together with a company's industrial applications. The goal is to empower industries with greater efficiency and reliability. This paradigm includes robotics and software-defined production processes. Industrial IoT is directly related to concepts such as Cyber-Physical Systems (Pivoto et al., 2021) and Industry *4.0* (Malik et al., 2021), as it is well analyzed by Boyes et al. (2018). Moreover, in certain contexts, they are identified as the same area, as declared in Munirathinam (2020): "IoT trend has created a subsegment of the IoT market known as the industrial Internet of Things (IIoT) or Industry *4.0*".

1.2.3 **Collaborative robotics as a disruptive technology**

The Industrial Internet of Things includes robotics and software-defined production processes. However, until recently, due to the prevalence of the Computer-Integrated Manufacturing (CIM) approach (Nagalingam and Lin, 2008), most robots function as simple manipulators coded under the control of (serving to) their human operators (Pan et al., 2012). While the concept of industrial collaborative robots (cobots) can be tracked back to 1999, many of today's hybrid human–machine assembly systems are merely weight compensators (Cherubini et al., 2016).

Collaborative robotics, that is, human–robot collaboration, stands as a foundational aspect of the Fourth Industrial Revolution and already has the basis for being projected into the Fifth Industrial Revolution (Baratta et al., 2023). Robots are becoming increasingly autonomous, coworking with their human counterparts (Semeraro et al., 2023). Human–robot interaction and human–robot collaboration will be crucial for enhancing the operator's work conditions and production performance by increasing efficiency, productivity, and flexibility at production lines and their corresponding workstations (Simões et al., 2022). In this regard, this key enabling technology opens new possibilities but also new technological (Kragic et al., 2018; Liu et al., 2022) and societal challenges (Bogataj et al., 2019).

As robots are increasingly used, the question emerges regarding their successful integration into human–robot teams, particularly within small- and medium-sized enterprises (SMEs). One of the principal barriers hindering SMEs from adopting robots to a greater extent is a lack of expertise (Buerkle et al., 2023). Easy software tools allowing robotic novices to program industrial tasks on a collaborative robot are a possibility (Schou et al., 2018). Alternatively, a more advanced or complementary approach involves the development of assistants supporting human–robot collaboration, a concept advocated by Angulo et al. (2023), especially focusing on collaborative cognitive skills (Chacón et al., 2021a). There is no doubt that safety is of paramount importance in industrial settings where humans and robots interact (Villani et al., 2018). However, human factors and cognitive ergonomics, including aspects such as cognitive workload, usability, trust, acceptance, stress, frustration, and perceived enjoyment, also play pivotal roles (Gualtieri et al., 2021). Unfortunately, these aspects are often underestimated or disregarded (Chacón et al., 2020b, 2021b).

To further highlight the impact of this disruptive technology on the labor market, let us check the statistics published by the International Federation of Robotics (IFR) about robot installation around the world. According to IFR, industrial robot sales exhibited a substantial 29% increase, reaching 229,261 units in 2014 compared to the preceding year, and the average annual growth rate for robot sales between 2010 and 2014 stood at an impressive 17% (Murashov et al., 2016). The advancement of robotics poses more questions about robot–human integration as advanced robotics takes expansion to an entirely new level (Richards, 2017b). In advanced industrial settings, robots are increasingly operating as part of a human-agent team, affording humans the opportunity to withdraw from monotonous, hazardous, or challenging tasks (Richards, 2017a). Conversely, individuals must cultivate a balanced proficiency in both soft and digital skills to thrive in a future characterized by technological advancements, as evidenced in Poláková et al. (2023). This study analyzed a dataset encompassing information pertaining to skill prerequisites extracted from job posts published on a job portal over five years, involving 19,000 distinct organizations. Furthermore, data on robot adoption and occupations by industry in thirty-seven countries for the period from 2005 to 2015 are analyzed by de Vries et al. (2020) to identify the impact of robot usage on employment. The findings, especially in high-income countries, indicate that an increase in robot adoption relates significantly with a decline in the employment share of routine manual task-intensive jobs.

Yet, as operators gain greater autonomy, the dynamics of the human–robot relationship will need an increased level of adaptability when considering the assignment of power allocation (Oosthuizen, 2022). Effective communication between humans and robots could be significantly enhanced if there were a formal system of control and assistance in place (Bhargava et al., 2021), as that proposed at the cognitive level in this book.

1.3 Artificial Internet of Things (AIoT)

The combination of the Internet of Things, Big Data and Analytics, and Artificial Intelligence leads to Artificial Internet of Things (AIoT) (Xhafa, 2023), that is, intelligent and connected systems capable of autonomous decision-making, evaluation of the results of these decisions, and self-improvement over time (Angulo et al., 2023). AIoT systems continuously gather all kinds of information in real time through sensors and employ machine learning for intelligent data analysis in the terminal equipment, edge domains, or cloud centers, including positioning, comparison, forecasting, scheduling, etc., which brings about the data security and privacy issues. AIoT is a mandatory area of expertise as the number of connected devices is growing exponentially.

The hyperconnectivity among devices generates a large volume of available data, which needs to be gathered, cleaned, analyzed, and converted into useful information for the end user (Hansen and Bøgh, 2021). AIoT is sometimes referred as AI-IoT (Al-Turjman et al., 2021) to stress the utilization of AI and ML algorithms, fog computing, and IoT (Sadri et al., 2022). Moreover, it is also named edge intelligence (Debauche et al., 2020) to highlight how near to the physical device the computation is performed. Lately, AIoT is employed in the form of Digital Twins (Lv, 2023) across several domains, from smart cities and construction (Gao et al., 2023) to agriculture and fish farming (Ubina et al., 2023). Data privacy being a major concern in connected systems, technologies as blockchain (Shen et al., 2023b) and federated learning (Rizwan et al., 2023) are considered as a general framework.

Moreover, Artificial Internet of Things (AIoT) should not only consider sensors but also encompass actuators, particularly autonomous and collaborative robots (cobots) within the Industry *5.0* domain, as mentioned in the list of disruptive technologies in Table 1.1 on page 6. Integrating industrial robots into an AIoT scenario allows the development of more efficient production systems, as it increases the potential of the robot's tasks alongside the human, and favors highly flexible and scalable scenarios (Muslikhin et al., 2021; Kuo and Wu, 2023). As an illustrative example, one application is presented in Tsai et al. (2020), which takes place in a manufacturing environment. In this scenario the AIoT architecture is described as a Cyber-Physical System Artificial Intelligence (CPS-AI) architecture.

As a general basis, a fundamental AIoT architecture can be defined as an interconnection between different layers, tailored to a specific context of application (Ansar et al., 2023). In the context of a cloud-based AIoT architecture, it typically comprises four layers:

1. Physical layer: This layer includes devices such as sensors, actuators, robots, and autonomous vehicles.

2. Connectivity layer: In this layer, field gateways play a key role in transporting information.
3. Cloud layer: This layer encompasses elements for data storage, processing, machine learning algorithms, and raw data visualization.
4. User communication layer: Components that can be found in this layer are dashboard, web or mobile applications, data interpretation tools, and user-friendly supporting visual interfaces.

This disruptive technology is employed across many industries in the context of Industry *5.0*. Here are a few examples of how AIoT is utilized in different sectors:

- Manufacturing: monitoring (Zhang et al., 2021), predictive maintenance (Matin et al., 2023), digital coworker (Slama, 2023);
- Healthcare: diagnostic assistance (Barnawi et al., 2021), quality of life of patient (Nozari et al., 2023; Pise et al., 2023), remote healthcare (Alshamrani, 2022);
- Agriculture: from farm to fork (Xu et al., 2022a), precision agriculture (Saranya et al., 2023), data mining (Krause and Bokinala, 2023);
- Smart city: self driving vehicles, sustainable and decarbonized solutions (Singh et al., 2020), situational awareness in urban environment (Li et al., 2022); and
- Education: smart learning environments that respond to students' needs and adapt to their learning styles (Lin et al., 2021).

In the case of manufacturing, the topic more related to the focus of our book, AIoT can offer various applications and benefits for different user profiles:

- a plant operator who needs to improve his skills (Tsai et al., 2021);
- a maintenance technician who needs to predict the behavior of sensors, actuators, and machines (Ubina et al., 2023);
- a plant supervisor who needs to integrate effective technologies in machine vision (Ullah et al., 2022) and robotics (Mourtzis et al., 2023);
- a cybersecurity technician who needs to improve network reliability and try to reduce the risk of cyber-attack (Parihar et al., 2023);
- a data science operator who assesses the most effective machine learning algorithm (Shang et al., 2021).

1.4 AIoT and Human-Centered Cyber-Physical System

In Industry *5.0*, not only are production lines and processes undergoing significant changes, but the role of humans is also subject to a profound transformation, turning out to be a milestone for the development of productive systems (Mark et al., 2021). Concerning the tasks and responsibilities of the operator in the smart factory, there exists an increase in the proportion of complex cognitive tasks. This growing demand accentuates the needs for coordination or organization of production resources, as well as the control and monitoring of complex production systems. Whether it is Industry *5.0* or Society *5.0*, the convergence of cyberspace and the physical world stands out as one of the critical enabling technologies. Humans as the most creative, flexible, and active factor within the system, should be closely involved in the cyber-physical interaction loop and the decision-making process, ultimately leading to the development of Human-Centered Cyber-Physical Systems.

A Human-Centered Cyber-Physical System (HCPS) is defined by Romero et al. (2016a) as a system that comprises humans and integrates computational and physical components, resulting in new levels of socio-technical interactions among humans, machines, materials, and objects. From a human-centered perspective, an HCPS is redefined by Chacón et al. (2020a) as a work system that enhances the capabilities of human operators through dynamic interactions between humans and machines in both the cyber and physical worlds, facilitated by smart human–machine interfaces. Therefore the objectives within an HCPS are achieved by means of interactions involving:

- the physical system or process to be controlled;
- cybernetic elements, such as communication links and software modules; and
- human workers who monitor and influence the functioning of the cyber-physical elements, including those from the AIoT.

A study of the associated literature shows that a significant change in this relationship from purely physical to cognitive refers to the human–machine interface, which encompasses the interaction between operators and a set of new forms of collaborative work (Prinz et al., 2017). Let us examine this new role of the human worker in human-centric smart factories (Wang et al., 2022; Zhang et al., 2023) from the perspective of all the involved elements:

- the human operator,
- the process, that is, the smart factory, and
- the cognitive assistant support.

1.4.1 The human operator

Since the increase in the degree of automation of factories reduces costs and improves productivity, we might think that people in the production hall will not be needed anymore, except for secondary tasks such as repair and maintenance. Theories of "unmanned factories" have been discussed decades, dating back to the Computer-Integrated Manufacturing (CIM) era. In practice, however, factories will not be without humans. Humans are indispensable resources in the workplace (Belkadi et al., 2019). People will work or operate alongside sensors, robots, machines, cyber-physical systems, and other humans (Müller and Oehm, 2019). The concept of Operator *4.0* (Romero et al., 2016a) emerges as a general definition for an operator in an industrial setting assisted by technological tools.

Most standard situations can be handled by automation through Cyber-Physical System (CPS) or Artificial Internet of Things (AIoT). However, operators must monitor and fine-tune the automated system to keep it functioning within specified bounds. Many visions and roadmaps about the future factory emphasize the critical role of humans in achieving better work performance. Automated systems are not capable of dealing with unanticipated situations (Müller and Oehm, 2019), whereas humans can learn from experience and compensate for incomplete knowledge. Humans can also adapt to different situations and prioritize different goals according to current demands. Thus human workers compensate for inevitable design shortcomings by learning and acting in flexible, context-dependent ways (Hollnagel, 2012).

Human operators remain key elements in manufacturing systems, yet the increasing degree of automation does not necessarily lead to enhanced operator performance. Humans can introduce variability (Chacón et al., 2020b) in the process or, even worse, make mistakes that have a direct influence on the cost of nonquality and delays. Some studies have demonstrated that human-caused nonquality is due to three main reasons (Chang, 2016):

- lack of appropriate guidelines,
- gaps in training, and
- the unavailability of documentation in production lines.

As a result of the disruptive technologies, the worker must deal with different working situations, which can arise due to changing workplaces in the production line or evolving production schemes and software products within the same workplace (Gorecky et al., 2014). Operators need to be aware of critical elements within each situation and interpret them correctly according to their specific task. Maintaining constant awareness of all these elements can be a challenging task for operators and may lead to cognitive overload, which needs to be minimized.

1.4.2 The factory in Industry *4.0*

On the other hand, continuous innovation in cyber-physical systems enables machines to handle tasks such as ensuring the adequate supply of materials, optimizing the production process for the actual product, or even autonomously devising new production plans (Wittenberg, 2016). Therefore this technological evolution generates, among others, the following impacts on the operator (Karre et al., 2017):

- the qualification of manual tasks decreases;
- the operator can access all the necessary information in real time to take decisions;
- intelligent assistance systems enable quicker decision-making;
- collaborative workspaces between machines and humans require less effort and attention;
- human implementation and monitoring are more relevant than ever.

Disruptive technologies in Industry *4.0* related to Artificial Internet of Things are enabling Cyber-Physical System systems oriented toward human–machine interaction (HCPS) to transition from a primarily physical interaction paradigm to also a cognitive one (Mizanoor Rahman, 2019; Bocklisch et al., 2022). Operators should be able to control and supervise automated production systems. However, the increasing information and communication capabilities of these systems introduce complexity beyond the comprehension of current standard user interfaces employed in the industry. Consequently, operators require support to maintain system stability.

Moreover, operators may need access to the factory's work plan (not just shift supervisors), needing additional information during field operations. This requires access to location-independent information, as well as a situation-oriented and task-oriented information interface (Hollnagel, 2010).

1.4.3 The cognitive assistant support

As a consequence of this paradigm shift, new forms of interaction are emerging in the field of Human–Machine Interface (HMI) in the Fourth Industrial Revolution. The interaction between human workers and Cyber-Physical System in smart factories is addressed by either direct manipulation or with the assistance of a mediating user interface. These intelligent user interfaces are referred to as Operator Support Systems (OSS), assistance systems, decision support systems, or Intelligent Personal Assistants (IPAs) (Rauch et al., 2020; Cimino et al., 2023). In the current industrial context, the operator interacts with a collaborative robot. This collaborative effort involves both parties working together to accomplish tasks. As the robot continues to enhance its skills and capabilities, such as autonomy, anticipation, and adaptation, it will evolve into an agent. This transformation will result in the robot becoming an artificial cognitive system or cognitive robot, enabling a more comprehensive interaction with the operator. This shift in interaction is a key point, as humans are inherently cognitive beings (Chacón et al., 2020a; Freire et al., 2023; Vernon, 2014; Cangelosi and Asada, 2022).

During the transition from a collaborative robot to a cognitive robot, assistance systems emerge. In the context of smart, people-centered service systems, cognitive systems have the potential to evolve from mere tools to assistants, collaborators, and even coaches. The perception of these systems may vary depending on the specific role they play within a service system.

Assistance systems provide support to the operator in the following ways (Nelles et al., 2016):

- From a human-centered design approach they consider the identification of user context, the specification of user requirements, the creation of design solutions, and their evaluation. Moreover, they provide an appropriate amount of information in a clear way.
- They are decision-makers in production control, involved in information acquisition, data aggregation/analysis, and operation choice.

At this point, it should be highlighted that the final decision always should remain in the human operator side, thus maintaining the principle of human centrality (Angulo et al., 2023).

Such a close interaction between humans and CPS raises socio-technological issues regarding autonomy and decision-making power (Read et al., 2015). Cybernetics (Rajanen and Rajanen, 2020) provides an answer on how a system that controls another system can compensate for more errors in the control process by having more operational variety. As the most flexible entity in the cyber-physical structure, the human will assume the role of a higher-level control instance. Through technological support, it is guaranteed that operators can develop their full potential and adopt the role of strategic decision makers and flexible problem solvers, thus managing the increasing technical complexity. Throughout this book, the inclusion of the human as a central element in the CPS will be presented, leading to the introduction of particular examples of Human-Centered Cyber-Physical Systems (HCPSs).

1.5 AIoT and human–robot team tasks in industry

Smart manufacturing is the primary application considered in this book. However, AIoT finds applications in several domains, including healthcare (Baker and Xiang, 2023), smart cities (Prabha et al., 2022), agriculture (Adli et al., 2023), and energy grids (Shen et al., 2023a). In the context of manufacturing, many publications related to the IoT and AI in Industry *4.0* have been released, primarily focused on larger enterprises. Nevertheless, it is increasingly important to be sure that small- and medium-sized enterprises (SMEs), considered the economic backbone of many countries, have easy access to these technologies and can effectively implement them (Hansen and Bøgh, 2021). In this situation, human factors play a critical role.

1.5.1 AIoT in human-centered smart manufacturing

Zhang et al. (2023) elaborated the concept of human-centric smart manufacturing (HSM) upon emphasizing its utilization of human flexibility, machine precision, and new-generation information technologies to establish a supersmart, sustainable, and resilient manufacturing system, all closely linked to the Industry *5.0* paradigm. Hence extensive research has been conducted on the concept, architecture, enabling technologies, and applications of smart manufacturing. However, research on HSM is still relatively scarce, although it is rapidly gaining momentum.

The human-centric perspective of the Fourth Industrial Revolution technologies was initially defended by Romero et al. (2016b), who presented early concepts and future projections of the so-called "Operator *4.0*", understood as a smart and skilled operator who performs work aided by machines and, if needed, by means of Human-Centered Cyber-Physical Systems, advanced human–machine interaction technologies and adaptive automation towards achieving human–automation symbiosis work systems. This is the main reason we prefer the use of the term Human-Centered Cyber-Physical System over the most recent Human-centric Smart Manufacturing System. However, both terms are accepted and used along the text, the latter term being understood as more restrictive than HCPS. We highly recommend reading of the papers in the recent special issue of Wang et al. (2023) for a deeper comprehension of this topic.

1.5.2 AIoT human–robot teamwork

In the context of smart manufacturing, particularly in component assembly, the conventional automation approach has encountered limitations. Tasks that can be automated have already been addressed, whereas the remaining tasks still rely on manual labor by human operators (Wang, 2022). To enhance working conditions and ensure consistent quality in manual work, human–robot collaboration (HRC) has gained popularity over the past decade.

Human–robot team-working in a manufacturing context aims to realize an environment where humans can work side by side with robots in close proximity. The main objective of the collaboration is to integrate the best of two worlds: the strength, endurance, repeatability, and accuracy of the robots with the intuition, flexibility, versatile problem solving, and sensory skills of the humans. Using HRC, higher overall productivity and better product quality can be achieved (Wang et al., 2019a). Human manual tasks are complemented, augmented, not replaced, with the help of collaborative robots. In teamwork the best skills of each team member, that is, human and robot, are combined (Othman and Yang, 2023).

As defended in Moniz and Krings (2016), since "intuitive" human–machine interaction (HMI) in robotic systems in the manufacturing industry becomes a significant objective of technical progress, new models of work organization are needed. Limits of cognitive and perceptual workload for robot operators in complex working systems exist. This is particularly relevant whenever more robots with different "roles" are to be increasingly used in the manufacturing industry. Human–robot interaction and human–robot collaboration will be crucial for enhancing the operator's work conditions and production performance (Gualtieri et al., 2022). The aim in this book is to describe progress on the integration of such complex socio-technical systems with regard to human-centered aspects of the technical dimension.

1.6 Problems statement and book questions

The introduction of different disruptive technologies, integrated through Human-Centered Cyber-Physical Systems (HCPS) in the workplace, forces the operator to acquire new knowledge, skills, and abilities to adapt to the evolving configuration of their work environment. The current trend is changing from the demand for physical abilities and skills toward sensory and cognitive abilities and skills, considered the latter of a higher level. However, operators are often not adequately trained in cognitive skills and abilities, resulting in situations of increased mental load, decreased performance, and therefore reducing the efficiency and effectiveness of the process (Chacón, 2022).

To address these demands and manage the increasing complexity of processes, it is necessary to provide support to operators. This support can be delivered through digital assistance systems, which help operators in performing their tasks across a variety of systems. The enhancement of operators' and engineers' cognitive skills is imminent to adapt the working environment to Industry *4.0*. Thus cognitive skills of smart operators are in higher demand than physical strength.

1.6.1　Human-centered AIoT

Human-centered AIoT refers to the design, development, and implementation of Artificial Intelligence of Things (AIoT) systems with a primary focus on enhancing user experiences, addressing human needs, and ensuring human well-being. It emphasizes placing humans at the center of AIoT technologies, considering their preferences, behaviors, and values (Angulo et al., 2023).

In a human-centered AIoT approach, the goal is to create intelligent IoT systems that are intuitive, adaptive, and responsive to human requirements. This involves understanding user contexts, gathering user feedback, and incorporating human-centric design principles throughout the AIoT development lifecycle.

Key aspects of human-centered AIoT may include:

- User-centric Design: Prioritizing the needs, goals, and expectations of users when designing AIoT systems. This entails conducting user research, usability testing, and incorporating user feedback to ensure systems are intuitive and user-friendly.
- Personalization and Context Awareness: Adapting AIoT systems to individual user preferences and contextual factors such as location, time, and situation. This enables tailored experiences and services that cater to specific user requirements.
- Transparency and Explainability: Ensuring that AIoT systems provide transparent explanations of their decisions and actions. This helps build trust, allows users to understand the system behavior, and facilitates effective human–AI interaction.
- Ethical Considerations: Addressing ethical challenges and considerations associated with AIoT, such as privacy protection, data security, fairness, and accountability. Human-centered AIoT strives to uphold ethical principles and protect users' rights.
- Human–AI Collaboration: Promoting symbiotic relationships between humans and AI technologies in IoT systems. This involves designing AIoT interfaces that facilitate seamless collaboration and cooperation between humans and AI algorithms, leveraging their respective strengths.

In embracing a human-centered approach to AIoT, the objective is to develop technologies that enhance human capabilities, improve quality of life, and provide meaningful experiences, all while upholding ethical principles and ensuring user empowerment.

1.6.2　Cognitive assistants

Cognition is a term referring to the mental processes involved in gaining knowledge and comprehension. In automation processes the application of solutions has mainly focused on the physical activities of the operator, with which automatic machines and robots have seen significant development. Currently, with the introduction of emerging technologies in the workplace (cobots, virtual reality, augmented reality, smart HMI), operators face the challenge of handling systems with a larger amount of data, which must be transformed into information and later into knowledge for decision-making. This transformation of information is facilitated by the cognitive abilities of the operator involving different functions such as analysis, memory, and planning.

Cognition is a concept that has been studied from various perspectives, including psychology, cybernetics, and neurology. To assist operators, it is important to establish certain characteristics of cognition. In this book, we focus on the concept of distributed cognition proposed by Hollan et al. (2000). Cognition refers to all the processes by which data is transformed, reduced, processed, stored, and utilized to address workplace events, including conditions monitoring, anomaly detection, optimization, and prediction of future states (Fischbach et al., 2020). Another perspective is the concept of cognition in work teams, as proposed by Fiore and Wiltshire (2016). This approach allows for the understanding of cognitive processes and functions beyond individual brains. Recognizing how cognition is distributed and enhanced through the actions of the different members of the team leads us to the concept of macrocognition, in addition to understanding that cognition is not a closed function.

It is also worth noting that artifacts can perform certain cognitive processes, giving rise to the concept of macrocognition in the workplace arising from the symbiotic relationship between human operators and technological operators. This macrocognition, when distributed in the workplace, enables human operators to develop their skills without experiencing mental overload or stress. Placing artifacts with the ability to perform cognitive processes within the Human-Centered Cyber-Physical System allows operators to have assistants in the workplace. In this study the work team consists of a human operator and a technological operator (H-R) collaborating in the workplace.

In the industrial domain, a significant research activity within cognitive robotics is the development of assistant or advisory robots designed for increasing productivity and optimizing work organization (International Federation of Robotics, 2018; Chacón et al., 2020a). In manufacturing work environments, providing assistance to skilled workers becomes increasingly essential. Industrial companies are now not only addressing ergonomic and safety concerns but also considering new qualification requirements and technical competencies for their operators. This involves effectively communicating decisions in the overall work process to operators with the goal of improving their information and skills (Moniz and Krings, 2016).

Moreover, the industrial robotics area is currently moving in specific human–robot interaction domains from industrial robots to collaborative robots (*cobots*), especially in small and medium enterprises (SMEs) because of affordable costs. Traditional industrial robots are designed primarily for tasks where safety and factory resources are priorities, usually enclosed in fenced areas to prevent human interaction (Groover et al., 1986). This is the case for mechanical robot arms.

The current transition from industrial to collaborative robotics scenarios is reshaping the safety model. Fencing is being replaced by shared workspaces where humans and robots can cooperate on tasks. Hence the first kind of interaction being under consideration in Industry is the physical one. By *physical interaction* we mean several scenarios involving humans and robots (Pervez and Ryu, 2011): space sharing, proximity, voluntary physical contact (limited in time), involuntary physical contact (collision), and reciprocal exchange of forces. At a mechanical level, robots should meet specifications for limiting force and speed to ensure safety. On the human side, aspects of biomechanics, risk prevention, and injuries associated with involuntary physical contacts should be analyzed.

One of the primary objectives of collaborative robotics development is to introduce robot-based solutions in small- and medium-sized companies (Gualtieri et al., 2020). Therefore it is convenient to find out the degree of maturity of the current industrial robotics area concerning new interaction models.

These human–machine interaction models encompass several functionalities to be developed (Sheridan, 2006): planning, monitoring, intervention, learning, facilitating interactions between humans and artificial agents (trained for dialogue with humans), assessing mental workload, and defining levels of automation (ranging from manual to shared and supervised control).

As the field progresses, industrial robotics evolves toward cognitive robotics. Moreover, considering progress in Artificial Intelligence, the integration of humans with artificial engineering systems presents an intriguing research area for exploration (Teo et al., 2019; Illankoon et al., 2019).

Research on workers and robots interaction is an emerging field evolving as the current robotics also does it within the framework of the new industrial paradigm called connected factory or Industry *4.0*. At the plant level, human operators are required to interact with several devices with changing capabilities as the synergy between Artificial Intelligence algorithms and electronic devices with fault diagnosis functionalities increases, necessitating communications using advanced protocols.

As research on increasing the social skills of future human operators continues to developed, it should be also checked that the design of work tasks promotes standardization (Secretary I.C., 2011; ISO Central Secretary, 2016a):

- Ensure that the human–robot team makes a significant contribution to task effectiveness and productivity.
- Provide individuals with an appropriate level of autonomy to make decisions and execute procedures and tasks.
- Create opportunities for novice operators to develop existing skills and acquire new ones.
- Offer sufficient feedback to keep the human operator engaged in the loop.

From a cognitive and social interaction perspective the advancement in algorithm development should enable intelligent robots or cognitive agents to understand the operator's work preferences, adapt to them, suggest improved or alternative ways of joint collaboration, and enhance the operator's skills. The dialogue between the operator and the robot should be changeable, fostering continuous learning by the operator and improving the overall comfort experienced while working with robots (Wang et al., 2019b).

Therefore one of the key functionalities of cognitive robots is cognitive assistance. However, it is worth noting that cognitive assistance, in the form of an automatic expert partner, is far from the functionality of today's collaborative robots, mainly focused on safety and physical assistance.

Once a cognitive automation platform understands how business processes work autonomously, it can also deliver real-time insights and recommendations on actions to take to improve performance and results (Romero et al., 2016a).

1.6.3 Book questions

This book focuses on the study of digital assistants that collaborate with the operator in performing cognitive tasks required in the workspace, in partnership with a technological counterpart, referred to as Human–Robot Teamwork. To guide this approach, the following questions are proposed:

Q1   What are the cognitive characteristics of a digital assistant in a Human-Centered Cyber-Physical System in the workplace?

Q2   How can a Human-Centered Cyber-Physical System be modeled as a Joint Cognitive System?

Q3   Which parameters should be considered to evaluate the human–machine team from a cognitive point of view?

Q4   How is the introduction of new technologies affecting human–machine system performance in the workplace?

The issues raised unfold sequentially throughout the book as shown in Fig. 1.1. Chapter 2 discusses AIoT in Human-Cyber Physical Systems and presents useful tools for assessing the cognitive side of the human operator. Chapter 3 shows the methodology in AIoT environments. Details are provided on workspace requirements, design aspects, and experimental setup. Chapter 4 deploys the workspace metrics and shows the summative and formative evaluations. Chapter 5 provides results based on statistical techniques for user research and graphical representation of performance. Chapter 6 promotes the discussion of results to obtain recommendations that can be made by the cognitive assistant. Chapter 7 synthesizes the main conclusions and provides future lines.

Within the context of this book, we delve extensively into the concept of *Cognitive Assistant*. A comprehensive exploration of this term is developed across several sections, each elaborating on distinct aspects. For a structured overview of these concepts, refer to the sections detailed in Table 1.2.

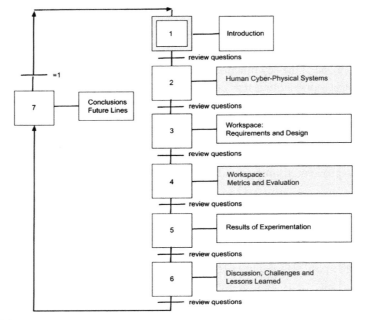

FIGURE 1.1

Reading guide recommendation.

Table 1.2 Cognitive Assistant concepts throughout the book.

Section	Concept
1.4.3	Cognitive Assistant Support
1.6.2	Cognitive Assistant Problem Statement
2.2	Cognitive Design Problem
4.3.4	Ontology for Cognitive Assistant
4.3.6	Cognitive Interaction
6.2.2	Cognitive Assistant as Recommender System
6.6	Conceptual Architecture of the Assistant System

1.7 Review questions

Chapters of the book are complemented by review questions and appendices to facilitate a didactic approach.

1. Identify part of the abilities of human operators in the form of a list of cognitive skills.
2. Define resilience in the context of Industry *5.0*.
3. Table 1.1 lists 12 disruptive technologies. Can you find an emerging technology that can be incorporated into this table?

4. Disruptive technologies need standardized documents for correct use by professionals. For instance, ISO/IEC 22989 (ISO Central Secretary, 2022b) covers AI concepts and terminology, and ISO/IEC 23053 (ISO Central Secretary, 2022a) describes a generic framework for using machine learning (ML) technology. Describe the main characteristics of these standards.

5. The ISO/IEC 30162 (ISO Central Secretary, 2022c) document specifies compatibility requirements and model for devices within industrial IoT systems. Describe the main characteristics of this standard.

6. What are the differences between industrial and nonindustrial AI solutions?

7. In view of the evolution of ChatGPT performance and efficiency: will it be effective and bring value when used to support operators and managers with generic activities?

8. Define human-centric smart manufacturing.

Human cyber-physical systems

2

Abstract

This chapter presents the synergy between socio-technical systems and joint cognitive systems, leading to the origin of Human-Centered Cyber-Physical System, an important component in the development of Industry *4.0*. In this environment, user assistance systems become increasingly necessary not as a tool but as a function that amplifies the capabilities of the operator in the work environment. From there the roles of humans in Human-Centered Cyber-Physical Systems are defined. The paradigm shift of doing to thinking has facilitated the emergence of cognition as a new perspective for intelligent systems. Among the different perspectives of cognition, in this book, we introduced the point of view of Joint Cognitive Systems (JCSs). The synergistic combination in the form of Artificial Internet of Things of different technologies such as Artificial Intelligence, (AI), the Internet of Things (IoT), and Multi-Agent System (MAS) allows the operator and the process to provide the necessary conditions to do their work effectively and efficiently. Hence the part of human cognition in the context of AIoT systems is discussed in more detail for the case of Human–Robot Interaction. For this purpose, the FRAM tool is presented, which allows the analysis of the performance of human–robot teams in industrial scenarios.

The continuous introduction of technology in the industrial environment is a main generator of changes in architectures, models, and work styles. Industry *4.0* signifies a great opportunity for operators to become a part of the new manufacturing systems (Lu, 2017). On the one hand, operators generate information and data, and on the other hand, they receive useful support for their work as well as effective cooperation with intelligent systems (Romero et al., 2016a). This bidirectional dialogue allows new types of powerful interactions between operators and machines. Hence a new kind of workforce should be trained to obtain a significant impact in industry (Ruppert et al., 2018).

The use of Artificial Intelligence, (AI) techniques to enhance the lifelong learning experience of humans has evolved in the literature from the early works on Intelligent Tutor Systems (Corbett et al., 1997), where AI is used as a tool to monitor and facilitate the user learning process, to the creation of Human–Computer Collaborative Learning (HCCL) systems (Dillenbourg and Baker, 1996), where AI entities become members of a group of mixed human and artificial learners. Through HCCL systems, humans acquire problem-solving or decision-making capabilities in a particular domain in simulated or real situations. Implementation of these systems in manufacturing pushes toward factories characterized by the symbiosis of human automation (Romero et al., 2015), where machines cooperate with humans, both parts having the opportunity to lead the cooperative task at hands.

The challenge motivating this chapter is to define a human-centered architecture to design, implement, and evaluate cognitive advisor agents in the framework of a Human Cyber-Physical Production System (HCPPS) (Romero et al., 2016a; Bunte et al., 2019), which supports the operator in Industry *4.0* to accomplish their job into an automation system (Rauch et al., 2020) in a more efficient and effective form.

2.1 Toward Human-Centered Cyber-Physical Systems

Industry *4.0* promises the fourth industrial revolution by integration of cyber and physical worlds through technology. Its implementation will result in human interactions with technical systems in a specialized manner. Therefore it will also be a socio (human-related) and technical (nonhuman-related) system in pursuit of a common goal (Sony and Naik, 2020). Socio-Technical Systems theory is concerned with the design of systems that contain both social and technical aspects that interact to pursue a common goal (Walker et al., 2008; Valette et al., 2023). The objective of a socio-technical system is to improve the relationship between the technology and the people involved in a defined project (Margherita and Braccini, 2021).

In the context of Socio-Technical Systems, the interactions between technology and human are mutual, as both of them influence each other (Baxter and Sommerville, 2010). Technology shapes human interactions, relations, and societies, and likewise technology is also shaped by social, economic, and political force (Reischauer, 2018). The rationale for adopting socio-technical approaches to systems design is that failure to do so can increase the risks that systems will not make their expected contribution to the goals of the organization. Systems often meet their technical "requirements" but are considered to be a "failure" because they do not deliver the expected support for the real work in the organization. The source of the problem is that techno-centric approaches to systems design do not properly consider the complex relationships between the organization (industry), the people (operators) enacting processes, and the system that supports these processes (machines). Industry *4.0* is predominant with technology such as connectivity and interaction technology such as smart products, smart machines, and smart operators. This causes a rethinking of relationships between human and machine. This interaction is a critical relationship, which will be governed by socio-technical transformation. As such, human-centric manufacturing systems need to have bidirectional empathy, proactive communication, and collaborative intelligence for establishing trustworthy human–machine coevolution relationships, thereby leading to high-performance human–machine teams (Lu et al., 2022b).

2.1.1 **Cyber-Physical Systems**

According to the US National Institute of Standards and Technology (NIST), Cyber-Physical Systems are intelligent systems, including interactive networks, designed of physical and computational components (Griffor et al., 2017). Cyber-Physical Systems (CPS) are one of the fundamental pillars in Industry *4.0* (Gorecky et al., 2014; Fletcher et al., 2019; Karnouskos et al., 2019). These systems integrate computing, communication, and control, known as the "3C" to provide real-time sensing, information feedback, dynamic control, and other services (Tao et al., 2019), including human interaction. The main drivers for the development and evolution of Cyber-Physical Systems are the reduction of development costs and time along with the enhancement of the designed products (Hehenberger et al., 2016). Conceived as components in the production system able of executing physical processes in cooperation with other entities, CPS allows systems to adapt independently to changing circumstances by learning from the additional information coming from the sensors (Bunte et al., 2019; Nguyen et al., 2022). As illustrative examples, 11 case studies of service innovations in manufacturing are investigated by Herterich et al. (2015) driven by digitalization and CPSs and their impact on the service ecosystem.

Usually, each component of the CPS autonomously takes the necessary control decisions related to the physical aspects of the underlying production system and communicates control decisions, system states, and behavior patterns (Hu et al., 2012; Villarreal-Lozano and Vijayan, 2020). Currently, the possibility to combine existing technologies such as Multi-Agent Systems (MASs), Service-Oriented Architectures (SOAs), Internet of things (IoT), cloud communication, augmented reality, big data, or Machine-to-Machine communication (M2M) (Weyer et al., 2015; Leitão et al., 2016) has empowered the features and functions of these systems so that levels of cognition in the cooperation beyond physical interaction can be also considered.

Cognitive Cyber-Physical Systems (C-CPSs) have gained significant attention due to the potential of such technologies to work robustly under complex scenes, which environmental conditions may vary, adapting to a comprehensive range of unforeseen changes, and exhibiting prospective behavior like predicting possible events based on cognitive capabilities that are able to sense, analyze, and act based on their analysis results (de Oliveira et al., 2019). As a consequence, there is now a greater demand for more effectively integrating, rather than eliminating, human cognitive capabilities in the loop of production related processes. Human integration in Cyber-Physical environments can already be digitally supported in various ways. However, incorporating human skills and tangible knowledge requires approaches and technological solutions that facilitate the engagement of personnel within technical systems in ways that take advantage or amplify their cognitive capabilities to achieve more effective Socio-Technical Systems (Emmanouilidis et al., 2019; Chacón, 2022).

In the approach with humans in the interaction, integration of HMI and ergonomics in cyber-physical productions system (CPPS) is needed (Stern and Becker, 2017; Garcia et al., 2019). Beyond these straightforward applications, new models of CPS have emerged focused on improving the capabilities of operators, such as cyber-physical human system (CPHS) (Madni and Sievers, 2018) and human cyber-physical production system (H-CPPS) (Romero et al., 2016a). CPHS is defined as "a class of socio-technical systems critical for security in which the interactions between the physical system and the cybernetic elements that control its operation are influenced by human agents". Our interest, however, focuses on H-CPPS, defined as "a work system that improves the capabilities of operators thanks to a dynamic interaction between humans and machines in the cyber and physical worlds through intelligent human–machine interfaces". The objectives for H-CPPS, rebranded as Human-Centered Cyber-Physical System (HCPS) latter in the literature, are achieved through the interactions between the physical system (or process) to be controlled, cybernetic elements (that is, communication links and software modules), and human agents that monitor and influence the functioning of the cyber-physical elements (Gely et al., 2020).

The result of the inclusion of disruptive Industry *4.0* technologies in the workspace has changed the role of the operator (Waschull et al., 2022). Fig. 2.1 shows the existence of a higher demand for the operator's cognitive skills as well as a lower demand for the operator's physical skills (Nardo et al., 2020).

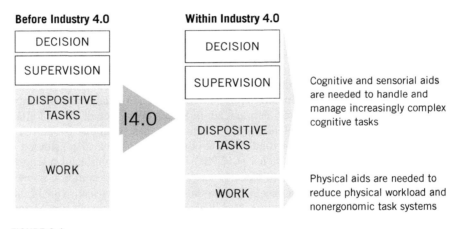

FIGURE 2.1

Change in the role of the operator in Industry *4.0*. Adapted from Rauch et al. (2020).

Moreover, the current development of technology allows us to deal at the level of cognition in Human-Centered Cyber-Physical Systems (HCPSs), as described in Fig. 2.2 (Krugh and Mears, 2018). Human centricity in Cyber-Physical System leads to reversing the pyramid of work intensity when designing new processes in smart manufacturing. More physical demanding lower levels require less time to be designed, as far as they are more standardized than higher cognitive levels where the interaction with soft skills of the operator are critical.

However, the understanding of cognition generates debates because it can be approached from several domains, mainly from psychology through mental models and from Cognitive Systems Engineering (CSE) to applications in practice. As far

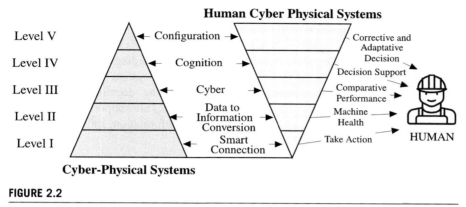

FIGURE 2.2

Levels in Cyber-Physical Systems (left) vs Human-Centered Cyber-Physical Systems (right).

as we are moving from digital manufacturing to a digital society in Industry *5.0*, a new mental modeling is required that can create value both for customers and enterprises (Skobelev and Borovik, 2017; Aslam et al., 2020). From our perspective, following the CSE approach in Jones et al. (2018), the right improvement is to treat human operators and automated systems not as autonomous agents but as team members in a Joint Cognitive System (JCS) (Hollnagel and Woods, 2005). A similar approach is also defended by Martín-Gómez et al. (2021), but the holonic proposal considers operators as CPS elements.

2.1.2 Human-Centered Cyber-Physical System as a Joint Cognitive System

A Joint Cognitive System (JCS) acknowledges that cognition emerges as goal-oriented interactions of people and artifacts to produce work in a specific context and at the level of the work being conducted (Kaasinen et al., 2022). It does not produce models of cognition, but models of coagency that corresponds to the required variety of performance and thereby emphasizes the functional aspects (Adriaensen et al., 2019). JCSs are characterized by three principles (Hollnagel and Woods, 2005):

1. goal-orientation,
2. control to minimize entropy (i.e., disorder in the system), and
3. coagency at the service of objectives.

In this situation, complexity emerges because neither goals, nor resources, nor constraints remain constant, creating dynamic couplings between artifacts, operators, and organizations. The Cognitive Systems Engineering (CSE) approach focuses on analyzing how people manage complexity, understanding how artifacts are used, and understanding how people and artifacts work together to create and organize Joint Cognitive System which constitutes a basic unit of analysis in CSE. Human and machine must be considered together, but different, rather than separate entities linked by human–machine interactions (Hollnagel and Woods, 2005).

In the domain of Cognitive Systems Engineering, the focus is on defining the mission that the Joint Cognitive System shall perform, avoiding ambiguities related to its human resemblances. As we can see in Fig. 2.3, this system performs cognitive work via *cognitive work functions* such as communicating, deciding, planning, and problem solving. These sorts of cognitive work functions are supported by *cognitive processes* such as perceiving, analyzing, exchanging information, and manipulating.

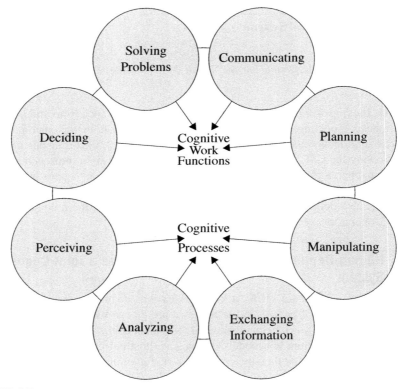

FIGURE 2.3

Cognitive work functions and cognitive processes in the domain of Cognitive Systems Engineering.

The importance of cognition, regardless of how it is defined, as a necessary part of the work has grown after the industrial revolution:

- Cognition is distributed rather than isolated in the human operator's mind.
- Operator does not passively accept technological artifacts or the original conditions of their work.

- Technological development is rampant; this entails the development of work with inevitably greater operational complexity.
- Technology is often used in ways that are not well adapted to the needs of the operator.

Pioneering work in the design of human–machine systems for process control and automation discussing the significance of Joint Cognitive Systems (JCS) paradigm in the design process can be found in Yurtseven et al. (2009). The discussion is presented within the framework of Cognitive Systems Engineering (CSE) in particular and in Socio-Technical System (STS) design framework in general. The discussion is focused on process control problems in process and manufacturing industries. The potential benefits offered by the JCS were also elaborated. However, it was discontinued until the CSE approach in Jones et al. (2018), employed also by Chacón et al. (2020a) and more recently by Bennett et al. (2023).

There is no turning back; the evolution of Information Technology, Digital Transformation and the Fourth Industrial Revolution requires that processes be more cognitive, automatic, and efficient. So one potential improvement is to treat human operators and automated systems not as autonomous agents but as team members in a Joint Cognitive System.

2.1.3 Human roles in a Human-Centered Cyber-Physical System

The dialogue between AIoT systems and the human must be modeled to allow AIoT systems to provide a human-oriented service. A starting point is the understanding of the role of humans in Human-Centered Cyber-Physical System (HCPS).

For the moment, the cyber and physical dimensions have been considered in our CPS-based approach. However, in a human-centered architecture, the roles of human, different to those of a CPS, in HCPS must be also defined. In the models of human–automation interaction, attention is paid to whether human assumes control of the system (Sheridan, 1992). In HCPS systems, however, human intervention is focused in more aspects: the dialogue with other agents, decision-making, and information supply. In this sense, one research line is about the definition of a human model as a part of the full HCPS model. However, human models defined as a transfer function lead to a poor approach. For instance, eight projections of enhancing operators are defined by Thorvald et al. (2021) according to technological augmentations: Super-Strength Operator empowered by exo-skeletons, Augmented Operator taking advantage of Augmented Reality, Healthy Operator making use of wearable devices, and so on. Some researchers expand this approach by developing analytic human models that reflect cognitive abilities in the interaction with cyber-physical systems (Madni and Sievers, 2018).

HCPS requires flexibility. An adaptive HCPS responds to unexpected or novel situations as replanning, setting new goals, learning from experience. Hence the definition of the roles of human (passive or active performer) are required. Using an academic approach, examples of human roles in HCPS are:

- Supervisor (human on the loop): approve CPS decisions; reallocate tasks between human and CPS.
- Controller (human in the loop, Operator *4.0*): interaction with sensors and actuators; use of augmented reality technology; collaborative task with a cobot.

Using a manufacturing approach, examples of human roles are:

- Production manager: skills in enterprise resource planning, optimization, maintenance, quality, and cyber-security;
- Production operator: skills for work with different robots and software application for robotics;
- Technicians: broad information technology skills to manage data generated by machines and interpret digital representations of physical machines;
- Engineers: expertise in Internet of Things communication protocols, electronics, and AI algorithms.

The status of the human operator must be studied in depth through systematic review, analysis of the job profiles that can be generated by new technologies and the human skills required so that the Operator *4.0* concept does not become just a conceptual label (Cunha et al., 2022).

Merging human roles with CPS roles to define the functional architecture of a HCPS leads our research to the design of a novel JCS model, its basic aim being to achieve a high level of successful performance managing the human cognitive load in the process.

2.2 Cognitive design problem

With the idea of designing Human-Centered Cyber-Physical Systems in mind, it is worth exploring the cognitive factor, which will be the core of the interaction between humans and AIoT systems (Angulo, 2022). This novel research area is currently explored, for instance, through the design of Intelligent Personal Assistants (IPAs) using Artificial Intelligence,. Hu et al. (2021) studied the interaction element is the core of the study. Mohamudally (2022) studied the emergence of collective intelligence from CPS units. However, an IoT Edge's vision is presented obviating humans in the interaction. Zolotová et al. (2018) referred the physical, sensing, and cognitive interaction in the Industry *4.0* concept and presented Human Cyber-Physical Production Systems in a laboratory environment based on the Operator *4.0* concept. This approach is in the line of human-centric smart factories (HSM), where cognition is in a similar level to physical interaction.

HSM is a human-centric system that takes advantage of cognitive science and personalized AI to construct a cognitive human–machine collaborative environment to achieve a high-level intelligence and super flexibility in the manufacturing process in Industry *5.0* (Zhang et al., 2023). In HSM, machines are mainly responsible for repetitive, boring, and high-risk work, and humans are more responsible for innovative work, thus realizing the personalized value of humans in this process and improving human's self-recognition and happiness. To know more about the HSM approach, the reader is invited to check Wang et al. (2020), Xifan et al. (2022), and Wang (2022).

2.2.1 Cognition in Human–Robot Collaboration

Since Human–Robot Collaboration is the main application in this book, let us introduce the cognitive factor in human–robot team working and in the assessment of human activities in the workspace. A comparison among several approaches introduced in recent published works is presented in Table 2.1. Columns show:

- the robotics *Approach* employed: Research, Social, and Industry;
- the interaction *Category* considered: Physical and Cognitive;
- the employed *Metrics*; and
- the main *Features* of the approach.

The column *Category* in Table 2.1 shows whether the interaction is Physical and/or Cognitive. When the Category's label for the interaction is Physical, the main concern is to establish a high level of safety in the use of collaborative robots. Hence, according to the ISO TS 15066 standard (ISO Central Secretary, 2016b), in Marvel (2013) the speed of the robot's terminal element is regulated, and the force exerted by the mechanical arm is limited. One step further, Bajcsy et al. (2017) considered that physical human interaction is not more a disturbance, but it is informative: it is useful information about how the robot should be doing its task. Concerning the human side, possible collisions between human and robot, as well as risk prevention of impact on various sensitive parts of the human body, are analyzed by Marvel et al. (2015).

The wide variety of scenarios, such as the type of terminal element used by the robot, the manipulation that the robot is performing on a part in a task, and the proximity of the human, makes very complicated to develop generic performance *metrics* (Marvel et al., 2019; Coronado et al., 2022). However, some of them exist. In the case of adding a collaborative robot in a manual workspace, the reduction of human physical fatigue should be measurable (Messeri et al., 2022). Some authors propose to establish a measure of the level of collaboration (Kolbeinsson et al., 2019). If the percentage of tasks performed by the robot in an H-R system increases, then the human workload decreases. In this form, physical stress and overuse during assembly tasks decreases, one of the main causes of musculoskeletal disorders of workers (Kuschan and Krüger, 2021).

When the *Category*'s label for the interaction is Cognitive, it is convenient to employ a measure of the performance of the automatic task planner: what tasks does the human do and what tasks are assigned to the robot (Lemaignan et al., 2017). For this kind of interaction, it is a key issue to enhance the perception of the environment. Using sensors, operators can be located, so other robots predict the human's intention to move, analyze the execution time of the human's tasks, and assess whether the robot can optimize subtasks initially assigned to the human. They can also identify

Table 2.1 A comparison among several Human–Robot Interaction metrics. Columns show the robotics approach, the interaction level, the employed metrics, and some particular features. Notations *H and R* mean human and robot (traded), whereas *H-R* means human and robot (shared).

Approach	Category	Metrics	Features
Research (Steinfeld et al., 2006)	Cognitive	H, R task effectiveness, Interaction effort, Situational awareness	Review and Classification of common metrics
Research (Marvel et al., 2019)	Physical and Cognitive	Human–robot teaming performance	Developing a metrology suite
Research (Bajcsy et al., 2017)	Physical	Subjective metrics in a 7-point Likert scale survey (seven heuristics)	Physical human interaction is modeled as informative and not as a disturbance
Research (Harriott et al., 2015)	Cognitive	Physiological, Task analysis	Model and comparison of H-H team, H-R team
Research (Hoffman, 2019)	Cognitive	Fluency	H-R teams research
Social (Di Nuovo et al., 2019)	Cognitive	System Usability Scale (SUS) questionnaire	Early detection neurological impairments like dementia
Social (Lemaignan et al., 2017)	Cognitive	Task effectiveness	H-R model with perception, knowledge, plan and action
Industry (Lasota et al., 2014)	Physical	Human localization, Latency, Performance	Prediction of future locations of H, R for safety
Industry (Kimble et al., 2020)	Physical	Completion task time	Robotic assembly systems
Industry (Marvel, 2013)	Physical	H-R distance, speed, performance; Time collision	Algorithm case studies, Standards ISO 13855, ISO TS 15066
Industry (Marvel et al., 2015)	Physical	H-R risk, Degree of collaboration, Task analysis	Assembly line with H-R shared tasks
Industry (Kolbeinsson et al., 2019)	Physical and Cognitive	Level of Collaboration; H, R fully controlled, cooperation	Holistic perspective in human–robot cooperation

human's working styles, the rhythm in which the human performs his/her tasks and changes in this rhythm. Hence the robot can suggest that operators change their working behaviors. For instance, the not so noticeable fatigue is mental fatigue (Muñoz-de Escalona et al., 2020; Blandino, 2023). Applying sensors for measuring heart rate, respiratory rate, for example, it is possible to collect data on the state of the human and recommend breaks (Lu et al., 2022a; Lin and Lukodono, 2022). All this sensory can become invasive, and traditionally questionnaires are employed when the task is finished to collect the subjective assessment of the operator. The NASA task load index (TLX) questionnaire measures mental load (Sotirios et al., 2023) and is suitable for assessing differences in cognitive load when the human is carrying out a main task and a secondary task is added (Steinfeld et al., 2006; Harriott et al., 2012). Other two possible questionnaires taking into consideration mental fatigue measurement are the subjective workload assessment technique (SWAT) defined by Reid and Nygren (1988) comprising scales assessing different workload components, i.e., time load, mental effort load, and psychological stress load; and the workload profile (WP) questionnaire defined by Tsang and Velazquez (1996) based on the multiple resources model in Wickens (1987).

The NASA-TLX questionnaire, considered in our study, comprises six combinations of relevant factors characterizing the subjective workload, as described by Hart and Staveland (1988):

1. mental demands: amount of mental and perceptual activity required,
2. physical demands: amount of physical activity required,
3. temporal demands: amount of pressure felt due to the rate at which the task elements occurred,
4. own performance: successful assessment in doing the task required and satisfaction assessment in accomplishing it,
5. effort: difficulty assessment in having to mentally and physically work to accomplish the level of performance, and
6. frustration: assessment of different feelings like insecure, discouraged, irritated, stressed and annoyed vs. secure, gratified, content, relaxed, and complacent during the task.

Thus an improved workspace setting should take into account the joint framework adopted by human, cognitive agent, and collaborative robot. In this context, we should distinguish two main roles for the human, *supervisor* and *operator*. In the case of a human with the role of supervisor, the cognitive agent assists her/him in deciding the best task planning. The cognitive robot can show the performance of the set of operators that work with collaborative robots and can provide guidelines for a better assignment of tasks to operators (Sparrow et al., 2022). Besides, for a human in the role of operator who works with the collaborative robot, the cognitive agent/robot can remind the operator about performance in previous days and can advise her/him on maintaining the working mode or changing to improve performance. In the case of new operators, the cognitive robot can provide feedback to enhance learning.

2.2.2 **The functional resonance analysis method**

As the automation of complex processes becomes more achievable, the need for engineering procedures that help decide what and how to automate becomes more important to the safety, flexibility, and performance of automation use. The implementation must satisfy general criteria such as (Wong and Seet, 2017; Hopko et al., 2022):

- minimizing workload,
- maximizing awareness of what is going on, and
- reducing the number of errors.

The basic problem therefore is reducing the cognitive demands of the tasks performed by the operators involved in the system while maintaining fully their ability to function within their given roles (Rauffet et al., 2015; Karakikes and Nathanael, 2023).

Adriaensen et al. (2022b) employed a socio-technical perspective to explore the potential of Joint Cognitive Systems to manage risk and safety in cobot applications, which can be extended to cognitive human–robot collaboration. Three systemic safety analysis approaches are presented for cobot applications:

- System-Theoretic Accident Model and Processes (STAMP) (Leveson, 2012);
- Functional Resonance Analysis Method (FRAM) (Hollnagel, 2017); and
- Event Analysis of Systemic Teamwork (EAST) (Stanton, 2018; Salmon et al., 2022).

The power of systemic methods for safer and more efficient cobot operations lies in revealing the distributed and emergent result from joint actions and overcoming the reductionist view from individual failures or single agent responsibilities. The safe operation of cobot applications can only be achieved through alignment of design, training, and operation of such applications (Adriaensen et al., 2022b).

Since the STAMP systemic analysis is too biased toward safety (Patriarca et al., 2022), the FRAM approach was selected by the authors over the novel EAST approach because the JCS perspective in developing the FRAM model allows understanding the effects of task and information propagation and eventual distributed criticalities, taking advantage of the functional properties of the system (Adriaensen et al., 2019). Hence FRAM has been also applied, for instance, to the risk assessment of organizational changes (Hollnagel, 2013) and extended to the use of Monte Carlo methods (Patriarca et al., 2017). However, as declared by Adriaensen et al. (2022b), with reference to cognitive agents, "to the best of our knowledge, Chacón et al. (2020a) and Jones et al. (2018) have been the only authors so far to propose a JCS perspective to design socio-technical systems for collaborative agents and CPS."

To understand the socio-technical system, the Functional Resonance Analysis Method (FRAM) is used, which allows us to have a model generated by the application itself. FRAM can be described as a method that is used to produce a model, and instead of a method derived from a model, this method is a way to interpret the phenomenon under study. The objective of FRAM is to build a model of how a set of activities is carried out in a given organization or workspace. It proposes that everyday events and activities can be described in terms of *functions* involved without predefined specific relations, levels, or structures, as we can see in Fig. 2.4. Instead, FRAM assumes that the behavior of functions, and hence the outcomes of an activity or process, can be understood in terms of four basic principles described in the following. Moreover, the nonpredefined functions can be characterized by means of six aspects named Input, Output, Preconditions, Resources, Control, and Time (Salehi et al., 2021b).

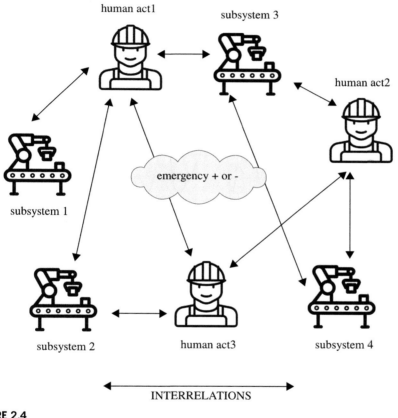

FIGURE 2.4

Success or failure emerges from the variability of system performance as a result of complex interactions and unexpected combinations of actions.

The principles of the Functional Resonance Analysis Method (FRAM) are:

1. The equivalence of successes and failures: acceptable and unacceptable outcomes are due to the ability of organizations, groups, and individuals successfully to adjust to expected and unexpected situations.

2. Approximate adjustments: things predominantly go well, but also they occasionally go wrong.
3. Emergent outcomes: the variability of two or more functions can be combined in unexpected ways that can lead to results unpredictable and disproportionate in magnitude, both negative and positive.
4. Functional resonance: The variability of one function may in this way come to affect the variability of other functions in analogy with the phenomenon of resonance (see Fig. 2.5).

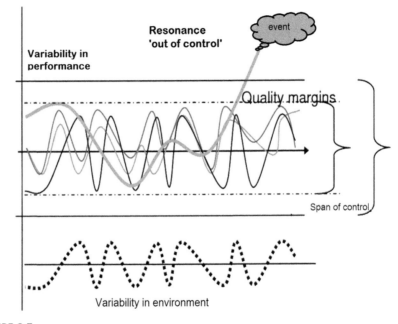

FIGURE 2.5

The resonance functional: Variability in one function propagates affecting variability of other functions.

In FRAM a function represents acts or activities – simple or composite – needed to produce a certain result. Examples of simple human functions are to triage a patient, to place a piece on a table, or to fill a glass with water. The organizational function of the emergency room in a hospital, for example, is to treat incoming patients (Sujan et al., 2023), whereas the function of a restaurant is to serve food. Finally, composite functions include, for instance, a flight's passenger management system (Havlíček et al., 2020).

In the description of functions an important differentiation can be made between tasks and activities, corresponding to the distinction between Work-as-Imagined (WAI) and Work-as-Done (WAD). A task describes work as designed or as imagined by managers. An activity describes work as it is actually performed or done. FRAM primarily focuses on activities as they are done or WAD but can of course also be used to model WAI (Tian and Caponecchia, 2020; De Nicola et al., 2023).

To basically illustrate the use of FRAM, a pick-and-place system showing human-robot team working is shown in Fig. 2.6. The task to be completed is filling boxes with cylinders. The cylinders supplier is in position "Warehouse" and the destination box in position "Box". FRAM should describe functions and their potential couplings for a typical situation, but not for a specific one. Hence it is not possible to certainly determine whether a function always will be performed before or after another function. It can only be determined when the model is instantiated. At the start, functions are identified in a first independent version from execution, as we can see in Fig. 2.7. Note in the lower element that "Pick cylinder" has as an Input having cylinders in stock, this production is under Control of the number of cylinders needed, and its Output is the Input for "Fill box". A similar analysis can be completed with the remaining FRAM activity/function representation.

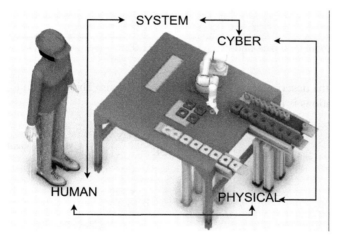

FIGURE 2.6

Example of a HCPS system: assembly task shared between human and robot.

The development of the model can continue in several ways – none of them being preferable over the others. One way is to look at the other functions in the same way and try to define as many of their aspects as seems reasonable and possible. Another way is to try to define aspects that are incompletely described in the current version of the model. The basis of FRAM is the description of the functions that make up an activity or a process. The functions of different tasks have been assigned depending on who does it, that is, human, cobot, and process, in the Human-Centered Cyber-Physical System (see Fig. 2.8). Relationships are neither specified nor described directly, and the FRAM Model Visualizer (FMV) in fact does not allow lines or connectors to be drawn between functions. Relationships are instead specified in-

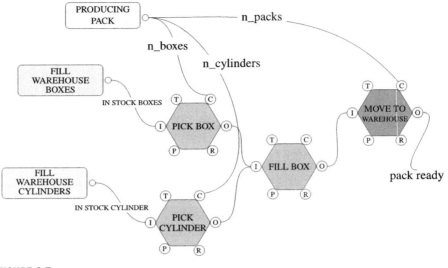

FIGURE 2.7

The FRAM model for a pick-and-place function (v1.0).

directly via the descriptions of the aspects of functions. The common technical term for such relations is *couplings*.

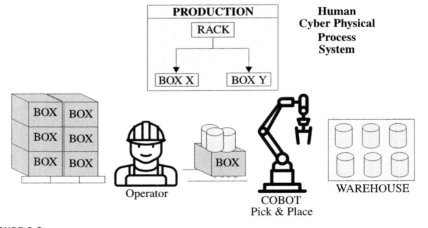

FIGURE 2.8

Example HCPPS system: product packaging.

Couplings described in a FRAM model through dependencies are called *potential couplings*. This is because a FRAM model describes the potential or possible relationships or dependencies between functions without referring to any particular situation.

In an instantiation of a FRAM model, only a subset of the potential couplings can be realized; these represent the *actual couplings* or dependencies that have occurred or are expected to occur in a particular situation or a particular scenario (Hollnagel, 2017).

Hence, basically, we can highlight the following useful features for our FRAM approach:

- Purpose: A FRAM analysis aims to identify how the system works (or should work) for everything to succeed (i.e., everyday performance) and to understand how the variability of functions alone or in combination may affect overall performance.
- Model: A FRAM model describes the system functions and the potential couplings among them. The model does not describe or depict an actual sequence of events, such as an accident or a future scenario.
- Instantiation: A precise scenario is the result of an instantiation of the model. The instantiation is a "map" about functions coupling, or how they may become coupled, under given – favorable or unfavorable – conditions.

The use of FRAM as a tool for the analysis of cognitive tasks would (will) allow us to understand about how JCS works, identify its critical points, the propagation of the relationships between functions, and understand the distributed cognition and coagency between the human and machine.

2.3 **Review questions**

1. The *International Federation of Robotics* has launched a series of positioning papers on robots, Artificial Intelligence, and automation. The report *Next generation skills* (IFR, 2020) establishes human manufacturing roles, new job profiles through automation, stakeholders, and government initiatives for next generation skills. Summarize the most important skills.
2. The *European Commission* shows the concept of Industry *5.0*: what this approach is focused on, how it will be achieved, and how it is already being implemented. Explain what Industry *5.0* is in features as planning digital transformation, industrial strategies and analyzing upskilling and reskilling of workers.
3. The *IoT European Large-Scale Pilots Programme* includes the innovation consortia that are collaborating to foster the deployment of Internet of Things (IoT) solutions in Europe through integration of advanced IoT technologies. Choose one project and briefly explain the technical details (smart living environments, autonomous vehicles, etc.).
4. Define what Cognitive Robotics is.
5. This chapter has linked the FRAM tool to the task of pick and place of products in automated systems. Another relevant task in the industrial context is the assembly of parts. In this task the human operator is relevant as she/he provides great

manual skills. Following the example presented in (Naeini and Nadeau, 2022), indicate the importance of the use of data gloves in the assembly task.

6. Read the cited paper and find out the soundness of the following statement: *FRAM should be applied as an assistive method in delivering recommendations and guidance for the safe design of systems involving human interaction with wearables and other components of an assembly system in the context of Industry 4.0.*

Workspace requirements and design

Abstract

This chapter introduces the first elements of the methodology used for design, implementation, and evaluation of workspaces where machines and humans coexist. In particular, requirements and practical modeling are presented. Moreover, methodology for the evaluation of the environment is also provided. A parallel study will be developed, with detailed findings in the next chapter, to experimentally evaluate the usability of the introduced methodology as a particular case. The developed research methodology is adapted from the User Centered Design approach. The Operator *4.0* is considered as the user on which the design is centered. This methodology promotes a framework developed in four steps divided into different sections in this chapter and the next one:

1. Understand and specify the *context of use*.
2. Specify the *user requirements*.
3. Produce the *design solutions* according to some metrics.
4. *Experimental evaluation* of the design solutions.

To understand the context of use and specification for the Operator *4.0*, the needs of the end user, around whom the design is centered, are taken into account. FRAM, Functional Resonance Analysis Methodology, is employed to complete this first step in the socio-technical system under consideration.

For industrial psychologists to analyze robot–human groups in the workspace only from a quantitative perspective is insufficient. Human relationships will be affected by robots in groups over a prolonged period if robots are present in a group. How will this affect trust within the organization? It may be that profitability increases initially but relationships within the group change as errors are perceived as becoming routine. The findings of investigations that emerge through human–robot collaboration may eventually become less fundamental. The rise of AI could lead to robots being viewed as social specialists. There is a risk that a group can become self-contained with "limited wisdom".

3.1 Introduction

Design, implementation, and evaluation of workspaces where machines and humans coexist, in the form of AIoT or any other kind of approach, needs the definition of a working methodology (Pizoń and Gola, 2023). From the early times starting approaches (De Santis et al., 2008), manufacturing companies are increasingly aware of these design needs (Hentout et al., 2019). Industry has started to heavily invest in "collaborative workspaces" where close interaction between humans and robots is present in the form of designed Human–Robot Collaboration (HRC) workspaces for humans and robots in industrial settings (Simões et al., 2022). One example of these efficient workspaces where both robots and human operators can work safely is the human–robot collaborative assembly workstation introduced by Bejarano et al. (2019), composed by the ABB YuMi robot that interacts with a human operation to assembly a product box as a part of a large-scale process. More recent publications refer also to more particular issues related to collaborative workspaces like to examining HRC acceptance in warehouses (Jacob et al., 2023) based on the Unified Theory of Acceptance and Use of Technology, or covering HRC in industrial settings achieved through robot learning strategies (Mukherjee et al., 2022).

For the case of the development of a user-centered methodology, the definition of the Operator *4.0* has been considered, understood as a smart, skilled operator who performs not only cooperative work with robots but also aided work by machines and if needed by means of human cyber-physical systems, advanced human–machine interaction technologies and adaptive automation toward achieving human–automation symbiosis work systems (Romero et al., 2016a). The different technologies associated with the Industry *4.0* create a novel work environment, which is much more technically qualified than in precedent situations. That means a more interesting working environment and greater autonomy and opportunities for self-development where the central element is the human (Kaasinen et al., 2020). Hence the focus of the research is moving toward the user, as the main executor of activities in the workspace.

The developed research methodology for the human–robot collaborative workspace is adapted from the User Centered Design approach (Pizzagalli et al., 2021; Prati et al., 2021). The Operator *4.0* is considered as the kind of user on which the design is centered (Longo et al., 2017). This methodology promotes a framework developed in four steps, as it can be observed in Fig. 3.1:

1. Understand and specify the context of use.
2. Specify the user requirements.
3. Produce design solutions.
4. Evaluate the design solutions.

By identifying needs of the Operator *4.0* using user centered design, it is possible to understand and specify the context of use. Next, through this understanding, it is possible to define a FRAM model considering the system as socio-technical and so specify the user (Operator *4.0*) and organizational requirements. A design is then produced for the Human–Robot Collaborative Workspace Experience, named HRCWE in Fig. 3.1, which can be simulated to work in the form of a digital twin (Malik and Bilberg, 2018; Pairet et al., 2019). Finally, the elaborated design is evaluated accord-

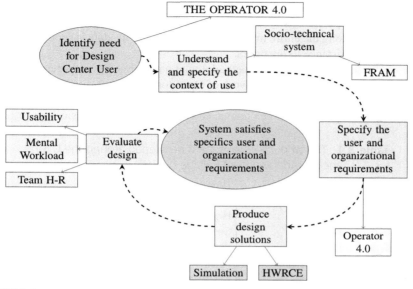

FIGURE 3.1

Proposed working methodology for the design, implementation, and evaluation of an AIoT-based workspace centered in the Operator *4.0.*

ing to some metrics and measures under consideration, in this case, usability, mental workload, and H-R teaming.

In this chapter, the two first elements of the methodology are defined, specifying the context of use and the user requirements. In the next chapter, a pilot study will experimentally evaluate the usability in a particular case: an operator is performing two tasks in a workspace. The objective in the study is determining how the mental workload of the operator is affected in the different situations that the operator is implied.

3.2 **Context of use**

The workspace can be considered as a set of working conditions, as shown in Table 3.1, and ergonomic principles and human factors, which can be considered as a space for improving the cognitive and physical abilities of the operator. The smart operator is collaborating with the machine, eventually a cobot, in a task with a high level of manipulation skills needed. A second level out of three of situational awarenesses is involved (Schömig and Metz, 2013), that is, a synthesis of disjointed elements through the processes of pattern recognition, interpretation, and evaluation. This level also requires integrating the information to understand how it will impact upon the goals. The speed considered in the working environment is very high. Decision making is performed by independent operators or work groups. Operator jobs are considered along the entire manufacturing tasks. Finally, data is supplied for real-time decision assistance to operators.

It will be necessary to develop methodologies and technologies to create a suitable working environment for efficient work of Operator *4.0*, which entails the concept of the workspace of the future (Gazzaneo et al., 2020). Section 3.3.1 shows in more detail the task allocation between human and robot in a shared physical space.

Table 3.1 The working environment developed around the Operator *4.0* concept. Adapted from Fallaha (2019).

Aspects	Description
Operator duty	Collaboration with the machine
Task complication	High
Situation awareness	Second level
Speed	Very high
Decision making dependency	Independent operators and work groups
Operator jobs	Entire manufacturing
Data supply	Real-time decision assistance to operators

For the development of the research, the Human-centered Cyber-Physical System (HCPS) has been identified as the unit of analysis (Hollnagel and Woods, 2005; Romero et al., 2016a) in a common framework. To develop our approach and work on the research questions, this HCPS is implemented, through a pilot trial, in the form of a case study named as Human–Robot Collaborative Workspace Experience (HRCWE).

To understand the context of use, the HCPS-based workspace has been conceptualized as a socio-technical system. The modeling is performed through the FRAM tool. Next, a first validation of the model through simulation and statistical assessment is performed. The study focuses on *work variability*, since it is a factor for unsafe work and errors. The next step is the implementation of the prototype in a laboratory and the design of experiments in the form of HRCWE, to collect data associated with the human part, such as usability, then the data of the machine through metrics, and teamwork data. These measurements enable understanding and evaluating performance from the perspective of the human–machine work team or, more specifically, in the experiment, the human–robot team.

3.3 **Workspace design**

The standard ISO10218-1:2011 (ISO Central Secretary, 2018b) defines the controlled space as one of the relevant aspects in the startup of an industrial robot. In this standard, within the controlled space, the *maximum space*, that is, the space swept by the movement of the robot with end effector and workpiece, coexists with the *restricted space*, defined as a subset of the maximum space, which can be the maximum space, and can be obtained by limiting the path of some robot joints (Mihelj et al., 2019).

This standard defines the concept of workspace associated with the idea of maximum and restricted space, together with the possibility that both robot and human can perform tasks simultaneously in the so-called cooperative workspace. The adjective cooperative is relevant, since industrial manufacturers prefer to call their new robots "collaborative" but do not call them "cooperative robots" (Yamaguchi and Inaba, 2023). Thus, according to the aforementioned regulation, the work that can be carried out by both humans and robots is called collaborative work.

3.3.1 Human–robot task allocation and use of the space

A collaborative robot manufacturer follows the indications of the current regulations and therefore reinforces in the user's manual the risk assessment, the intended use of the robot, and the nonpermitted use. In the opinion of the authors, the list of tasks for which the collaborative robot is designed can be added to the manual (assembly, quality inspection, welding, material inspection, material handling, machine tending, among others) together with a recommendation of the task and the task assignment to the human or robot based on skills, experience, complexity, and risk. If the robot is to work with the human, then it is necessary to know the degree of cooperation that the robot will provide for each of the mentioned tasks depending on the user's profile (Müller et al., 2017; Liau and Ryu, 2020).

So, first of all, once the robot is installed collaboratively and reviewed the maximum space and possible limitation of movement with respect to the total volume possible, the workspace should be designed. For this purpose, several possibilities are considered. The space provided for working is either single-use or fragmented into different areas, and these fragments can be combined for different uses. To go into detail, as a specific case, let us suppose that the space is fragmented into three parts (see Fig. 3.2):

1. Restricted space: this is a space for the tasks to be performed by the robot.
2. Transit space: the robot and human use this space for secondary tasks, but not at the same time.
3. Cooperative space: the robot and human can perform tasks simultaneously.

By observing Fig. 3.2, in Space 1 (restricted) the main concept is production throughput, the task is 100% automated, and the robot speed is high. In Space 2 (transit) the relevant concept is the input of raw material by the operator to the station, or product output: the robot deposits the finished product coming from Space 1. In Space 3 (cooperative) the robot and human can perform a task together, so the robot speed is reduced, manual guidance of the robot is feasible, it is necessary to limit the force exerted by the force exerted by the mechanical arm, and a monitored stop (ISO Central Secretary, 2018b) must be performed if necessary.

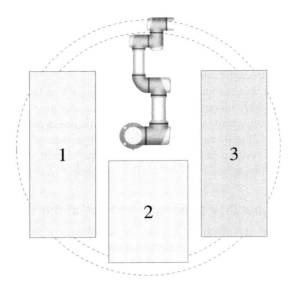

FIGURE 3.2

Space design with (1) restricted space for the robot, (2) transit space for shared asynchronous collaboration, and (3) shared simultaneous collaborative space.

The configuration shown in Fig. 3.2 is a particular case of a broader problem, the flexibility of space use (Ranz et al., 2018). Thus by defining the operational modes (automatic, semiautomatic, collaborative, manual) a generic redistribution of space use can be realized, as shown in Table 3.2.

Table 3.2 Operational modes and space use. AUT, SEM, and COL stand for Automatic, Semiautomatic, and Collaborative, respectively.

Mode	Space use	Description
AUT	Spaces 1 and 3 for robotic tasks.	Automatic station
	Space 2 as stock of raw material; product delivery.	
SEM	Space 1 for automated robotic task.	Semiautomatic station
	Space 3 for robot collaborative task.	
	Space 2 as stock of raw material; product delivery.	
COL	Spaces 1, 2, and 3 for collaborative tasks.	Collaborative station
	The operator can add raw material and withdraw product in any of the following spaces.	
Manual 0	Spaces 1, 2, and 3 for quality control, maintenance, and startup.	Maintenance station

Beyond the particular case of a specific robotic application, where the type of the end effector and application must be addressed, the operator must recognize the mode of operation of the station incorporating a collaborative robot and the segmentation of the use of space helps in this recognition. The manufacturers of collaborative robots indicate in the user manuals the robot work envelope and numerical indications of time and stopping distance, but it would be advisable to include in that robot work envelope aspects of anthropometrics and human reach (horizontal, vertical) related to the dimensions of the robot.

3.3.2 **Layout**

In the previous aspects of the startup of a robotized station, it should be also taken into account the conditioning of the workspace, the type of drive (electric, pneumatic), the possibilities of input and output connections, etc.

As a whole, the design of the station entails making it easier for the operator to perform various types of tasks, and hence the access comfortable to each of the devices is one of the criteria followed for the design. In an early design, Fig. 3.3 shows the arrangement of some of these devices. The robotic equipment consists of a mechanical arm, the cabinet control, and the programming console arranged in two levels. On the table, there is a beacon for the display of the station status, along with a strip to facilitate the connection of the end effector, sensors, and other actuators to the cabinet control, on the lower floor of the table. The table shown is fixed, but wheels can be added for transport, if necessary.

FIGURE 3.3

Station design for a cobot.

The station is complemented by an industrial control panel and an emergency stop button for generic stop of the station, which is complemented by the emergency stop of the robot arranged in the programming console. As a whole, the functionality allows the input of operator commands (buttons, selectors, touch screen), the programming of robotized tasks, and the reception of information through the console screen programming and beacon.

The space near the mechanical arm has been empty to facilitate the use of the space explained in the previous subsection. The arrangement of the robot implies that it can complete, optionally, on the back, a table with a desktop computer. The station is self-sufficient, adding a computer table can facilitate access and remote control tasks in a didactic environment of a teaching laboratory.

3.3.3 Industrial control panel

The design of the control panel takes into account the next vertical functionality: startup (station power supply) and modes of functioning. Fig. 3.4 also shows details with a horizontal layout: a display top with lights and a lower control part with selectors and buttons.

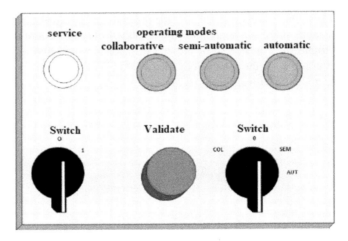

FIGURE 3.4

Industrial control panel design.

In industrial automation, a mode selector manual / automatic is very usual. In collaborative robotics, the operator can cooperate with the robot (COL tag, SEM tag), so the terminology is different from the usual one. Once the operator has selected the operational mode of work, he/she validates it by pressing a button (Validate label). This identification of the operational mode has its impact to know at all times the behavior of the season. Since there may be various types of robotic and automated stations in an industrial environment, it is desirable for the operator to easily recognize such behavior.

For both undergraduate engineering students and novel plant operators who have the first contact with new technologies, it is important to facilitate the understanding and recognition of functionalities. Managing the transition from one operational mode to another allows the operator to adapt her/his learning pace to the incorporation of new robots in a workspace initially not automated. Another important purpose for the use of operational modes on the control panel is that they contribute as digital input signals to the programming of the robot. Therefore the panel adds flexibility in the programming of robotic tasks, as will be discussed in a further section (Palmiter and Elkerton, 1987).

3.3.4 Beacon

The beacon endowed in the robotized station can provide additional information. A first proposal is a vertical beacon with four lights providing the information presented in Table 3.3: green color for normal behavior, orange light for asking for operator's attention, red light for shutdown, and blue color lighting as an indicator of remote robot control activated. It is defined in ISO Central Secretary (2018c) remote access with manual interventions for robot diagnostics. The connectivity of the robotic equipment to a LAN or wireless network is provided by the manufacturer, and the following aspects must be considered:

- the operator must set the selector switch on the right in Fig. 3.4 to "mode 0" and validate the selection;
- the operator must activate the remote mode on the robot programming console interface;
- A visual indicator is also activated on that screen;
- The beacon indicates the remote status by activating the blue light;
- The local operator must be synchronized with the remote operator to monitor tasks and minimize hazards to people and equipment.

The end of the remote task requires the operator to restore local access to the station. Local access to the station is reestablished by disabling that option in the robot's programming console. Thus technological advances in remote access to equipment

Table 3.3 Design and use of the beacon.

Beacon color		State of the station
Green (gray in print version)		Normal behavior.
Orange (light gray in print version)		Alarm (warning of robot finishing automatic task).
Red (mid gray in print version)		Device failure. Requires shutdown of the station.
Blue (dark gray in print version)		Remote robot control has been activated.

and machines, involve, in the case of collaborative robotics, the definition of two user profiles, the local and remote operators. The role of the local operator is well defined as illustrated in this subsection and in the following one, whereas the role of the remote operator should be analyzed using cognitive traversal techniques to clearly elicit the possible useful tasks and associated mental workload for the remote operator (Zimmer et al., 2022).

3.3.5 Programming

This subsection describes the generic structure of a robot program taking into account that the operator's decisions are transmitted in the form of actions on the control panels and as logic inputs in the code. The structure of the program coded according to functionality makes it possible to bound the behavior of the robot. For instance, the operator must adjust the reduction / increase of speed and the use of force control according to the operational mode. A generic code structure template allows us to initiate the plant operator / engineering student training in the use of collaborative robots, as we can see in the example in Fig. 3.5.

The template is consistent with the task assignment and operational mode. Modeling this code favors for easy scalability toward a structured design that allows us to upgrade the performance of the robot. The template is intended for use by the local operator. In turn, if remote access is necessary, then the remote operator must understand the context in which this programming has been performed, so the template is a meeting point between operators who may have different approaches to task programming, but who must understand how to correctly diagnose problems with the use of the robot.

3.4 Designing solutions in AIoT environments

We will consider along this book the premise that, from the concept of Industry *4.0*, the operation of a process or a processing plant requires the participation of an operator (Hollnagel, 2012). The objective is therefore to analyze the social construction of robots as coworkers in collaborative work environments to better understand how the distribution of tasks and the organization of work will be affected by the introduction of this new form of robotics. The characteristics of the workspace to be implemented, related to operator skills, tasks, and management of abnormal situations, are shown in Table 3.4. It can be observed that we are considering novice or low-skill operators, in the sense that they were not specifically trained for the dedicated job. Moreover, it is supposed that no training is performed, and experience is gained through job development. Tasks to be considered are related to keep the production going in a high-frequency high-repetitive line, that is, an easy production line, where abnormal situations are easily detected with a fast and easy recovering procedure. Working conditions are not challenging operators, no complex interac-

----

Before start

//sequence that is started before executing the main program
(values, variables, I/O status, counter, etc.)

Robot Program

if Startup = 1

if switch = aut and validate = 1   // human operator selects automatic mode and validate

if sensor = 1   // emulation of activation of the
signal of a sensor
elseif switch = sem and validate =1   // human operators select semiautomatic mode and validate

call subprogram_sem

elseif switch = col and validate=1   // human operators select collaborative mode

call subprogram_col

elseif switch = 0 and validate=1   // human operators select manual
mode and validate
// Robot stopping

else
// Sequential program (For instance: pop-up
message to the human operator)

Program_name_auto   // Subprogram inside the robot program
// Subprogram sequence for automatic task in spaces 1,3

Program_name_sem   // Subprogram inside the robot program
// Subprogram sequence for automatic task in spaces 1
// Subprogram sequence for collaborative task in spaces 3

Program_name_col   // Subprogram inside the robot program
// Subprogram sequence for collaborative task in spaces 1,2,3

FIGURE 3.5

Robot program template.

tions or dynamics are considered, the goal state is fully specified, but time pressure
is high. Summing up, this is a workplace requiring limited operator skills inside a
high-frequency production line.

Table 3.4 Organization of work in the workspace.

Operator qualification and training	
Level of education	Low (no dedicated job training)
Training contents	Brief introduction to the machines and tasks
On-the-job training	Often the only source of training
Conditions for learning	Poor (few permanent jobs)
Routine task characteristics	
Content	Keeping production going, meeting specifications, quality control, dealing with faults
Specificity of interventions	Qualitative, few instrumental measurements
Human–automation task sharing	Operators provide the preconditions and collaborate with assembly
Frequency of interventions	High
Repetitiveness	High
Types of control	Production control, compensatory control, corrective control
Monitoring	Vigilance and scanning, need for mental models, perceiving effects of process in products, reacting to alarms
Dealing with abnormal situations	
Detecting	Easy
Dealing with faults	Compensatory control (stopping, restarting), often just removing symptoms, procedural knowledge gained from experience
Challenges for operators	
Understanding the process	Basic
Complex interactions	No complex system dynamics but limited understanding of interconnections between machines, product properties, and environment
Goal state	Fully specified, clear hierarchy of constraint
Time pressure	High

3.4.1 Value-sensitive design

Future production workspaces will be augmented with multiple types of worker assistance systems that will combine technologies such as collaborative robotics, voice interaction, augmented reality, and more, thus giving rise to digital assistants (Wang et al., 2021; Longo et al., 2020). In part, this drive toward these new types of symbiotic technologies is a consequence of increased needs in manufacturing industries, with a consequent increased need for production workers. However, like all technologies, these systems also embody human values (Gazzaneo et al., 2020). More specifically, the design decisions made in the engineering of HCPSs imply a series of human values, even if they are not explicit (Terziyan et al., 2018). The philosophy of technology has long held that technologies are neither value-neutral, nor purely instrumental, nor purely deterministic (Miller, 2021). The Value-Sensitive Design (VSD) approach (Vernim et al., 2022; Gazzaneo et al., 2020) is a principled framework to illustrate how technologies enabling human–machine symbiosis in the Factory of the Future can be designed to embody elicited human values (Longo et al., 2020). The question is how to align humans, technology, and organization to ensure human well-being and system performance in industrial work systems in the transition to Industry *4.0*? For this research purpose, VSD identifiers are shown in Table 3.5.

Values under consideration are:

- Accessibility: making all workers successful users of technology. For instance, accessibility to the AR/VR headsets used by the Operator *4.0* (Gazzotti et al., 2021; Eswaran and Bahubalendruni, 2022; Álvaro Segura et al., 2020).
- Conformity: supporting workers to respect rules and expectations, thus demonstrating social discipline and loyalty (Cialdini and Goldstein, 2004). At the same time, it will restrict one's actions and / or conditioning one's choice, inclinations, impulses, and desires.
- Human Welfare: ensuring workers' health thanks to a proper work-life balance, a balanced workload, and a comfortable and pleasant work environment (Wilcock, 1998).

Table 3.5 Values from VSD for Human–Robot Collaborative Workspace Experience.

Value	Definition
ACCESSIBILITY	Making all workers successful users of technology.
CONFORMITY	Supporting workers to respect rules and expectations, thus demonstrating social discipline and loyalty.
HUMAN WELFARE	Ensuring workers' health: physical well-being and peaceful psychological state.

To support the development of human values, Fig. 3.6, Fig. 3.7, and Fig. 3.8 propose a set of specifications in accordance with the standard established for the corresponding value. The Accessibility, Conformity, and Human Welfare values lead to the list of technical specifications (right columns of Fig. 3.6, Fig. 3.7, and Fig. 3.8). This book will show in detail, in later chapters, the specifications: human–cobot task allocation and assistance to reduce mental workload.

3.4.2 Variability analysis using FRAM

The natural variability of human behavior during plan execution poses a difficult challenge for human–robot teams (Harriott et al., 2015). Some researchers use the Theory of Mind (ToM) or the ability to infer beliefs, desires, and intentions of others (Hiatt et al., 2011) to analyze how this variability affects the human–robot collaboration. The previously introduced Functional Resonance Analysis Method (FRAM) allows modeling complex socio-technical systems by collecting data from real / simulated work practices. It provides a tool to describe system outcomes using the idea of reso-

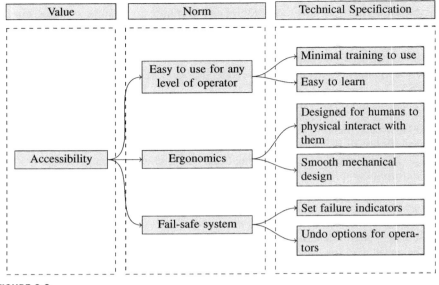

FIGURE 3.6

Accessibility refers to making all workers successful users of technology.

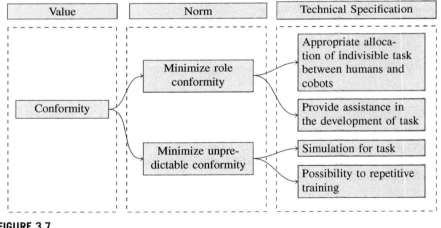

FIGURE 3.7

Conformity is a value supporting the workers to respect rules and expectations.

nance arising from the *variability* of everyday performance (Salehi et al., 2021a). By understanding sources of human variability using FRAM it is possible to design cognitive assistant robots with the aim to balance this variability (Chacón et al., 2020b; Chacón, 2022).

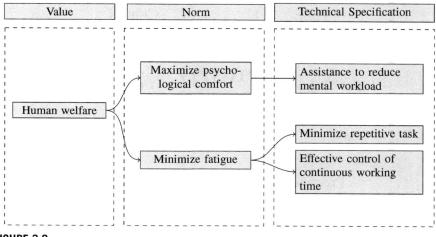

FIGURE 3.8

Human welfare refers to ensure workers' health through a balanced workload and proper environment.

In the context of human–robot interactive systems, the application of FRAM when modeling H-R tasks to get task allocation / configuration between human operator and robot allows us in a straightforward form to evaluate variability as a performance measure (Adriaensen et al., 2022a). Whit this aim in mind, some analysis steps are necessary:

1. Identify and describe system activities into a task and characterize each one using six basic characteristics (*aspects*): *Resource, Precondition, Input, Time, Control, Output*. See Fig. 3.9 and Table 3.6.
2. Check the completeness / consistency of the model. In this point, a discussion about the work of human–robot teams is required.
3. Characterize the potential variability of the activities in the FRAM human–robot model.
4. Define useful variability metrics.
5. Identify an effective task allocation / configuration between human and robots.

The variability of an activity output is revealed by the variability occurred in its outputs and is referred to the deviation of one or several of the following dimensions such as timing, duration, magnitude, object, and so on, with respect to an expected value. Thus the variability occurred in the upstream functions affects the performance of the downstream function. The subsequent propagation of the variability in the system may lead to a nonlinear effect called *resonance* generating unexpected/uncontrolled consequences. However, the impact of such variability over the system cannot be determined by observing the variability of the upstream function output only. In fact, it also depends on the variability acceptance capacity of the function receiving

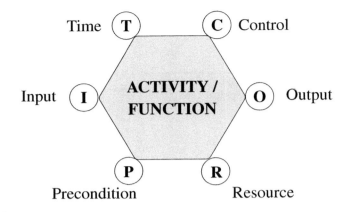

FIGURE 3.9

FRAM activity / function representation (Hollnagel, 2012) to graphically represent instances in a FRAM study.

Table 3.6 Aspects related to an `<ACTIVITY>`.

Aspects	Description
Input (I)	It activates the activity and/or is used or transformed to produce the Output. Constitutes the link to upstream activities.
Output (O)	It is the result of the activity. Constitutes the link to downstream activities.
Precondition (P)	Conditions to be fulfilled before the activity can be performed.
Resource (R)	Components needed or consumed by the activity when it is active.
Control (C)	Supervises or regulates the activity so that it derives the desired Output.
Time (T)	Temporal aspects that affect how the activity is carried out.

inputs (downstream). Thus the functional resonance effect is triggered by the output variability of the upstream function exceeding the variability dumping capacity of the downstream function (Bellini et al., 2020).

All the elements have been now defined: human and robotics activities will be modeled using FRAM, because this methodology allows the evaluation of the variability in quantitative measures. Modeling configures a task in several activities, which will be simulated using FlexSim (Gelenbe and Guennouni, 1991), RoboDK (Garbev and Atanassov, 2020), and UR robot simulator URSim (Kebria et al., 2016) and executed to get information about this variability in the measure. According to the obtained performance, feedback is provided to improve human skills and robot behavior. Eventually, this feedback will generate new interaction models for the task. In the next section, all these elements will be implemented in the form of a manual assembly task, and results obtained from the executed simulation will be analyzed.

3.5 Environment modeling and simulation

This section provides a precise description of the experimental setup in the form of collaborative manual assembly: metrics under consideration, mainly variability depending on user preferences and selected process strategies, impacting on product / process quality; modeling of the task, using the FRAM method, in the form of activities; obtained results in a simulated environment; and their interpretation and experimental conclusions drawn from the simulated experiences of the manual assembly task. For easiness of the discussion, FRAM principles of failures and emergence are out of the scope in this chapter.

3.5.1 Experimental setup: a manual assembly task

The production process to be automated is an assembly system for a turning mechanism, which is part of the whole production system. In Fig. 3.10 the components of the assembly task are shown in a simulated layout. On the left, there are warehouses dispatched for three types of components: base, bearing, and cap. Some automated system feeds the stocking places where either robot or human is picking the parts. Next, going to the right, there is the shared workspace where the different elements are assembled. Finally, on the right, the product is stored in a stock, usually by the robot.

The product to be assembled, as we can see in Fig. 3.11, requires three parts: a *base* (blue part, dark grey in print version), on which a *bearing* (round red part, grey in print version) is placed, and finally the assembly is sealed with a *cap* (green part, light grey in print version). As an initial stage, it is assumed that the raw material

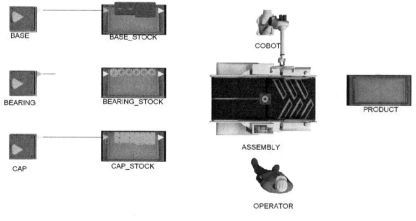

FIGURE 3.10

Simulated layout of an assembly task.

is always available on stock. The workstation process is described as follows (Work as Imagined, WAI (Hollnagel, 2012)):

1. It is verified that there is a base, a bearing, and a cap from the stock to start the assembly.
2. Get a base from the stock, get the bearing, and preassemble on the base.
3. Get the cover and assemble the product.
4. Take the assembly and store it in a stock.

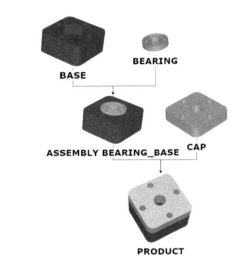

FIGURE 3.11

Product to be produced in the assembly line is a Turning mechanism. The assembly steps are indicated.

This process of assembly will continue until completing the production order or until the end of the work shift. Input and output stocks can be in either the same or different location.

3.5.2 Activities modeling for the manual assembly task

The goal of the FRAM model is the allocation of functions needed to perform product assembly and assigning functions to the operator or robot within the workspace in a collaborative human–robot environment. For the modeling, first, a basic model of the necessary functions of the process is created, without considering who performs the function. Three possible scenarios are established for the execution:

- Scenario 1. Fully manual task.
- Scenario 2. Fully automated task with a robot (a cobot by default).
- Scenario 3. The process is executed in a collaborative manner, human–robot shared task.

The FRAM methodology (Nemeth, 2013) is followed for modeling the activities in the manual assembly task, based on the four steps describe above.

3.5.2.1 Scenario 1. Fully manual task

In this scenario the functions are executed only by a single operator, within the work shift, who performs assemblies according to the production orders that arrive at the workstation. For the execution of the activities, a new function is added to the basic model, called <OPERATORS>, which oversights the resource operator, as shown in Table 3.7.

Table 3.7 Function <OPERATORS>. Description, Type, and Aspects.

Name of Function	<OPERATORS>
Description	Oversight resource operator
Function Type	Human
Aspect	**Description of Aspect**
Input	Assembly process
Output	OPERATOR
Control	Work permit

According to the FRAM methodology, the functions executed by the operator are of "Human" type. Therefore the Function Type characteristic, initially labeled as "Not described initially", now changes according to the options shown in Table 3.8. Hence all the seven functions are declared as "Human".

Table 3.8 Function Type defined as "Human" for all the activities in the manual assembly task (Scenario 1).

Function	Function Type
<ASSEMBLY PRODUCT>	Human
<ASSEMBLY BEARING_BASE>	Human
<GET BASE>	Human
<GET BEARING>	Human
<GET CAP>	Human
<OPERATORS>	Human
<CHECK PRODUCT>	Human

3.5.2.2 Scenario 2. Fully automated task with a robot

In this scenario, functions are executed by a single robot, within the work shift, which performs the amount of assemblies possible according to the production orders. For the execution, the function called <OPERATORS> is redefined in Scenario 2 as shown in Table 3.9.

Table 3.9 Function `<OPERATORS>`. Description, Type, and Aspects.

Name of Function	`<OPERATORS>`
Description	Oversight resource operator
Function Type	Human
Aspect	**Description of Aspect**
Input	Assembly process
Output	ROBOT
Control	Work permit

Now the functions executed by the robot are of "Technological" type, and the "Function Type" characteristic changes according to those shown in Table 3.10. In this case, all the functions are declared Function Type "Technological", except `<OPERATORS>`, which is always "Human".

Table 3.10 Function Type defined as "Technological" for most of the activities in the Scenario 2.

Function	Function Type
`<ASSEMBLY PRODUCT>`	Technological
`<ASSEMBLY BEARING_BASE>`	Technological
`<GET BASE>`	Technological
`<GET BEARING>`	Technological
`<GET CAP>`	Technological
`<OPERATORS>`	Human
`<CHECK PRODUCT>`	Technological

3.5.2.3 Scenario 3. The process is executed in a collaborative manner, Human–Robot shared task

In this scenario the functions will be executed collaboratively by either an operator or a robot, within the work shift, performing assemblies according to the production orders. For the execution, the function `<OPERATORS>` is in charge of changing the type of function within the model according to the strategy established by a human agent or by a technological agent. As a result, now the functions executed by the robot are of "Technological" type, and the functions executed by the operator are of "Human" type. The characteristic changes according to those are shown in Table 3.11.

The choice between "Technological" and "Human" for this scenario has been determined to mix both types for `<ASSEMBLY XX>` functions and `<GET XX>` functions for illustrative purposes. It has been assumed that the base-bearing assembly is a delicate one from a decorative perspective. Hence introducing dexterous human abilities will improve final quality of the product from a decorative / customer perspective that the robot is not able to perform always with the current sensor setting or programming.

Table 3.11 Function Type defined as "Human" or "Technological" depending on the activities to be performed in Scenario 3.

Function	Function Type
`<ASSEMBLY PRODUCT>`	Technological
`<ASSEMBLY BEARING_BASE>`	Human
`<GET BASE>`	Human
`<GET BEARING>`	Human
`<GET CAP>`	Technological
`<OPERATORS>`	Human
`<CHECK PRODUCT>`	Technological

3.5.3 Identifying variability

For the identification of the variability, the type of the function defined in the model is considered. The objective of the study is to determine the variability according to the type of an agent used to perform the functions. Based on the FRAM methodology, to check the variability of the performance of the output of the functions, the characteristics *Time* and *Quality* are selected.

The measurement of the output characteristics will be performed through the "Time to Task" and "High-Quality Product Percentage" KPIs (Sauro and Lewis, 2010), as we can see in Table 3.12.

Table 3.12 KPI quantitative variables definition.

Characteristic	KPI	Description
Time	Time to Task	Time to complete a product (total assembly)
Quality	High Quality Product Percentage	Ratio of high-quality products to total production expressed as a percentage

Based on the definitions, Eqs. (3.1) and (3.2) show how they are calculated:

$$\text{Time to Task} = \sum_{i=1}^{5} T_{A_i} \tag{3.1}$$

with T_{A_i} being the time to complete activities A_i: `<GET BASE>`, `<GET BEARING>`, `<ASSEMBLY BEARING_BASE>`, `<GET CAP>`, and `<ASSEMBLY PRODUCT>` for $i = 1, \dots, 5$, respectively, and

$$\text{High Quality Product Percentage} = \frac{N_{High\,Q\,Product}}{N_{Total\,Products}} \cdot 100 \tag{3.2}$$

with $N_{HighQProduct}$ being the quantity of products exceeding standard quality and $N_{TotalProducts}$ being the total quantity of completed products. There is usually a collaboration between human and robot skills, allowing the production of high-quality products, which would impossible to obtain with only humans or only robotics processes.

However, this improvement in quality standards because of the collaboration between humans and robots has a cost. As a general concept, for each planned scenario, the characteristics of the operator are considered as sources of *Time* variability. Conversely, *Quality* of the final product will vary and be reduced when robots are integrated into the process (Evjemo et al., 2020). All the products have, at least, Standard quality, but most of them are of High quality in some sense for the customer, not affecting functioning but, for instance, addressing decorative issues. For example, the parts for the assembly arrive at the process without any orientation, the process assembles its products with high efficacy and typical quality, but if the operator aligns them by changing their orientation, then the customer perceives a better quality of the product. This alignment is an easy task of decision for the human operator, whereas for the robot, it would require the use of extra sensors, for example, artificial vision and program code, which could be unavailable or too costly.

3.5.4 Variability in the Human–Robot Collaborative Workspace Experience

For the case under study, variability in Time and Quality due to the presence of humans and robots in teamwork, the same three scenarios defined for general assembly tasks are established:

- Scenario 1. Fully manual task.
- Scenario 2. Fully automated task with a robot (a cobot by default).
- Scenario 3. The process is executed in a collaborative manner, human–robot shared task.

3.5.4.1 Scenario 1. Fully manual task

In this scenario the variability is considered to depend on the type of operator performing the process, defined as *Expert*, *Standard*, or *Novice*. Based on the FRAM methodology, Table 3.13 and Table 3.14 show the characteristics considered for the study. Operators' Time used for assembly of the product varies from fast and robust for experts to slow and variable for novice operators. Similarly, for Quality, expert operators produce a higher percentage of high-quality product than novice operators.

3.5.4.2 Scenario 2. Fully automated task with a robot

Based on the FRAM methodology, Table 3.15 and Table 3.16 show the characteristics considered. The "Type Operator" is a cobot than can be considered in a Basic version or an Optimized one, which are faster processing parts. Hence the optimized robot process parts in a fast pace and the basic option work at a sufficient pace. Similarly,

Table 3.13 Potential output variability for *Time* in Scenario 1.

Function	Type Operator	Output
<ASSEMBLY PRODUCT>	Expert	Too early: Time to Task down and keep regular in time
	Standard	On Time: Time to Task is according to design
	Novice	Too Late: Time to Task increases with irregular variations

Table 3.14 Potential output variability for *Quality* in Scenario 1.

Function	Type Operator	Output
<ASSEMBLY PRODUCT>	Expert	High-Quality Product Percentage value is high
	Standard	High-Quality Product Percentage value is typical
	Novice	High-Quality Product Percentage value is low

Table 3.15 Potential output variability for *Time* in Scenario 2.

Function	Type Operator	Output
<ASSEMBLY PRODUCT>	Optimized	Too early: Time to Task down
	Basic	On Time: Time to Task is the same all the time

Table 3.16 Potential output variability for *Quality* in Scenario 2.

Function	Type Operator	Output
<ASSEMBLY PRODUCT>	Optimized	High-Quality Product Percentage value is high
	Basic	High-Quality Product Percentage value is typical

for Quality, the optimized robot is able to produce more high-quality products than the basic version.

3.5.4.3 Scenario 3. The process is executed in a collaborative manner like a Human–Robot shared task

In this scenario the total variability is the result of the multiple possible combinations of the variability of the human-type functions and the technological functions; the result depends on the strategy of assignment of the activities. In this first version, the MABA-MABA (Men-Are-Better-At / Machines-Are-Better-At) method is considered (Dekker and Woods, 2002) as declared in Table 3.17. Therefore it is assumed that the human operator better develops the function <ASSEMBLY BEARING_BASE>, and the robot better develops the function <ASSEMBLY PRODUCT>. Table 3.18 and Table 3.19 show the characteristics considered for different activities.

3.5.5 Human–robot collaborative workspace in laboratory

A collaborative robot is defined by Krüger et al. (2009) as a mechanical device enabling human–machine cooperation through direct physical interaction with fellow

Table 3.17 MABA-MABA strategy human–cobot.

Human is better than the cobot	Cobot is better than the human
Ability to improvise and use flexible procedures	Ability to respond quickly to control signals and to apply great force smoothly and precisely.
Ability to reason inductively.	Ability to perform repetitive, routine tasks.
Ability to detect changes in part quality	Ability to maintain on time
Ability to replanning time	Ability to maintain precision

Table 3.18 Potential output variability for *Time* in Scenario 3.

Function	Type Operator	Output
<ASSEMBLY	Expert	Too early: Time to Task down and keep regular in time
BEARING_BASE>	Standard	On Time: Time to Task is according to design
	Novice	Too Late: Time to Task increases with irregular variations
<ASSEMBLY PRODUCT>	Optimized	Too early: Time to Task down
	Basic	On Time: Time to Task is the same all the time

Table 3.19 Potential Output variability for *Quality* in Scenario 3.

Function	Type Operator	Output
<ASSEMBLY	Expert	High-Quality Product Percentage value is high
BEARING_BASE>	Standard	High-Quality Product Percentage value is typical
	Novice	High-Quality Product Percentage value is low
<ASSEMBLY PRODUCT>	Optimized	High-Quality Product Percentage value is high
	Basic	High-Quality Product Percentage value is typical

humans. The area where human and robot work and can coexist is the workspace observed in Fig. 3.12, while each robot and human has a space where they can move during performance of job, which is called the work zone in the work-envelope. Within each work zone, there can be additional zones depending on the interaction type.

According to the architecture model for human–robot collaboration shown in Fig. 3.13, the Human–Robot Collaborative Workspace Experience can be described in the three dimensions:

- *HRC team composition.* In this case, we consider one human and one robot. A robot assists a human in accomplishing the tasks.
- *HRC interaction levels.* The interaction level under consideration is Cooperation. Human and robot both have shared tasks in the shared workspace, but they do not work on the same component. Human and robot have a common shared workspace, and they are present in the workspace at the same time. However, each of them works on a separate workpiece. This is implemented in a sequence.

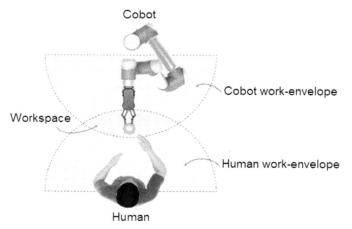

FIGURE 3.12

Human robot collaboration spaces according to Malik and Bilberg (2019b).

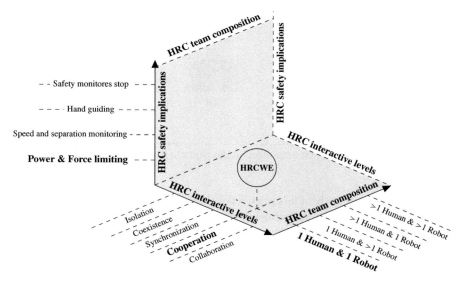

FIGURE 3.13

Architecture model for human–robot collaboration adapted from Malik and Bilberg (2019b). The interactive level is Cooperation, the safety implication is power and force limiting, and the team composition is one human and one robot.

- *HRC safety implications.* Power and force limiting is the safety element under consideration for HRCWE. The cobot follows the safety limitations for human–

robot interactions as described in ISO 15066 standard (ISO Central Secretary, 2016b).

Assembly can be performed according to the combination of components (base, bearing, cap) to produce three different products, without changing the robot programming. The different possibilities are shown in Fig. 3.14: (1) base-bearing-cap, (2) cap-bearing-cap, and (3) base-bearing-base. The activities shown have been initially distributed according to the grasping conditions of the objects.

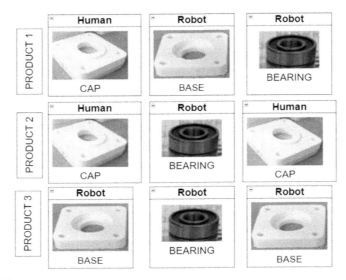

FIGURE 3.14

Three different products can be assembled in the Human–Robot Collaborative Workspace Experience.

The experimental study of this work is developed in the laboratory scenario shown in Fig. 3.15. A laboratory scenario has great adaptability for the identification of human–robot solutions, development of new methodologies, application of algorithms and evaluation of collaborative human–robot workstations (Gualtieri et al., 2020).

The human supervisor plans the activities with one or more human operators, with one or more collaborative robots, tuning the task allocation between human and robot, giving visual feedback of the robot behavior to the human (using visual color lights) and information using pop up windows into the robot teach pendant.

Fig. 3.16 shows the workspace, which is divided into two areas. The "Work Area 1" is where the operator executes the primary task, the Tower of Hanoi game with five disks (TOH5), with a high demanding cognitive workload. It is considered as the "Task 1", the main task for the operator. The "Work Area 2" is where the operator executes the Collaborative Assembly (CA) of the product with the robot. It is

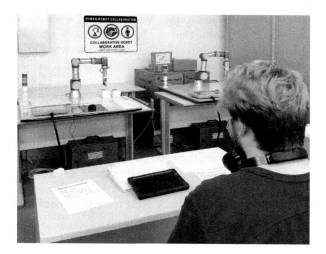

FIGURE 3.15

Laboratory resources: the main task developed on a tablet and the secondary collaborative task of assembly with the robot on the left in the background.

FIGURE 3.16

Human–robot collaborative workspace: "Work Area 1" is on the right, with the primary task, demanding cognitive skills. "Work Area 2" is on the left, a collaborative assembly task with low demanding cognitive and physical skills.

named "Task 2", the secondary one, only executed when the operator is asked for the robot. In the "Work Area 1" the human is in the loop. The information processing system provides participants with visual feedback of the task being developed. The participant can plan strategies and make decisions about when and in which intensity attend the request of the robot. The participant executes physical actions in a touch screen when performing the "Task 1".

If the participant pays attention to the 'Work Area 2', then the human is in the loop. The visual orange color light alert to the participant if a human collaborative task is required by the robot. The participant can decide whether to leave "Work Area 1" momentarily to go to "Work Area 2". In this case the human is in the loop attending the assembly station.

Inside the "Work Area 1", it is possible to design cognitive tasks regarded with human capabilities. The Tower of Hanoi with five disks (TOH5) task is an example of problem solving (high-level reasoning capabilities) where people use mental skills and learning ability to achieve a successful solution (Havur et al., 2013; Hardy and Wright, 2018), whereas the collaborative assembly task in "Work Area 2" is a good example of pick-and-place task in industrial environment. It shows the eye-hand human coordination to achieve a successful solution. Hence this work illustrates the idea that a human–robot collaborative task must include physical and cognitive aspects together.

3.5.5.1 Task 1. Tower of Hanoi (TOH5)

The objective of the task is to move the tower of disks from the first support on the left to any other support with the help of an intermediate support (see Fig. 3.17). The tower is segmented into disks, which are actually moved to rebuild it again in the final position. This task must be performed in as few movements as possible and with as few errors as possible. Disk movements are conditioned by two constraints:

- It is not allowed to place a larger disk on top of a smaller one.
- The disks can only be moved in the order in which they are placed in the tower, starting with the one at the top first.

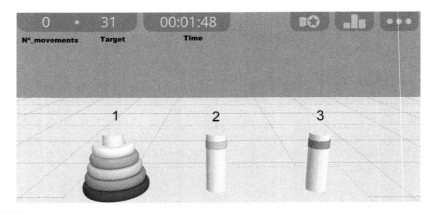

FIGURE 3.17

Digital version of the Tower of Hanoi with five disks (TOH5) task.

In this study, the Tower of Hanoi is performed only by the human, using a digital version of this problem, available at Google Play HANOI 3D. This software allows the manipulation of the disks and records the number of moves and total time in seconds required to complete the task. It is proved that there is no experimental cognitive variation if either wood pieces or a digital version are used in experimental sessions (Robinson and Brewer, 2016; Hardy and Wright, 2018). Following the workload level evaluation scale in Gervasi et al. (2020), this task is classified as appreciated mental workload because a human without a previous expertise in this game must develop a plan and effective strategies. In fact, as a first contact with the Tower of Hanoi problem, the case with three disks is a challenge for many users. The difficulty of this task was previously tuned according to several early participants, and a medium level of difficulty with five disks was decided.

For the solution of the TOH task, the minimum number of moves is 2^{n-1}, where n is the number of disks on tower number 1 at the beginning of the test (Szegedy, 1999). Hence the TOH5 task can be optimally solved with 31 moves.

3.5.5.2 Task 2. Collaborative Assembly (CA)

The assembly area ("Work Area 2") is where robotic work takes place in the process. Humans and robots should cooperate to simplify the job and make the overall system more efficient and productive (Fasth-Berglund and Stahre, 2013). The objective of this task is to collaborate in the assembly of a product composed of three components: a base, a bearing, and a cap, as shown in Fig. 3.11 (page 60). The task is a priori classified as low mental workload, from a human-centered perspective, because eye-hand coordinated skills are more relevant in the activity (Fournier et al., 2022). The collaborative assembly task shows a low level of risk for the human, and no action is required to decrease this risk.

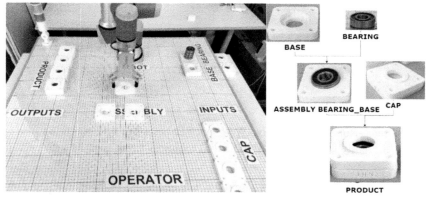

FIGURE 3.18

Assembly process: on the left, the working area; on the right, the parts to be assembled into the product.

Fig. 3.18 shows the implementation of the assembly process using a collaborative robot from the company Universal Robots, model UR3 (Universal Robots, 2015).

The difficulty of the programmed robot task was previously tuned experimenting with early participants and a medium level of difficulty for robot velocity was decided. The purpose is to allow the participant to approach the station and be able to intervene physically without compromising safety and performance.

3.5.5.3 Cycle of work

In the workspace the distribution of activities between the human operator and the collaborative robot (cobot) is shown in Table 3.20. Task 1, as a cognitive demanding activity, is completely assigned to the human. In Task 1 the human is placing the cap to finish and check the quality of the product. The human is also in charge of reloading the storage, making sure that parts are located in the right position. The cobot is assigned to the collaborative task 2, where it first places base and bearing, then assembles the product after the human intervention, and finally palletizes the product for the next workstation.

Fig. 3.19 shows an instance of the cycle of work for a participant. Upper pictures represent activities to the collaborative robot. Lower pictures show human intervention in the collaborative assembly task.

Table 3.20 Tasks and activities allocation in the human–robot collaborative workspace's experiment.

Task	Activity	Operator
Task 1	Solve problem TOH5	Human
Task 2	Get base	Cobot
Task 2	Get bearing	Cobot
Task 2	Get cap	Human
Task 2	Reload storage	Human
Task 2	Assembly product	Cobot
Task 2	Palletize product	Cobot

3.5.5.4 Safety conditions

In the Human–Robot Collaborative Workspace Experience, safe conditions are considered differently from traditional industrial robotics. These specific safety requirements are:

1. Universal Robot's UR3 cobot has been designed to work in direct cooperation with humans within a defined workspace according to the ISO Central Secretary (2018b) standard (Universal Robots, 2015).
2. Maximum speed and torque have been reduced for the normal mode and the maximum value as it can be seen in Table 3.21.
3. Virtual safety planes are defined for the cobot to reduce the workspace.
4. Visual indicators alert the operator of the robot's operating condition.

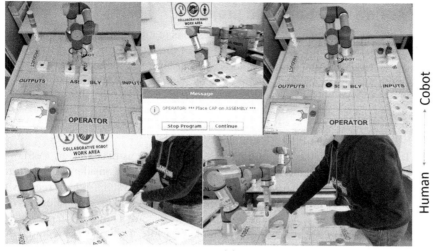

Assembly

FIGURE 3.19

Cycle of work in the Collaborative Assembly (CA) task.

Table 3.21 Motor operating conditions for the UR3 cobot.

Variable	Normal mode	Maximum
speed	1500 mm/s	5000 mm/s
torque	150 N	250 N

Because safety issues are similar to those reported by Scalera et al. (2020), in this approach the authors do not consider strategies and possibilities of collision between the robot and human operators, because the human operator and robot do not physically coincide in the same spatial location at the same time in the case study. In fact, the robot can wait the ending of the human operator activity before starting its work (Zanchettin et al., 2019).

Now, the Human–Robot Collaborative Workspace Experience has been designed. It is time to declare the measurements to consider and develop the experiment to get information. These are the topics for Chapter 4. Moreover, results about how variability is affected by the teamwork between human and robot are presented in Chapter 5.

3.6 **Review questions and project**

In this section the readers will find some questions to check their level of knowledge about the experience gained. In addition, some of these questions pose research challenges, such as search for formal methods or scenarios in which the reader has to plan which methodology to use and how to proceed with experimental measurement.

3.6.1 **Questions**

1. Briefly define what is the Operator *4.0*.
2. Table 3.5 shows the selected values of Value Sensitive Design (VSD) for Human–Robot Collaborative Workspace Experience. Consider, in the current design, the operator being monitored by a camera system, which records the movement of each operator. In this scenario, we can add a new value, privacy. Briefly explain why the data from the camera system is not used to measure the individual and data processing is completed while maintaining the anonymity of the operator.
3. In Section 3.4.2 the FRAM methodology is presented with the aim to model the human–robot team and characterize the potential variability. Examine the usefulness and applicability of the Fuzzy Logic theory to demonstrate and visualize the propagation of variability in FRAM applications.
4. Lists a set of tasks that can be performed by the Operator *4.0* at a collaborative robot workstation.
5. Do you see a need for skill-based instruction in the transformation of the Operator *4.0* from novice to expert?
6. Workplace design can be approached in two ways. In the first case, it is designed from the outset with the possible sharing of space between human and robot in mind. In the second case, the workspace is already being used for human tasks, and the decision has been made to add a robot. Guidelines are provided for workspace design.
7. What is a mobile cobot?
8. Consider the Operator *4.0* working with a mobile cobot. Show an architecture model for human–mobile robot collaboration.
9. Let us assume that the task to be performed at the station is the Tower of Hanoi in a shared human–robot manner. A movement by the human is followed by a movement by the robot. Indicate what type of technology is needed to visualize the Tower of Hanoi game and to know the position of each piece. Indicate what type of terminal element you would use to pick up the pieces that form the Tower of Hanoi.
10. Suppose you know the behavior rules and the Tower of Hanoi Algorithm. Explore how the use of recursive approach can simplify robot programming.
11. In relation to Safety, define the meaning of the following collaborative applications: Safety Monitored Stop, Hand guiding, Speed and separation monitoring, and Power and force limiting.

3.6.2 **Project**

In a factory in the food sector (product packaging and distribution), the aim is to transform the manual task of a conventional operator into a semiautomated task and facilitate the acquisition of skills to become the Operator *4.0*.

1. *Resource identification.* In the context mentioned above, identify the needs of human operator roles, automation technology, and types of products to be manufactured, packaged, and distributed.
2. *Workspace design adding a collaborative robot.* Products arrive via various conveyor belts. The operator's task is to sort products and place them in different boxes. This task is repetitive and tiring. Consider redesigning the workspace and task by adding a collaborative robot. Tasks can now be shared between operator and robot.
3. *Gripper selection.* Some products are fragile and require careful handling. Indicate which type of terminal element may be most suitable for this type of product.
4. *Picking assistance.* The operator comments that some products arrive at the pick point with different orientation and this is a problem for the robot. Do you know any vision system and machine learning algorithm that can help the robot to identify the exact point where to pick up the incoming product on the conveyor belt?
5. *Interaction.* The operator observes the robot behavior but would like to know in detail when the robot is working at low or high speed, or when the robot is waiting for some operator action. Design a set of alerts/warnings in the form of lights or screen messages to assist the operator.
6. *Human–machine interface.* By adding a robot the operator can pay more attention and time to maintenance, safety, and production targets. To do this, the operator asks for a human–machine interface (HMI) that sends commands to the robot and receives useful information. Define the main functionality that you think the HMI should have to be useful.
7. *Training programme.* The operator can manually guide the robot and can thus record points and learn how to carry out robot programmes. Plan a training programme that will enable the operator to acquire skills in programming robotic tasks.
8. *Remote access.* In terms of preventive maintenance, it is necessary to monitor the temperature of the robot's motors and the number of working hours performed by the robot. Find out what type of IoT device can be inserted to acquire this data and send it for web monitoring, allowing remote access to the robot.

Workspace metrics and evaluation

4

Abstract

The methodology that is used for design, implementation, and evaluation of workspaces where machines and humans coexist was introduced in the previous chapter. Moreover, a concurrent study was presented to assess the usability of the introduced methodology. The objective in the study using two tasks, main and secondary, is to determine how the mental workload of the operator is affected in the different situations where the operator is involved.

The developed research methodology is divided into four steps, which determine the different sections in the previous chapter (the first two steps) and this one (steps 3 and 4):

1. Understand and specify the *context of use*.
2. Specify the *user requirements*.
3. Produce *design solutions*.
4. *Evaluate* the design solutions.

Coronado et al. (2022) presented a literature review of the different aspects concerning the problem of quality measurement in Human–Robot Interaction (HRI) applications for manufacturing environments. To help practitioners and new researchers in the area, this chapter presents an overview of factors, metrics, and measures used in the robotics community to evaluate performance and human well-being quality aspects in HRI applications.

Now, following the proposed application related with the operator's mental workload in an assembly task, the last two steps in the methodology are defined. Finally, it is checked whether the system satisfies the specified user and organizational requirements from the previous chapter.

4.1 Introduction

In the previous chapter, a research methodology was defined for Human–Robot Collaborative Workspace Experience, adapted from the User Centered Design approach. The Operator *4.0* is considered as the user on which the design is centered. This methodology promotes a framework that is developed in four steps,

1. Understand and specify the context of use.
2. Specify the user requirements.
3. Produce design solutions.
4. Evaluate the design solutions.

The two first elements of the methodology were deployed in the previous chapter. To check the use of FRAM, a study was defined focused on work variability. The results for this study will be presented in Chapter 5, alongside the results for the particular case where an operator performs two tasks in a workspace. The objective of the study designed in this chapter is to determine how the mental workload of the operator is affected in various working situations where he / she is involved. Once the implementation of the prototype in a laboratory and the design of experiments in the form of HRCWE have been completed, the data from the interaction through several metrics should be experimentally developed. These measurements allow understanding and evaluating performance from the perspective of the human–machine work team or more specifically in the experiment the human–robot team.

4.2 Metrics

To evaluate the latter proposed experiments around HCPS, standardized metrics are used in human work. In our case, we will consider two metrics, usability and mental workload, where fluency will play a special role.

4.2.1 Usability

To evaluate the performance of the work carried out by a human–robot team, the use of usability as an evaluation metric is proposed, based on the experience of human–computer interaction systems (Chacón et al., 2021b). However, in human–robot work, there are some differences (Yanco et al., 2004). Robots represent dynamic systems with varying levels of autonomy that operate in real-world environments. In addition, there are differences in the types of interactions and their roles: the physical nature of the robots, the number of systems with which the user may have to interact at the same time, and the environment in which these interactions can occur (Scholtz, 2003). Hence, for instance, a very popular evaluation framework specifically designed for Human–Robot Collaboration with humanoid robots addressing usability, social acceptance, user experience, and societal impact (USUS) as evaluation factors is proposed by Weiss et al. (2009).

User research is the systematic study of the goals, needs, and capabilities of users (Schumacher, 2010). Usability testing is a basic element for determining whether the users accomplish their goals (Barnum, 2011). Following the international standard definition ISO 9241, Part 11 (ISO Central Secretary, 2018a), usability is the extent to which a product can be used by specific users to achieve specific goals with:

1. *Effectiveness* refers to the number of errors the number of successfully completed activities.
2. *Efficiency* relates with the task time, physical effort, fatigue, and cognitive workload.
3. *Satisfaction* is usually measured using subjective questionnaires and refers to a specified context of use.

A diagram about the different elements impacting usability is depicted in Fig. 4.1.

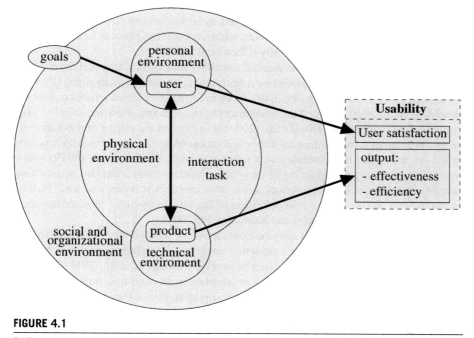

FIGURE 4.1

Definition of Usability according to standard ISO9241-11 (ISO Central Secretary, 2018a).

It is worth noting that other researchers as Chowdhury et al. (2020) include the usability in a broader methodological framework focused on user experience. A pleasurable user experience is an essential design target of human–collaborative robot interaction, and more goals can be added such as fellowship, sympathy, inspiration, and accomplishment.

To evaluate the usability of collaborative workspace between humans and robots, in this research, we present a usability test plan. It is developed through a concrete Human–Robot Collaborative Workspace Experience (HRCWE) to illustrate how this usability test plan can be applied in a real environment. A description of the experience is provided, specifying objectives, roles, and responsibilities of all involved and associated timelines. Note that the main outcomes are not the results obtained for this illustrative usability test plan, but rather the design of the plan itself.

4.2.2 Mental workload

A key element in the manufacturing transformation toward Industry *4.0* is the emphasis on both a human-centered approach and full automation. This human-based transformation implies a paradigm shift from independent automated and human activities toward a human–automation symbiosis characterized by the cooperation of machines with humans in workspaces, which are designed not to replace (eventually, overcome) skills and abilities of humans, but rather to coexist and assist humans in increasing human well-being and production performance (Romero et al., 2016a). In recent reports, such as the Good Work Charter of the European Robotics Industry (EUnited, 2021), fusion skills are defined as an interesting challenge: skills that draw on the fusion of human and robots within a business process to create better outcomes than working independently (Chen et al., 2020).

In manufacturing systems the manual assembly task is a routine activity that has been tried to be completely replaced by robotics, unsuccessfully many times (Pfeiffer, 2016). In the case to be developed in this work in the form of human–robot collaboration, Arai et al. (2010) detailed the assessment of the operator stress induced by robot collaboration in assembly. Hinds et al. (2004) investigated the effects of robot appearance and relative status on human–robot collaboration to the extent to which people relied on and ceded responsibility to a robot coworker. Welfare et al. (2019) investigated negative impact reduction of integrating human–robot teams by maintaining human aspects as social interaction, autonomy, problem solving, and task variety. Hence further studies on the role definition of the human operator in manufacturing applications are required (Gallo and Santolamazza, 2021).

Cognitive skills should not only be considered for the operators, but also for the robotics systems. Human–robot interaction design at a cognitive level is a key element for the success of the collaborative workplace (Mutlu et al., 2016). In some cases the operator could get help from an assistant with cognitive skills to improve the operator's understanding of technology equipment. Hence Pacaux-Lemoine et al. (2022) applied a cognitive work analysis method for the design of an assistance system to support human in the control of intelligent manufacturing systems. Tsarouchi et al. (2017) developed an intelligent decision making method that allows human–robot task allocation using the robot operating system (ROS) framework. With the aim to decrease the workload of the human and maximize the user adaptation, Kim et al. (2007) developed a set of cognitive models enhancing Human–Robot Interaction for service robots: task model, truth-maintenance model, interaction model, and intention rule-base. A mathematical model is introduced by Rabby et al. (2019) relating human low workload (physical, mental) to high performance in a human–robot collaboration framework depending on the complexity of the task and on whether the robot task is performed successfully or with errors (human intervention is required). Finally, considering the current hot topic approach of digital twins, a cognitive digital twin framework for smart manufacturing and especially for human–robot collaboration cases is proposed in Shi et al. (2022).

For cognitive interaction between an operator and a station, what type of interface allowing efficient dialogue should be considered? Marvel et al. (2020) developed a framework defining methods, metrics, and design recommendations for the study of effective interface designs in collaborative human–robot interaction. Moreover, when collaborative robots progress toward cognitive robotics, the human operator should be trained to be at that same level of competence. In this context, cognitive architectures for human–robot teaming interaction must be developed and tested (Seidita et al., 2019). A prospective vision and research topic for future work in the human-centric smart manufacturing era is proposed by Li et al. (2023c). Proactive robot control would allow multiple human and robotic agents to collaboratively operate manufacturing tasks, considering each others' operation needs, desired resources, and qualified complementary capabilities.

From the cognitive point of view, workload and attention must be assessed. A priori, semiautomatic systems (collaborative systems) should facilitate effective teamwork between robots and humans. The human task must be adequately balanced so as not to excessively increase the assigned load. However, existing HRC development mainly undertakes either a human-dominant or robot-dominant manner, where human and robotic agents reactively perform operations by following predefined instructions, thus far from an efficient integration of robotic automation and human cognition (Li et al., 2023c).

With regard to attention (Pereira et al., 2019), it is necessary to analyze what type of attention is appropriate for the performed tasks (sustained, selective, divided) (Gray et al., 2016). If a task has high priority, then sustained attention is preferable: the human is focused and motivated to continue and complete this task. In other cases, selective attention is preferable: the human develops the task even when there are distractions around him. In some situations the operator needs to have attention in multiple places. Divided attention helps the human retain information while successfully completing two or more tasks at the same time.

Having to intervene in various places can cause stress for the operator and make it difficult for the chosen task to be carried out successfully. To understand in detail how humans behave when faced with the challenge of completing a task or interrupting it to carry out a direct intervention at the station, the following section shows how to prepare a laboratory scenario of performing and evaluating human–robot collaboration tasks.

4.2.2.1 Fluency

In the collaborative approach, the incorporation of collaborative robots (cobots) has transformed the dynamics in modern smart factories. These robotic agents work in conjunction with human operators, collaborating hand-in-hand in the execution of tasks. Since cobots are designed to be more than just tools, seamless interaction between operators and their robotic counterparts becomes essential to ensure compliance with employee responsibilities and, ultimately, to achieve high performance (Paliga, 2022). The fluency measure refers to the ability of a system or entity, whether a collaborative robot (cobot) or a human being, to perform a task or activity smoothly and without apparent problems. This measure is used in various contexts to evaluate how well a system or individual can execute a specific task.

In the context of cobots, fluency refers to the robot's ability to perform collaborative tasks efficiently and without interruption, such as working alongside humans on an assembly line or performing manipulation tasks. A cobot that exhibits fluidity in its movements and actions is capable of safely and effectively interacting with humans in a shared work environment (Hoffman, 2019).

The extent of fluency between a cobot and a human will depend on several factors, including the technology and design of the cobot, the training of the human operators, and the nature of the task they carry out together. In general, a high measure of fluidity between a cobot and a human implies that they can work together efficiently and harmoniously as a team, which is desirable in robotic collaboration applications.

4.3 Evaluating the design solutions

Periodically, researchers carry out the validity of methodological proposals in human–robot interaction using several measures (Steinfeld et al., 2006; Murphy and Schreckenghost, 2013). According to the increasing presence of collaborative and intelligent robots in industry, standardized metrology for the performance measurement of human–robot (H-R) systems (Marvel et al., 2019) is still needed in the manufacturing environment.

Along with the development of robotic interfaces, there has been an increase in the evaluation of these systems. HRI researchers have employed a variety of evaluation styles in their work (Marvel et al., 2020). They can evaluate their systems summatively (i.e., after-the-fact) or formatively (i.e., during system development) (Clarkson and Arkin, 2006).

Various emerging technologies affecting the Operator *4.0* work environment and the very concept of human centrality motivate the need to search for a methodology that considers human values as part of the design process of any human–automation-type system.

4.3.1 Summative evaluation

Summative usability is an evaluation method used to assess the overall usability of a product or system after it has been developed and is close to being released to users. The goal of summative usability is to identify any remaining usability issues and to evaluate the effectiveness of the product or system in meeting its intended goals.

According to Clarkson and Arkin (2006), the HRI Heuristic Validation is useful to make a summative evaluation, according to which eight heuristics are established.

1. *Sufficient information design*: The interface should be designed to convey "just enough" information: enough so that the human can determine if intervention is needed, and not so much that it causes overload.
2. *Visibility of system status*: The system should always keep users informed about what is going on, through appropriate feedback within reasonable time. The sys-

tem should convey its world model to the user so that the user has a full understanding of the world as it appears to the system. The system should support the user's situational awareness.

3. *Appropriate information presentation*: The interface should present sensor information that is clear, easily understood, and in the form most useful to the user. The system should utilize the principle of recognition over recall, externalizing memory. The system should support attention management.

4. *Use natural cues*: The language of the interaction between the user and system should be in terms of words, phrases, and concepts familiar to the user, rather than system-oriented terms. Follow real-world conventions, making information appear in a natural and logical order.

5. *Synthesis of system and interface*: The interface and system should blend together so that the interface is an extension of the system, the user, and the world by proxy. The interface should facilitate efficient and effective communication between the system and user and vice versa, switching modes automatically when necessary.

6. *Help users recognize, diagnose, and recover from errors*: System malfunctions should be expressed in plain language (no codes), precisely indicate the problem, and constructively suggest a solution. The system should present enough information about the task environment so that the user can determine if some aspect of the world has contributed to the problem.

7. *Flexibility of interaction architecture*: If the system will be used over a lengthy period of time, the interface should support the evolution of system capabilities, such as sensor and actuator capacity, behavior changes, and physical alteration. Sensor and actuator capabilities should be adequate for the expected tasks and environment of the system.

8. *Aesthetic and minimalist design*: The system should not contain information that is irrelevant or rarely needed. The physical embodiment of the system should be pleasing in its intended setting.

To validate these eight heuristics, the questionnaire shown in Table 4.1 is proposed.

4.3.2 Formative evaluation by HRI metrics

Regarding HRI metrics, the usual human-centered interaction metrics consider *Effectiveness*, *Efficiency*, and *User satisfaction* (Prati et al., 2021) for the measurement of usability. Metrics to be considered are, for instance, "Degree of success in completing a task", "Total task time", "User physical load", or "Mental workload". These starting HRI metrics should be augmented with metrics associated with the robot behavior, which in the industrial field are known as Key Performance Indicators (KPIs), such as "Percentage of use of the robot", "Tasks successfully completed by the robot", or "Task time". Some standardized metrics for task effectiveness and task efficiency are listed in Table 4.2.

For measuring user satisfaction in the interaction, qualitative questionnaires are the main approach. In the application of satisfaction questionnaires, the need to adapt

Table 4.1 Questionnaire to evaluate HRI heuristics validation.

Heuristic	Question
H1. Sufficient information design	Has the designer considered all tasks and activities in the design?
H2. Visibility of system status	Is the operator informed about the progress of the system with the appropriate response and within an acceptable time?
H3. Appropriate information presentation	Does the system use concepts and language familiar to the operator rather than technical terms?
H4. Use natural cues	Do design elements, such as objects and actions, have the same meaning or effect in different situations?
H5. Synthesis of system and interface	Are the task methods efficient?
H6. Help users recognize, diagnose, and recover from errors	Is appropriate help provided and is the information easy to find and focused on the operator's task?
H7. Flexibility of interaction architecture	Can the operator customize frequent actions or shortcuts?
H8. Aesthetic and minimalist design	Does the dialogue contain irrelevant or rarely used information?

Table 4.2 Task effectiveness and task efficiency metrics for measuring performance of human–robot interaction.

Metric	Detail
Task effectiveness	
TSR	(H, R) Task Success Rate with respect to the total number of tasks in the activity
F	Frequency with which the human requests assistance to complete their tasks
Task efficiency	
CAT	Concurrent Activity Time (H-R): percentage of time that the two agents are active in the same time interval
TT	Time to complete a task (H, R)
IT	Idle Time: percentage of time the agent (H, R) is idle
FD	Functional Delay: percentage of time between tasks when changing the agent (H, R)

the existing questionnaires in Human–Computer Interaction (HCI) to a broader scope should be addressed. As a starting point, a first approach is to adapt questions from questionnaire models, such as the Technology Acceptance Model (TAM) (Davis, 1989), the System Usability Scale (SUS) (Brooke, 2013), the Fluency (Subjective Fluency Metrics) (Hoffman, 2019), and the Part C questionnaire on comfort in ISO 9241-420 Table D.1 (ISO Central Secretary, 2011). To facilitate the use of these heuristics, a consensus scale is required. For example, a 5-point Likert scale, where in many of the heuristics the ends of the scale are "Strongly disagree" and "Strongly agree" (Schrum et al., 2020, 2023). These cited qualitative metrics for measuring interaction from the user satisfaction perspective are partial since once an H-R task is defined, the synergy between each of the agents involved leads to a broader model that must consider the overall performance and teamwork fluency (Hoffman and Breazeal, 2007; Hazbar et al., 2019), that is, quantitative measures used for effectiveness and efficiency.

Our proposal advocates for quantitatively measure both the overall satisfaction of the interaction, that is, user satisfaction, and "task satisfaction", by using *variability* in the task efficiency metric, *TT*. In other words, we propose to move from both direct quantitative robotics and qualitative human measures to the overall product or process quality evaluation.

4.3.3 Metrics for quality evaluation: variability

The product or process quality evaluation aims to investigate if a task or an activity requires improvements in terms of standardization and reduction of process instability or variability (Gualtieri et al., 2020; Nwanya et al., 2016). From a manufacturing approach, variability is defined as an inherent process deviation from a nominal value. Gualtieri et al. (2020) identify the process variability as the coefficient of variation CV defined as

$$CV = \frac{\sigma}{mv}, \tag{4.1}$$

where σ is the standard deviation, and mv is the mean value of time data or success rate data. As a consequence, the variability is a negative situation, which requires a more controlled condition to achieve the designed process and product quality values (Sanchez-Salas et al., 2017). To ensure the product quality and save manufacturing costs, growing attention has been paid to the problem of the stability of the manufacturing process with unknown probability distribution and trend (Xia and Zhu, 2016). It has been also employed for risk assessment when introducing collaborative robotics (Jocelyn et al., 2023).

The collaboration of workers in automated tasks using cobots improves product quality and process results but introduces some kind of unknown/unpredictable variability, especially in time execution for activities (Gambao, 2023; Keshvarparast et al., 2023). Once all activities are mapped and measured, it is useful to identify a list of those presenting a high level of process variability PV (see Fig. 4.2). The amount of process variability can be categorized ("Low PV", "Medium PV", "High PV") according to either previously registered dispersion in the measures (data-driven), or activity modeling in simulation (model driven), or both in the case of digital twins (Caputo et al., 2019; Kadir and Broberg, 2020). In case of detecting a certain amount of variability, cognitive assistance to the worker can be employed to provide a set of recommendations related with timing, checking accuracy, training for novice workers, modifications in the order. In a qualitative manner, as defended by Chacón et al. (2020b), cognitive assistance is related to process variability. After a new exe-

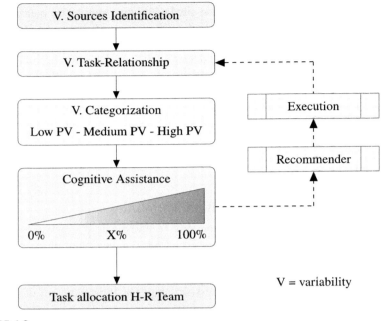

FIGURE 4.2

Analyzing process variability in human–robot collaborative tasks and task allocation.

cution phase and collected data, the variability is again measured and task allocation is reconsidered.

4.3.4 Ontology for cognitive assistants

To understand how a cognitive assistant can be integrated into a human–robot team, we can design an ontology for cognitive assistants. Previously, we have seen that there are various types of workers: the Operator *4.0* and the collaborative robot at the plant level; and at the control room level, we would have the supervisor. By classifying the Operator *4.0* into the categories of Novice, Standard, and Expert we can model these categories as instances of the Operator *4.0* concept (see Fig. 4.3). The relationship between ontology and cognitive assistants is clear if we consider the cognitive assistant as an agent that can be modeled in terms of problem-solving tasks (Tecuci et al., 2016). Following guidelines in Tecuci et al. (2016) from knowledge engineering, we can adapt the ontology of knowledge-intensive problem-solving tasks for the cognitive assistant. The collection of experimental data, in fact, the dynamic variation of these data, allows the association between objects and subconcepts in the analytic task part of the ontology. As we can see in Fig. 4.4, elements to be considered in this analytic task are:

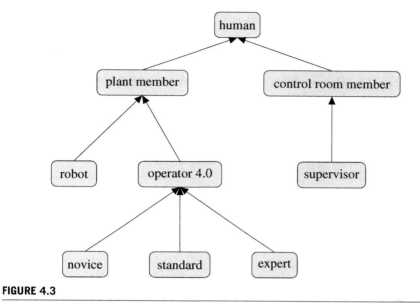

FIGURE 4.3

Ontology person and objects (plant member, control room member) inside a hierarchy model.

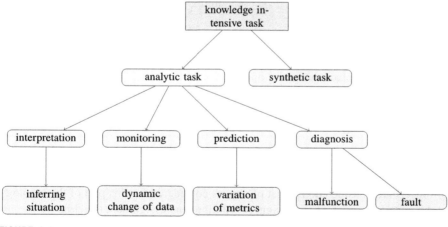

FIGURE 4.4

Ontology of knowledge-intensive problem-solving tasks applied to cognitive assistant. Analytic task part.

- *Interpretation.* It refers to the subconcept of *inferring situation*. The supervisor may need to know the state of the system consisting of operator and robot, and the cognitive assistant can provide this state so that the supervisor can interpret the system.

- *Monitoring.* After data gathering, data is under treatment so that dynamic changes can be visualized on a dashboard. It allows the supervisor to monitor the system.
- *Prediction.* This element refers to the transformation of data into information, and this information written in the form of metrics and key performance indicators can facilitate support for short-term prediction of the evolution of the system.
- *Diagnosis.* It leads to inferring system malfunctions. In electromechanical systems, it can be useful to know defects and failures. Moreover, it is also useful to know human errors in the operator when he is developing the task.

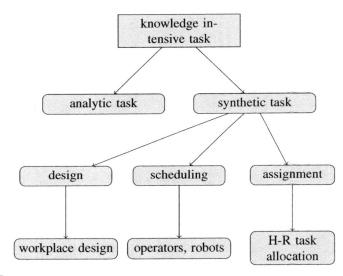

FIGURE 4.5

Ontology of knowledge-intensive problem-solving tasks applied to cognitive assistant. Synthetic task part.

A synthetic task is one in which the requirements for the preparation of the design of objects are considered. The list of objects considered for this part of the ontology of the cognitive assistant are design, scheduling, and assignment (see Fig. 4.5).

- *Design* means the subconcept of *workspace design*. The design of the workspace for H-R tasks must consider ergonomic aspects that benefit the team.
- *Scheduling* means allocating sequences of activities. Plan how many operators and how many robots are required and the sequence of subtasks to perform between them.
- *Assignment* means creating a mapping between the objects. The *H-R task allocation* is a subconcept useful for identifying the capabilities of each one.

In Section 5.2, we will see a fragment of the application of this ontology for cognitive assistant focused on the objects of interpretation, monitoring, and prediction.

4.3.5 Usability test plan

When a new collaborative robot is introduced into production, tasks under development change from the point of view of the human operator. It is necessary to evaluate how these changes affect human operator behavior and measure and analyze human–robot collaboration tasks in detail. With this goal in mind and taking advantage of the experience in the field of human–computer interaction, a *Usability evaluation* is carried out (Jordan et al., 1996).

In our study, we follow some guidelines for its planning and execution from the Norman Nielsen Group in their paper "Checklist for Planning Usability Studies", available at https://www.nngroup.com/articles/usability-test-checklist/. Fig. 4.6 depicts this planning.

4.3.5.1 Define goals for the study

The purpose of a usability test is, giving a specific context of use, to measure the performance of a system in terms of task effectiveness, efficiency, and satisfaction. Thus the necessary feedback is provided to help decision-making in the redesign of systems. In particular, in this work a collaborative workspace is considered where the operator is developing a main task. It is supposed that the operator has some experience in this main task and the workspace is correctly designed. Next, the operator is required for developing a secondary task, implying collaboration with a robot. The general objective of the usability test in this scenario would be to evaluate the usability of the workspace when a secondary collaborative task with cobots is added to the operator.

The usability of the proposed Human–Robot Collaborative Workspace Experience (HRCWE) is evaluated on the basis of the international usability standard ISO 9241-11 (ISO Central Secretary, 2018a), which takes into account both objective and subjective metrics. According to this standard, the effectiveness and efficiency of usability is evaluated through the measurement of *Task to Time*, that is, the time in seconds to complete a task and *Task Completion Rate* as the percentage of tasks that users complete correctly, performed by each participant while performing the tasks. In addition to these objective measures, a questionnaire has been developed to evaluate subjective usability using the System Usability Scale (SUS) (Brooke, 1996), whose definition is based on psychometric methods (Lewis, 2006).

What the usability test is not designed to achieve

Our proposed usability test is not oriented to evaluate the design characteristics of the implemented prototype or its productive performance. Moreover, this test is focused on early steps of design and not on the final launch of products to the market. Human factors and ergonomics use the same orientation in early steps of design. The aim is to use the collaborative robot as a partner and not as a substitute of human operator.

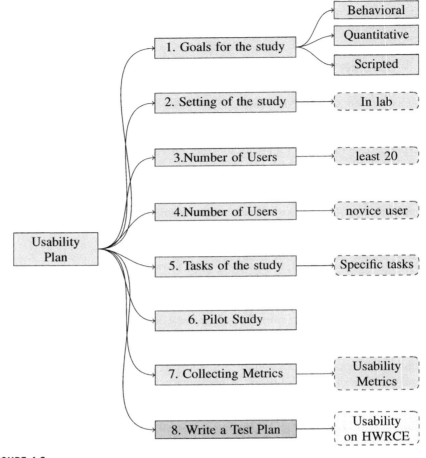

FIGURE 4.6

Usability Test Plan for HWRCE.

Thus the context implies the formation of human–robot teams, each contributing with their best skills (Tekniker et al., 2017).

4.3.5.2 Determine format and setting of the study

Specifying the study characteristics is the first step in a study of usability, to specify the context of use where the experimental study will be carried out, the description of the process, the type of participants, and the academic purpose of the workspace (Kalmbach et al., 2018; Masó et al., 2020).

Context of use

In this case, the experience is designed in a University laboratory, participants being recruited among students and teaching staff laboring in this environment. The laboratory endows two identical robot stations and a set of computer workspaces. It is designed to introduce students in the managing of collaborative robots in two training steps: the first one is understanding the robot and its programming, and the second step is adopting the role of human operator in a realistic scenario.

The Human–Robot Collaborative Workspace Experience (HRCWE) is based on a prototype implemented in the laboratory with the aim of developing teaching and research on the relationships between humans and robots. In particular, in collaborative mode, with a focus on the cognitive and mental tasks of the human operator. Certainly, the use of a collaborative robot facilitates physical interaction with humans. However, the cognitive and mental aspects should not be underestimated. The human's perception of the task complexity or their trust in the robot are also relevant elements to consider.

Location and dates

The address of the test facility is Automatic Control Department, FIB Faculty, Automatic Control Department Laboratory C5-202, Universitat Politècnica Catalunya Barcelona Tech. Authors plan to test participants according to the schedule shown in Table 4.3.

Table 4.3 Schedule of experiments.

Time	Monday	Wednesday	Thursday
09:00–11:00	Pilot Testing	Participant	Participant
11:00–13:00		Participant	Participant
14:00–16:00		Participant	Participant

Test facilities

The experimental equipment under consideration is shown in Table 4.4.

4.3.5.3 Determine the number of users

This experiment is quantitative, so 20 participants, characterized as novice users, were chosen for this usability test.

4.3.5.4 Recruit the right participants

The roles involved in a usability test are as follows. It is worth noting that an individual may play multiple roles and tests may not require all roles.

Participants

They are University's bachelor students and some teaching staff. The participants' responsibilities are attempting to complete a set of representative task scenarios presented to them in a manner as efficient and timely as possible and to provide feedback

Table 4.4 Experimental equipment.

Name	Description	Use
Tablet	Android system with digital version of TOH5 (HANOI3D)	Task 1 TOH5
Collaborative Robot	Robot Model UR3 with controller CB3. Manufactured by Universal Robot	Task 2 Collaborative Assembly (CA)
Laptop	Intel Core i5, Windows 10 Operating System	Data collection and logging
Web Cam	External, high definition	Get video of the experiment
Software	Cam video recorder, Visual Components v4.2	Record video of the experiment and record data of the collaborative robot

regarding the usability and acceptability of the experience. The participants are addressed to provide honest opinions regarding the usability of the application and to participate in postsession subjective questionnaires. These participants have good skills in engineering methods, computer science, and programming. They do not have previous knowledge about collaborative robots and how manage human–robot activities.

A recruitment form *Participants* is used to recruit suitable participants. The more relevant elements in this form are questions about:

- Participant inclusion,
- Participant exclusion,
- Participant experience.

Main facilitator

General facilitator's responsibilities are to:

- Write the test plan,
- Organize the recruitment of suitable participants,
- Preserve ethical aspects,
- Prepare the workspace for the development of the experimentation,
- Show the task instructions to the user,
- Record the data of the experiment,
- Analyze usability test data,
- Summarize the results in a usability report.

The facilitator must supervise the ethical and psychological consequences for research participants. Any foreseeable effect on their psychological well-being, health, values, or dignity must be considered and, in the case of judging it negative, even to a minimal degree, eliminated (ETSI, 2000). From a robotic perspective, roboethics has as objective the development of technical ethical tools, which can be shared by various social groups. These tools aim to promote and encourage the development of robotics and to help preventing its misuse against humankind (Veruggio and Operto, 2008; Tzafestas, 2018).

The facilitator must ensure that the test can be carried out effectively. To do this, previously set the level of difficulty for the Tower of Hanoi solution, in this case, 5 disks, adjust the speed of the collaborative robot's movement, and program the cobot's task.

Ethics

All participants involved with the usability test are required to adhere to the following ethical guidelines:

- The performance of any test participant must not be individually attributable. Individual participant's name should not be used in reference outside the testing session.
- A description of the participant's performance should not be reported to his or her manager.

Considering that this study involves work with humans, the usability plan has been endorsed by the Ethics Committee of the Universitat Politècnica de Catalunya with the identification code 2021-06.

4.3.5.5 Write tasks of the study

To evaluate the effects on the human operator when a collaborative human–robot task is added in the original workspace, a workplace composed of two tasks is defined, in particular, with a focus on assembly tasks. The workplace tasks are:

- Task 1: Tower of Hanoi. The original/principal/main task for the human operator is about solving the Tower of Hanoi with five pieces (TOH5). This problem consists of five perforated disks of increasing radius stacked by inserting them into one of the three posts fixed to a board, as seen in Fig. 4.7. The objective is to move one disk from the first pole to another one, making only one move at a time and placing a larger disk on top of a smaller one. The Tower of Hanoi puzzle was established as a robotics challenge as a part of EU Robotics coordination action in 2011 and IEEE IROS Conference in 2012. In our experiment the Tower of Hanoi is performed only by the human operator.
  A digital version of the TOH is used, available at Google Play, HANOI 3D. This program allows manipulating the disks and records the number of moves and total time in seconds required to complete the task. It has been reported that no experimental cognitive variation exists if either wood pieces or a digital version is used (Hardy and Wright, 2018).
- Task 2: Collaborative assembly of a product. The introduced secondary task consists of collaborative assembling (CA) of a product composed of three components: a base, a bearing, and a cap, as shown in Fig. 4.8. This task is determined as adding a low cognitive workload, from a human-centered perspective, because eye-hand coordinated skills are more relevant in this task. Moreover, the assembly

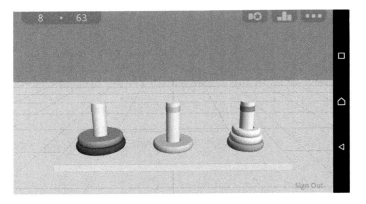

FIGURE 4.7

Digital version of the Tower of Hanoi problem with five disks, TOH5.

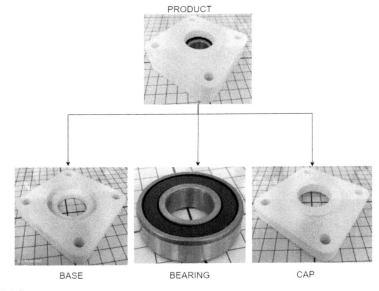

FIGURE 4.8

Collaborative assembly elements in the secondary process.

task shows a low level of physical risk for the human, and no action is necessary to decrease this risk.

4.3.5.6 Pilot testing

The purpose of the pilot test is to identify and reduce potential sources of error and fix any technical issue with the recording equipment or with the experiment that might cause delays to the current experiment. It is expected that the pilot test takes two hours at maximum. The problems found would be immediately fixed. Observers are not invited due to the nature of the pilot.

4.3.5.7 Collecting metrics

In a benchmark test the usability of products is made measurable and enables a comparison with the competition. Based on different metrics, the usability dimensions, that is, effectiveness, efficiency, and user satisfaction (ISO Central Secretary, 2018a), are assessed and summarized into a meaningful overall score.

Data collection and metrics

A dataset with data collected from experiments is organized as shown in Fig. 4.9. A set of statistical measures and tests available in the tool Usability Statistics Packages[1] (Zazelenchuk et al., 2008) are used for dataset analysis.

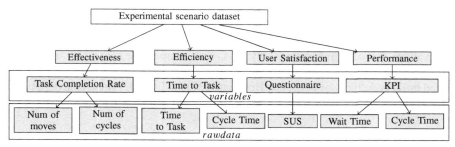

FIGURE 4.9

Organization of the dataset for the experimental study.

4.3.5.8 Test plan: task effectiveness and efficiency

The quantitative component involves handling of numerical variables and use of statistical techniques to guard against random events. This quantitative component includes information about the statistical significance of the results.

Effectiveness

The efficiency is evaluated using the *Task Completion rate* measure. For this binary variable, a maximum error of 10% of the optimal number of moves needed to solve the problem is set. Hence it is coded with 1 (pass) for participants who solve the task and 0 (fail) for those who do not solve it.

---

[1] Jeff Sauro's formulation available in http://www.measuringusability.com/products/statsPak.

Efficiency

To evaluate efficiency, the *Time to Task* measure is obtained from dataset associated with TOH5. Only participants who completed the task are considered, and the analysis is made with the mean values obtained from each participation.

Satisfaction

The System Usability Scale (SUS) is used to evaluate the level of user satisfaction (Sauro, 2011). The advantage of using SUS is that it is comparatively quick, easy, and inexpensive, whilst still being a reliable way of gauging usability. Moreover, the SUS questionnaire allows to provide us with a measure of people's subjective perceptions of the usability of the experience in the very short time available during evaluation sessions.

However, interpreting SUS scoring can be complex. The participant's scores for each question are converted to a new number, added together, and then multiplied by 2.5 to convert the original scores ranged in 0–40 to 0–100. Though the scores are 0–100, these are not percentages and should be considered only in terms of their percentile ranking (Sauro and Lewis, 2016). A way to interpret SUS score is to convert it into a grade or adjective (Bangor et al., 2008), as shown in Fig. 4.10.

Key performance indicators for cobot

To evaluate the cooperative assembly (CA) task, that is, the secondary task in the experimental scenario, some Key Performance Indicators (KPIs) have been collected, based in KPIs defined for cobots by Bouchard (2017). Table 4.5 shows the definitions used in this work for these KPIs.

Table 4.5 KPIs referred to cobots.

KPI	Definition
Cycle Time	Cycle Time measures the duration of one cobot sequence
Cycled Completed	How many cycles have been performed by the cobot in a particular time period
Per Utilization	How long a cobot is being used compared to how long it could
Per Efficiency	It defines the percentage of time that the cobot performs productive work while running a program
Wait Time	The percentage of time that the cobot is waiting while it is running a program

The data gathering procedure to calculate cobot's KPIs has been implemented through a tool for obtaining the values of the variables recorded in the robot through the communication protocol with an external desktop. The values for *Cycle Time*, *Wait Time*, *Products* as the number of assembled products, and *Bases* as the number of bases, are acquired using this tool. In Fig. 4.11, we show an example employing Visual Components software where this information is saved as an electronics sheet for KPI analysis. *CapTime* in Fig. 4.11 is the operator's time to place the cap. This

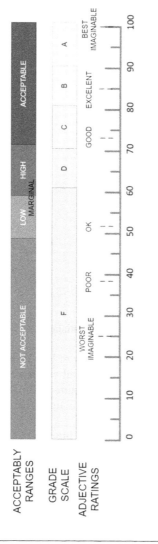

FIGURE 4.10

Grade rankings of SUS scores. Adapted from Bangor et al. (2008).

value will be considered as the idle time of the robot as well as the *Human Operator Time*, since the robot is stopped.

Video recording

Experimental sessions are recorded on video, and hence the facilitator can later measure events like operator travel time from one task to another, how many times the

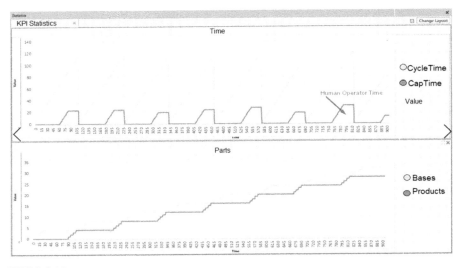

FIGURE 4.11

Time data and raw material sent from cobot UR3.

operator check whether the robot has finished, and the right development of user actions in the assembly task.

While the user is developing the Tower of Hanoi task, the robot is working placing bases and bearings (red light). The vertical column of lights indicates with a green light when the presence of the user is required. The video recording can show if the user is paying attention to the column of lights or concentrating on the Tower of Hanoi task.

As a further analysis in collaborative human–robot stations, video recording allows the observation of repetitive hand and arm movements that allow risk analysis and physical ergonomic assessment of the task.

4.3.5.9 Experimental sessions

Each participant session will be organized in the same way to facilitate consistency. The users will be interviewed at the end of the tasks.

Introduction

The main facilitator begins by emphasizing that the testing is being carried out by a PhD student. This means that users can be critical of the experience without feeling that they are criticizing the designer. The main facilitator is not asking leading questions. The main facilitator explains that the purpose of the testing is to obtain measures of usability, such as effectiveness, efficiency, and user satisfaction, when working with collaborative robots. It is made clear that it is the system, not the user, that is being tested, so that if they have trouble, it is the workspace problem, not theirs.

Pretest interview

At the beginning of the experiment, it is explained to the participant about the experience, which are his/her tasks, how the experiment is developed (a document is used for this), and that at the end of the experiment, there is one questionnaire to be answered.

Participants will sign an informed consent that acknowledges: participation is voluntary, participation can cease at any time, and session will be videotaped, but their privacy of identification will be safeguarded. The facilitator will ask the participant if they have any questions. The form *Consent form* is used for this aim. The more relevant aspects of this form are:

• Description of objectives in the experiment,
• Safety explanation for the participant,
• Participant's rights.

Next, the facilitator explains that the amount of time taken to complete the test task is measured and that exploratory behavior outside the task flow should not occur until after task completion. Time-on-task measurement begins when the participant starts the task.

The facilitator presents a demonstration to the user according to the guide *Demonstrations*, also elaborated by the facilitator. The more relevant aspects of this form are:

• Demonstration of the use of the Tower of Hanoi game on the tablet,
• Demonstration of operator involvement in product assembly.

After all tasks are attempted, the participant completes the posttest satisfaction questionnaire.

Case study

The experimental scenario is composed of two tasks within the HRWCE. The main task is Task 1 TOH5; a secondary task is added, Task 2 Collaborative Assembly (CA), as an additional human–robot collaboration task (see Fig. 4.12). Table 4.6 shows the conditions of performance for the tasks. Time allocated for this scenario is 15 minutes.

The objective for the participant in the task TOH5 is to perform as many replays as possible. The secondary task, Collaborative Assembly, is related to responding to requests for collaboration from the cobot, which are indicated by the green light of the beacon in the assembly area. Both the time taken by the human takes to place caps, recorded as *Wait Time*, and *Cycle time* are saved in a data table as the one shown in Table 4.7, jointly with figures for Task 1 when the operator is in the experimental scenario. In the collaborative assembly task, the activities of the participant are:

• performing quality control of the assembly process,
• place the caps on the subassembly zone,
• feeding the base and bearing warehouses.

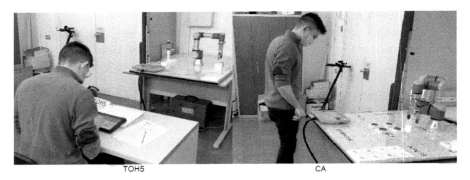

TOH5   CA

FIGURE 4.12

Scenario of the experience. Left, the TOH5 task, the main one, is performed. Right, the CA secondary collaborative Assembly task is being developed.

Table 4.6 Experimental scenarios.

Task	Performance	Total time
TOH5	Maximum number of TOH5 replays with 31 moves	15 minutes
CA	At least 7 work cycles completed	

Table 4.7 Form to Experimental Scenario (TOH5+CA). Tasks: Solve problem (main) and Collaborate with cobot (secondary).

Operator			Cobot		
Replay	N_moves	Time to Task (sec)	Cycle	Wait Time (sec)	Cycle Time (sec)
1			1		
...			...		

Adapted posttest questionnaire

At the end of the experience, the participant answers the adapted System Usability Scale (SUS) as the satisfaction questionnaire. As it has been demonstrated by Cowley (2006), SUS can be applied to a wide range of technologies. This feature allows the questionnaire to be adapted to this particular experiment. In the SUS standard questionnaire, the word "system" has been changed to "human–robot collaborative workspace" because it is not a human–computer task but a human–robot task. A medium or low SUS score indicates the need for discussion and effort to redesign the experiment.

4.3.6 Cognitive interaction

The evaluation of mental workload is a key issue to research and develop for human machine interfaces, as well as to find levels of comfort, satisfaction, efficiency, and security in the workspace (Rubio et al., 2004). Moreover, some researchers explain in detail how important the cognitive load and the mental workload are in the design of workspaces for assembly tasks (Ustunel and Gunduz, 2017). A laboratory scenario in a manufacturing context has been designed to create an environment where humans can work side-by-side with robots in close proximity (Wang et al., 2019b). The human operator facilitates the assembly task carried out by the robot since it feeds the station with parts, collects the products, and attends to any possible malfunction. The variation of the human operator's mental workload is evaluated when switching from a main task into a secondary task in this human–robot collaboration workspace scenario. The general objective of the test in this scenario is to evaluate the variation of mental workload when the mental workload of the operator is increased due to regular time-constrained collaborations with a robot. Our hypothesis is that when the operator performs the collaborative task with the robot, the mental workload value is not very far from the mental workload of the main task. Moreover, both values would be in an intermediate comfort zone of mental workload. If tasks are designed in which the perceived mental workload is in an intermediate zone, then quality in performance and decision-making in problem solving are guaranteed (Soria-Oliver et al., 2018).

4.3.6.1 Experiment on cognitive workload

Following the hypothesis explained at the beginning of this section and the tasks detailed in Table 3.20 (page 72), two working scenarios are designed:

- Working Scenario 1 (TOH5): The participant only executes Task 1, without distractions, using a tablet for this end, as seen in Fig. 4.13.
- Working Scenario 2 (TOH5+CA): The participant executes a combination of the two tasks. The main task is TOH5 and also collaborates with the cobot in activities of Task 2 according to the work cycle in Table 3.20 (see Fig. 4.14).

FIGURE 4.13

Working Scenario 1 (TOH5): the operator works on Task 1 (TOH5) without distractions.

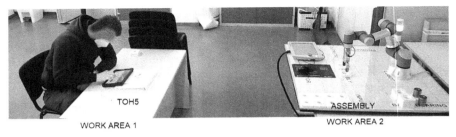

FIGURE 4.14

Working Scenario 2 (TOH5+CA): the operator works with divided attention on the main task (TOH5) and a secondary task (CA).

4.3.6.2 Participants

Data in both scenarios were collected from 18 participants. Among the participants, there were undergraduate students, vocational students, and teaching staff. Details about them are shown in Table 4.8. Nobody had previous experience working with cobots.

Table 4.8 Participants.

Type	Number	Gender	Age (Years)	Percent
2*Undergraduate students	10	male	22–26	55%
	2	female	22–24	11%
Vocational students	2	male	18–20	11%
Teaching staff	4	male	40–50	23%
Total	18	–	–	100%

4.3.6.3 Procedure

The participant's study is composed of two main steps, demo and test.

- Demo. As a first step, a facilitator provides each participant with a brief demonstration, usually about 2–3 min long, about the main functionalities of the experience.
- Test. For each test, the participant works on the two defined working scenarios.

During the test, both scenarios are considered by the participant: firstly, Scenario 1 for 6 min, then Scenario 2 for 15 min, fulfilling the objectives described in Table 4.9.

A facilitator supervised the test and took notes about the time expended by the participants during the performance of each task. When tasks were completed, each participant was invited to fill a NASA TLX index questionnaire form about the proposed experience.

Table 4.9 Experimental tasks and activities.

Scenarios	Task	Activities	Goals	Time
Scenario 1	TOH5	The participant solves the TOH5 problem	Solve the problem with 31 moves	6 min
Scenario 2	TOH5+CA	The participant solves the TOH5 problem and responds to requests for collaboration from the robot	Solve the problem with 31 moves and complete 9 cycles of work with cobot	15 min

4.3.6.4 Measure

There are several mental workload physiological metrics to be taken into consideration, for instance, heart rate, pupil dilation, respiration rate, skin temperature, and fundamental frequency (Heard et al., 2019; Muñoz-de Escalona et al., 2020). In the participants' study presented in this research, the authors used a subjective mental workload measure through the adoption of the NASA-TLX index standard questionnaire. The questionnaire form was derived from the app NASA TLX index v1.8.2 (see Fig. 4.15 and Fig. 4.16). It allows deriving the overall workload score based on a weighted average of ratings on six subscales: mental demand, physical demand, temporal demand, performance, effort, and frustration level. This questionnaire is an effective tool for the study of the mental workload. As shown in Fig. 4.15, the participant must fill in the two questionnaires, one for the working scenario 1 (TOH5) and the other for scenario 2 (TOH5+CA).

A description for each of these subscales was provided to help participants answer accurately. They are rated for each task within a 100-point range with 5-point steps. These ratings are then combined with the task workload index. These scales and descriptions are shown in Table 4.10.

FIGURE 4.15

NASA TLX index app with the two forms defined.

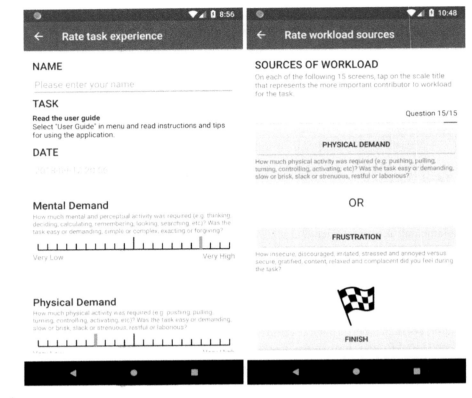

FIGURE 4.16

Example NASA TLX index app. On the right, the range of subscales, and on the left, the weight of the pair of subscales.

4.4 **Review questions**

In this section the reader will find some questions to check their level of knowledge about the experience gained. In addition, some of these questions pose research challenges, such as search for formal methods or scenarios in which the reader has to plan which methodology to use and how to proceed with experimental measurement.

1. Find information on metrics applicable to human–robot teams.
2. Section 4.2 discusses the use of objective and subjective metrics for the evaluation of operator and robot performance. At the local scale, at the station where the cooperation between the operator and robot takes place, examples of these metrics include task effectiveness and time to task. In manufacturing processes, these objective metrics are encompassed in operational key performance indicators. Complete the list of metrics by adding examples of strategic key performance

Table 4.10 Rating scale definitions for the NASA TLX index standard questionnaire.

Subscale	Endpoints	Descriptions
Mental Demand	Low/High	How much mental and perceptual activity was required? Was the task easy or demanding, simple or complex?
Physical Demand	Low/High	How much physical activity was required? Was the task easy or demanding, slack or strenuous?
Temporal Demand	Low/High	How much time pressure did you feel due to the pace at which the tasks or task elements occurred? Was the pace slow or rapid?
Overall Performance	Low/High	How successful were you in performing the task? How satisfied were you with your performance?
Effort	Low/High	How hard did you have to work (mentally and physically) to accomplish your level of performance?
Frustration Level	Low/High	How irritated, stressed, and annoyed versus content, relaxed, and complacent did you feel during the task?

indicators (oriented to a general scale focused on organization, business, and management).

3. Imagine that the operator works with an intelligent assistant. Redesign the Usability Test Plan presented in this chapter according to the new scenario to define data gathering, build metrics, and assess the quality of the assistance.

4. Complete the previous question by adding user experience functionality, that is, measures of trust, explainability, and emotional aspects of the interaction between the operator and the intelligent assistant.

Results of experimentation

5

Abstract

This chapter shows the results of the experimentation, the discussion of which will be presented in the next chapter. In Chapters 3 and 4 the research methodology for the Human–Robot Collaborative Workspace Experience was developed in four steps. In the first two steps the FRAM methodology was introduced as a form to measure variability in the shared workspace. The three possible scenarios, three possible final products, and several kinds of operator and robot skills were defined. Now it is time to get the results of this experimentation. At the experimental level, simulated tests and academic laboratory tests for the HRCWE prototype have been carried out. In the tests with collaborative robot in assembly task for variability measurements, different operational modes (manual, automatic) and different operator profiles (novice, standard, expert) have been considered. Practical statistics for user research and graphical representation are used in the quantification of the user experience.

Next, a study about mental workload focuses on defining objective variables (e.g., effectiveness, efficiency) and subjective variables (e.g., satisfaction, mental workload) and providing metrics. The metrics used come from the field of human–computer interaction and from research work developed by other authors, such as fluency metric. The purpose of using these metrics is to collaborate in the development of H-R metrics that can be shared with the scientific community. In turn, the methodology outlined in the previous chapter together with this presentation of quantitative results can help other scientists to plan experimental studies on H-R teams.

5.1 Introduction

In Chapters 3 and 4 the research methodology for the Human–Robot Collaborative Workspace Experience was developed in four steps. Now it is time to get the results of this experimentation.

Metrics have been chosen, some of them derived from the state of the art, and are now shared with the scientific community. Moreover, the methodology outlined in the previous chapters together with this presentation of quantitative results can help other scientists to plan experimental studies on H-R teams.

Our proposal is defending to quantitatively measure the overall satisfaction of the interaction, that is, user satisfaction, and also "task satisfaction" by using *variability* in the task efficiency metric, Time to Task *TT*. That is, we propose to move from both direct quantitative robotics and qualitative human measures to the overall product or process quality evaluation.

5.2 Results for task satisfaction. A simulated experiment

This section shows the results obtained through the simulation of the three scenarios specified in Section 3.5.2 (page 60) for the Manual Assembly task:

- Scenario 1. Fully manual task.
- Scenario 2. Fully automated task with a robot (a cobot by default).
- Scenario 3. The process is executed in a collaborative manner, human–robot shared task.

5.2.1 Execution in an AIoT simulated environment

Experimentation in the Manual Assembly task is performed as described in Chapter 3 according to their associated activities. The variabilities for process *Time* and product *Quality* are evaluated. Following the FRAM approach, the task is simulated using a Flexsim software (Nordgren, 2002) scenario under several contexts of use. Some distribution functions for variability will be used to perform a realistic simulation of an industrial assembly task.

The FRAM model for the analysis of collaboration tasks is analyzed through the instantiation of different states. The existing relationships are observed in Fig. 5.1, which presents an instance of the model for the case of the Scenario, the one that mixes actions from the robot (blue elements, grey in print version) and operator (green element, dark grey in print version). The function <OPERATORS> provides the cobot and operator as resources and uses them depending on the type of task performed in the state; the <GET CAP> function in this case is carried out by the human operator, whereas the others are carried out by the cobot.

Before starting the simulation, a virtual basic version of the process has been created using the RoboDK simulation software (Garbev and Atanassov, 2020) to obtain realistic completion times for each activity. These values are considered as references for the process, as shown in Table 5.1.

Using the FRAM methodology, two variation characteristics are considered in a straightforward form: *Time*, expressed as for Time to Task (in seconds), and *Quality*, defined as the Percentage of High-Quality Product Percentage, as it was defined in Section 3.5.3 (page 63). Let us remember that Time to Task is a measure of efficiency, the time to complete a product (total assembly). Similarly, High-Quality Product Percentage is the ratio of high-quality products to total production expressed as a percentage.

For the simulation, two types of distribution functions are used. The operator takes different time periods to perform operations about take and place the different parts for the assembly. The time for these operations tends to be greater than the average

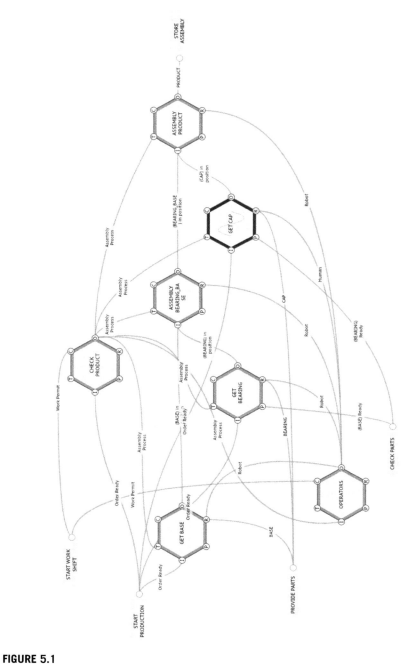

FIGURE 5.1

Model of the Scenario 3 on FRAM for Human and Cobot collaboration.

Table 5.1 Time to Task values obtained from the RoboDK virtual model.

Function	Time
<ASSEMBLY PRODUCT>	3.3 s
<ASSEMBLY BEARING_BASE>	1.0 s
<GET BASE>	1.9 s
<GET BEARING>	2.0 s
<GET CAP>	2.3 s
Time to Task, mv_t	10.6 s

value for the robot, thus affecting downstream in the assembly process and increasing the total production time of the parts. Following the recommendations of experts in manufacturing modeling (Piera, 2004), a *lognormal* distribution is used for this type of cases (see Table 5.2). The mean variation value, $\Delta mv = 0$ s, that is, how much time, in mean, is used for different operators for each activity, is not modified. Hence there is not difference in how fast are operators completing activities. However, standard deviation increases as expertness operator decreases. In this form, for the study, only variability is affecting *Time* process.

Table 5.2 Values used in distribution functions for *Time*, the same for all the functions.

Function	Type Operator	Value
Log-Normal()	Expert	$\Delta mv = 0$ s, $\sigma = 3$ s
	Standard	$\Delta mv = 0$ s, $\sigma = 4$ s
	Novice	$\Delta mv = 0$ s, $\sigma = 5$ s

Variations in the assembly process affect product Quality, in this case, between High quality and Typical quality values. For this case, according to Piera (2004), a Bernoulli distribution function is the best option. Hence, as we can see in Table 5.3, different percentages are considered depending on the level of the operator's expertise. It is considered that 98% of products are High quality when activities are performed by an expert operator. This percentage decreases to 90% and 80% for the case of standard and novice operators, respectively.

Table 5.3 Values used in distribution functions for *Quality*, the same for all the functions.

Function	Type Operator	Output
Bernoulli()	Expert	98% High-Quality products
	Standard	90% High-Quality products
	Novice	80% High-Quality products

The simulation in the Flexsim software has been configured with a working time of 3600 s, that is, one hour, and a total of 30 replicates per experiment, to avoid bias from the probability distribution.

5.2.2 Results on task indicators

In this section the results for task indicators, Time to Task and Percentage of products finished with high quality, are shown using simple statistics, mean and standard deviation.

For data collection, three types of models (Scenario) are used in the collaborative work environment. The model represented in Fig. 5.2 corresponds to Scenario 3. The control panel displays the simulation results, including the "Time to Task" values and the quality of the produced products. In addition, it allows obtaining a vision of the distribution of tasks between the operator and cobot.

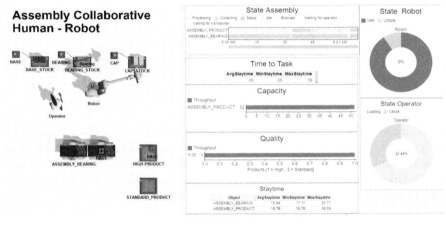

FIGURE 5.2

Simulation of the collaborative human–robot assembly workspace for Scenario 3.

On the left panel the collaborative human–robot assembly is simulated. The middle panel, from top to down, presents the action being executed, statistics about the Time to Task measure, the total quantity of assembled products, the percentage of high-quality assembled products, and statistics about the lasting time performing actions. Finally, on the right panel, the percentage of use of the robot (up) and the percentage of collaboration of the operator (down) are illustrated. Since only one task is being performed, most of time the robot is in "idle" situation. This is not very time efficient, but will allow to obtain higher percentages of high-quality products. The same can be said for the operator side.

5.2.2.1 Scenario 1. Fully manual task

For the first scenario, it is considered that only one operator develops the different activities associated with the assembly task. It can be observed in Table 5.4 how the mean time mv_t and its standard deviation σ_t for completing the task increases as the level of expertise decreases. Note that it was supposed that all the operators are identically fast performing activities, $\Delta mv = 0$. Thus it is evident that the only presence of variability introduces delays in the task performance from 11.87 seconds to complete a task, in the case of an expert operator, to 13.77 and 15.20 seconds for the other two cases. In this form, an expert operator is able to complete 173 products in one hour; a standard one is completing 152 products, and a novice operator is only completing 138 products. This difference in effective production is also reported when observing how much time operators are active, that is, performing an activity. This percentage ranges from 89% to 72% and 63% for Expert, Standard, and Novice operator, respectively.

Table 5.4 Scenario 1: Results for *Time* (mv_t, σ_t) and *Quality* (mv_Q, σ_Q).

Type Operator	mv_t (s)	σ_t (s)	mv_Q (%)	σ_Q (%)
Expert	11.87	0.43	98%	3.01
Standard	13.77	0.57	90%	3.79
Novice	15.20	0.81	80%	4.03

As it could be expected, the mean quality mv_Q is similar to the default percentages assigned for each type of operator, specified in Table 5.3. However, it is worth noting how standard deviation for high product quality σ_Q gets significantly high values for all the types of operators, showing clearly how time variability also impacts on the final product *Quality*.

5.2.2.2 Scenario 2. Fully automated task with a robot

For this fully automated scenario, it is considered for the cobot that starting from the typical / normal condition, an optimization upgrade allows increase its speed by 20% and so is translated to the result for mv_t, as displayed in Table 5.5. Besides, no time deviation is considered for the execution of the activities, as it is the usual high-precision case in industrial robotics. Therefore the standard deviation σ_t gets the null value as a result.

Table 5.5 Scenario 2: Results for *Time* (mv_t, σ_t) and *Quality* (mv_Q, σ_Q).

Type Operator	mv_t (s)	σ_t (s)	mv_Q (%)	σ_Q (%)
Basic	11.0	0.0	79%	3.50
Optimized	10.0	0.0	79%	3.14

Our hypothesis is that the cobot is not well prepared for this new task, because some decorative specifications are asked for the user that the robot is not able to accurately sense. This is the reason why human operators are helping in the assembly process in Scenario 3. Consequently, the mean value used in the distribution function for high-quality products is 79%, below that of a novice operator. As it could be expected, a similar mv_Q is obtained as result for both types of cobots, the basic and the optimized one. It is worth noting that the standard deviation is higher for the basic robot than for the upgraded (faster) one. Hence it is demonstrated that the percentage of high-quality products is not downgraded because of faster processing.

5.2.2.3 Scenario 3. Collaborative human–robot task

The implementation of the MABA-MABA (Men-Are-Better-At / Machines-Are-Better-At) strategy (Sheridan, 2000) has been carried out in this scenario. As a result of three kinds of operator skill levels, from novice to expert, and two kinds of robots, basic and optimized, there are six possible cases to be considered, as observed in Table 5.6. For the implementation of the cases, the Efficiency-Thoroughness Trade-Off (ETTO) (Hollnagel, 2009) principle has been maintained.

Table 5.6 Scenario 3: Results for *Time* (mv_t, σ_t) and *Quality* (mv_Q, σ_Q).

Operator (R)	Operator (H)	mv_t (s)	σ_t (s)	mv_Q (%)	σ_Q (%)
Basic	Expert	11.03	0.18	98%	2.96
	Standard	11.93	0.25	89%	2.99
	Novice	12.43	0.50	79%	3.39
Optimized	Expert	10.93	0.25	98%	3.07
	Standard	11.03	0.18	90%	3.04
	Novice	11.80	0.41	79%	3.43

For this collaborative scenario, mv_t values for time employed to complete the assembly task are higher than those for the fully automated scenario. No significant time increase is observed when the Basic cobot is used, that is, humans are not delaying too much the product completion. However, this is the case where the optimized cobot is employed for all types of human operators. As a first conclusion, optimizing cobots' speed is not worthy for the collaborative scenario in this assembly task because the speed difference between robots and humans is increasing too much. The standard deviation σ_t is reduced in comparison with the totally manual scenario, as it was expected because cobots are not inserting variability.

For the measure of *Quality*, it is important to highlight how percentages of high-quality products mv_Q in this collaborative scenario are very similar to those in the totally manual scenario. That is, the collaborative human–robot shared task allows us to significantly outperform the low percentage when using only cobots, due to the dexterous expertise of the human operators. At the same time, the total quality is very near to the totally manual scenario, showing that the introduction of robots allows faster completing tasks at almost no cost in the quality performance.

In Fig. 5.3 the boxplot for the variation of the Time to Task for 30 repli-cates is shown in a workspace composed of a Human Operator (Expert, Standard, Novice) and the Robot Operator set Basic. We can observe a greater variability (grey whiskers) for the novice operator than for the other two cases.

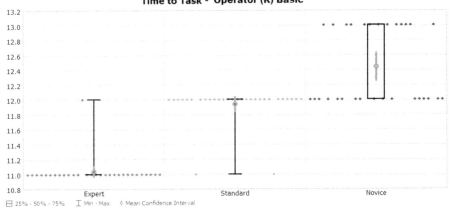

FIGURE 5.3

Time variation according to the variable Time to Task considering Operator Robotic Basic in Scenario 3.

A similar boxplot is displayed in Fig. 5.4 for the percentage of high-quality as-sembled products. For this scenario, quality is more related to the characteristics the operator imposes on the process, which is why there is greater, but similar, variability for each case. Mean value is where differences can be better appreciated, depending on the operator skill level.

5.3 Results from real experimentation in HRCWE

Results from real experimentation in Human–Robot Collaborative Workspace Expe-rience are presented according to the planned methodology introduced in the previous Chapters 3 and 4.

Let us recall that in Chapter 3, Fig. 3.16 (page 69) showed the workspace divided into two areas. The "Work Area 1" is where the operator executes the primary task, the Tower of Hanoi game with five disks (TOH5), with high demanding cognitive workload. It is considered as the "Task 1", the main task for the operator. The "Work Area 2" is where the operator executes the Collaborative Assembly (CA) of the prod-uct with the robot. It is named "Task 2", the secondary one, only executed when the operator is asked for the robot. In the "Work Area 1" the human is in the loop. The information processing system provides the participant with visual feedback on the task being developed. The participant can plan strategies and make decisions about

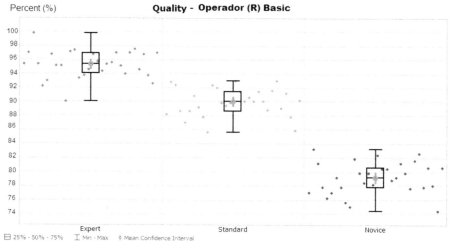

FIGURE 5.4

Quality variation according to the variable High-Quality Product Percentage considering Operator Human Standard in Scenario 3.

when and in which intensity attend the request of the robot. The participant executes physical actions in a touch screen when performing the "Task 1". In Chapter 4 the Human–Robot Collaborative Workspace Experience experimentation design, the metrics to be used, and measurement tools were presented.

Fig. 5.5, shows the organization of the presented results in this chapter. For *usability*, the variables effectiveness, efficiency, and user satisfaction are considered, the last one measured using the SUS questionnaire. The results for *cognitive workload* are based on the concept of mental workload, measured using the NASA-TLX questionnaire. Finally, *human–robot teaming* is measured using several key performance indexes and the fluency concept introduced in this research.

5.3.1 Results from heuristics evaluation in HRCWE

Prior to the real implementation of the Human–Robot Collaborative Workspace Experience, the evaluation of the proposed preliminary design is carried out through the questionnaire shown in Table 5.7.

A review of the responses obtained suggests some considerations. For question H1, the answer suggests a detailed approach on the part of the designer but could benefit from greater specificity and clarity as to how the reviews and analyzes were conducted. Additionally, clearly defining what is meant by "all tasks and activities" could help avoid misunderstandings.

For question H2, the response provides specific information on how feedback is communicated to the operator using the robot's LED tower and technology pendant.

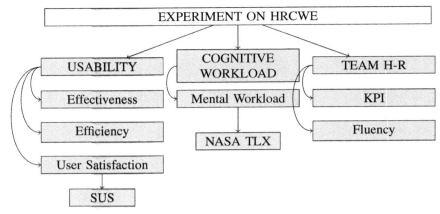

FIGURE 5.5

Organization of results presented for the Human–Robot Collaborative Workspace Experience.

Table 5.7 Questionnaire to evaluate heuristics for the design of Human–Robot Collaborative Workspace Experience.

Heuristic	Question	Answer
H1. Sufficient information design	Has the designer considered all tasks and activities in the design?	All task are analyzed and all activities review
H2. Visibility of system status	Is the operator informed about the progress of the system with the appropriate response and within an acceptable time?	Feedback is send to operator by LED's tower and techpendant on robot
H3. Appropriate information presentation	Does the system use concepts and language familiar to the operator rather than technical terms?	The names of piece and activities are standard
H4. Use natural cues	Do design elements, such as objects and actions, have the same meaning or effect in different situations?	Pick and Place is defined in the same manner for all activities.
H5. Synthesis of system and interface	Are the task methods efficient?	The activities have low workload for operator
H6. Help users recognize, diagnose, and recover from errors	Is appropriate help provided and is the information easy to find and focused on the operator's task?	The errors are minimal and easy to recover from error
H7. Flexibility of interaction architecture	Can the operator customize frequent actions or shortcuts?	The operator is free to decide which activities to perform.
H8. Aesthetic and minimalist design	Does the dialogue contain irrelevant or rarely used information?	The minimal additional intervention is necessary.

However, it does not directly address the adequacy of the response or the delivery time. It would be valuable to add additional details on these aspects for a more complete evaluation of the original question. In H3 the response indicates that the system uses standard part and activity names rather than technical terms, suggesting that language familiar to the operator is used. However, it might be beneficial to provide more details on how this choice was arrived at and how operator understanding is ensured. For H4, the response indicates that "Pick and Place" is defined the same across all activities, suggesting a search for consistency in the interpretation and application of this design element. However, it might be valuable to provide more information on how this consistency is maintained and why it is considered important for a more complete evaluation.

For H5, the response suggests that attention has been paid to the efficiency of task methods by designing the activities so that they have little workload for the operator. This is a positive approach to ensure efficient operation, but additional details could be provided on the specific strategies used to achieve this efficiency.

In H6 the answer focuses on error minimization and ease of recovery, which is important in the context of usability. However, it does not directly answer the question of whether adequate help is provided and whether the information is easy to find and focused on the operator's task. For a more complete evaluation, it would be beneficial to provide specific details about the help and organizations of information in the system.

In H7 the answer emphasizes the freedom of the operator to make decisions about what activities they can perform but does not directly address the question about customizing common actions or shortcuts. It would be beneficial to provide more details or clarifications on this aspect for a more complete evaluation. In H8 the response suggests that the dialogue has been designed in such a way that minimal additional intervention is necessary, which implies that the inclusion of irrelevant or little-used information in the system has been minimized. However, it might be beneficial to provide more detail on the specific methods or approaches used to achieve this efficiency in dialogue.

Overall, the answers provided appear to address the questions in general terms, but in some cases, they could benefit from additional details for a more complete evaluation. Furthermore, some of the aspects mentioned, such as efficiency and customization, are considered positive in terms of usability and user experience. From the answers obtained in the questionnaire it is established that the standardization of terms, activities, and tasks is necessary, minute detail is a strategy that will be useful to avoid ambiguous interpretations by the operator.

With the provided results, a validated design is obtained to start working with.

5.3.2 Results on usability in HRCWE

Seventeen (17) participants were completing the experiment; however, three (3) are discarded as they have not correctly completed the proposed questionnaires displayed in Appendix A.1. For this reason, the results on fourteen (14) participants are presented, so the sample space is $n = 14$. For the statistical analysis of the results, the following values are configured: the statistical significance level is set to $p < 0.05$, and the confidence level is declared 95%.

5.3.2.1 Effectiveness

The measure of effectiveness refers to the task success rate with respect to the total number of tasks in the activity. Hence "pass and fail" histograms show the results in solving the tasks within the Human–Robot Collaborative Workspace Experience. Histogram in Fig. 5.6 displays eleven (11) participants solving Task 1, the cognitive demanding Tower of Hanoi with five disks (TOH5), and three (3) participants failing. Histogram in Fig. 5.7 shows the results of the human–robot (H-R) team in solving Task 2. As expected, collaborative assembly being a less demanding cognitive task and also low physical demand, Task 2 (CA) is more successfully completed than Task 1 (TOH5).

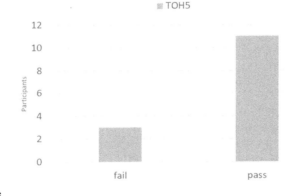

FIGURE 5.6

Histogram of fail and pass for Task 1 – TOH5.

Values for *Task Completion rate* are calculated using the formula

$$Task\ Completion\ rate = \frac{Number\ of\ participants\ with\ successfully\ task}{Total\ number\ of\ participants\ undertaken}. \qquad (5.1)$$

In this form the calculated values for the experimental results are shown in Table 5.8.

The results for the *Task Completion rate* for TOH5 have a mean value of 78.6%. The Benchmark value represents the null hypothesis, that is, there is no significant difference between the actual completion level and the reference value. In this case the Benchmark value is $\mu = 56\%$, where μ represents the population mean of the completion level. Since the *Task Completion rate* is 78.6% and the Benchmark value is 56%, the p-value $= 0.044$ is obtained. Therefore the calculated p-value of 0.044 is lower than the common significance threshold of 0.05. This suggests that there is sufficient statistical evidence to reject the null hypothesis and conclude that the observed value is significantly different from the Benchmark at the 0.05 significance

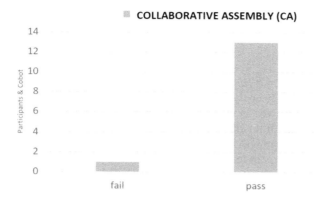

FIGURE 5.7

Histogram of fail and pass for Task 2 – CA (Collaborative Assembly).

Table 5.8 Statistics for the measure *Task Completion rate.*

	TOH5		CA	
Success	11		13	
n	14		14	
Task Completion rate	78.6%		92.9%	
Confidence Interval	Low	High	Low	High
	51.70%	93.2%	66.5%	100%
Benchmark	56			
p-value	0.044		0.002	

level. In other words, the results suggest that the observed value of 78.6% is statistically significantly different from the Benchmark 56%.

Results for the *Task Completion rate* level for CA have a mean value of 92.9%. Again, the null hypothesis is the same, leading to a *p*-value $= 0.002$. In this case the *p*-value reinforces the idea that the observed completion level is significantly different from the reference value. This suggests that there is sufficient statistical evidence to reject the null hypothesis and conclude that the observed value is significantly different from the Benchmark at the 0.05 significance level. In other words, the results suggest that the observed value of 92.9% is statistically significantly different from the Benchmark 56%.

Sauro and Lewis experience (Sauro and Lewis, 2010, 2016) states that a *Task Completion rate* lower than 56% could indicate a very low level of trustness for this variable. The results show a superior level in both tasks, 78.6% and 92.9% with p-values 0.044 and 0.002, respectively. This value is acceptable as it is a first experience of the participant. However, for a continuous work, it would be necessary to improve this value. The *Task Completion rate* level for the CA around 70% could be considered standard given the characteristics of human participation in a so easy human–robot task.

5.3.2.2 Efficiency

To evaluate efficiency, the *Time to Task* variable is analyzed. Recall that this is a variable that was previously analyzed for the case of variability in the simulated manual assembly task. Now, two parallel tasks, collaborative assembly and TOH5 are considered. Firstly, with all the data obtained from the experiment, a percentile scale is generated with five (5) ranges for the variable. They are defined as shown in Table 5.9, according to the time spent in solving the task under consideration.

Table 5.9 Percentiles in Time to Task to resolve TOH5 and CA.

Percentile	Time to Task (s)	
	TOH5	CA
10%	23	102
50%	44	107
75%	66	113
90%	93	116
98%	>94	>120

Task 1 (TOH5) is firstly analyzed. Statistical results for *Time to Task* are shown in Table 5.10, displaying a mean value of 56.2 seconds, which is above the percentile 50%. This table also shows the value for the coefficient of variation (CV), a measure calculated according to Eq. (5.2) for the *Time to Task*, representing a weighted standard deviation in comparison with the mean value. Task 1 (TOH5) with a value of 0.42 represents a very high level of variation, as a result of solving the task only with human participation.

$$CV = \frac{\text{standard deviation}}{\text{mean value}}. \tag{5.2}$$

Table 5.10 Statistics of *Time to Task* for Task 1 (TOH5).

	TOH5	
Mean Value	56.2 (s)	
sd	25.9	
n	14	
Confidence Interval	Low	High
	43.34	72.89
CV	0.42	

For Task 2, *Time to Task* is defined as a result for the overall human–robot teaming, as shown in Eq. (5.3). This time is composed by the human's time (t_H) plus the

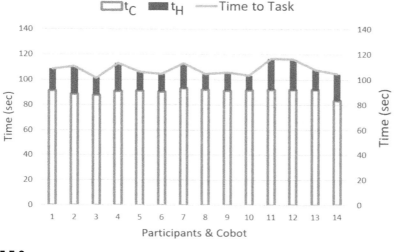

FIGURE 5.8

Time to Task for Task 2.

cobot's time (t_C) when completing the collaborative assembly task.

$$Time\ to\ Task = t_H + t_C. \tag{5.3}$$

Fig. 5.8 shows the results obtained from each participant. We can observe the time addition of the task, the cobot's time being the most important part of the total time.

For the statistical analysis of the *Time to Task* variable, we consider t_C equal to *Cycle Time* for the cobot and t_H equal to *Wait time*, the values obtained directly from the cobot controller.

Results in Table 5.11 show a *Time to Task* of 108.9 seconds as mean value. This corresponds to a percentile of 50% according to Table 5.9 when times for CA and TOH5 are added. CV value is 0.04, equivalent to 4% of variation, which can be considered as very low. Going in deep to each one of the parts composing the Time

Table 5.11 Statistics times in Task 2.

	Time to Task	t_H **(s)**	t_C **(s)**
mean value	108.9	17.05	90.58
standard deviation	4.8	4.5	2.5
n	14	14	14
Confidence Interval			
Low	105.36	14.7	89.10
High	110.89	19.79	92.08
CV	0.04	0.25	0.027

to Task, for t_H, the time employed by the operator, the mean value is 17.05 sec, with CV value of 0.25 equivalent to 25%, which in this case is considered as high, a typical conclusion for human tasks. Finally, for t_C, the mean value is 90.58 sec, and CV is down to 0.027, equivalent to 2.7%, that is, a minimum variation, as expected considering the high stability of the cobot.

5.3.2.3 System usability scale score results

Table 5.12 provides an overview of the mean value, standard deviation, number of incomplete questionnaires, and checking the coding of the questionnaires as well as the values of reliability indices (Cronbach's alpha) for the obtained measures.

Table 5.12 Statistics SUS scoring and reliability test.

Mean SUS Score	81.1		
sd	13.3		
Nonblank	14	Coding Check	Values appear to be coded correctly from 1 to 5
Cronbach Alpha	0.814	Internal Reliability	Good

Table 5.13 shows the results of SUS in the form of percentiles and a descriptive adjective of its value. The value of 81.1 qualifies the Human–Robot Collaborative Workspace Experience as *Excellent* and the degree of acceptability as *Acceptable*.

Table 5.13 SUS results interpretation.

Raw SUS score	81.1	Percentil Rank	88.1%
SUS Benchmark	Hardware	Adjective	Excellent
		Grade (Bangor)	B
		Grade (Sauro&Lewis)	A-
		Acceptability	Acceptable

Extrapolating HRCWE as a hardware system, following the Sauro–Lewis classification, the benchmark of the experience with such hardware shows that a raw SUS score of 81.1 has a higher SUS score than 88.14% for Hardware.

The main value from SUS is providing the single total score. However, it is still necessary to look into detail the individual score for each statement (Bangor et al., 2008). This information is presented in Table 5.14. Sercan Caglarca suggested taking into account individual evaluation by verifying the shape of a "five-pointed star" visualization (Hariyanto et al., 2019). Hence raw scores from Table 5.14 corresponding to responses to individual statements of the SUS questionnaire have been transformed into a radial chart, as shown in Fig. 5.9. Caglarca also concluded that the more the five-pointed star looks, the more positive the usability will get. Although it tends to be a subjective assessment, it is worth noting that the five-pointed star shape is almost in perfect form in this study (Chacón et al., 2021b).

Table 5.14 Responses to individual statements of the SUS questionnaire.

	Statements	Raw Score
1	I think that I would like to use Workspace Collab (HRCWE) frequently.	3.86
2	I found Workspace Human–Robot Collab (HRCWE) unnecessarily complex.	1.64
3	I thought Workspace Human–Robot Collab (HRCWE) was easy to use.	4.29
4	I think that I would need the support of a technical person to be able to use Workspace Human–Robot Collab (HRCWE).	1.57
5	I found the various functions in Workspace Human–Robot Collab (HRCWE) were well integrated.	4.0
6	I thought there was too much inconsistency in Workspace Human–Robot Collab (HRCWE).	2.07
7	I would imagine that most people would learn to use Workspace Human–Robot Collab (HRCWE) very quickly.	4.21
8	I found Workspace Human–Robot Collab (HRCWE) very cumbersome (awkward) to use.	1.50
9	I felt very confident using Workspace Human–Robot Collab (HRCWE).	4.29
10	I needed to learn a lot of things before I could get going with Workspace Human–Robot Collab (HRCWE).	1.43

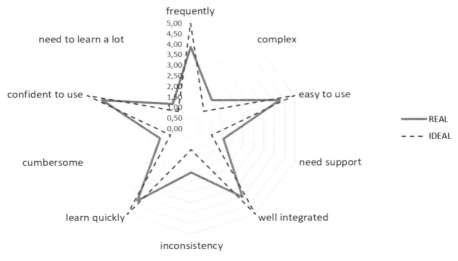

FIGURE 5.9

Evaluation of SUS questionnaire responses in the form of a five-pointed star.

5.3.2.4 Cobot performance

To finalize the experiment about usability, using data from *Cycle Time* and *Wait Time*, the key performance indexes (KPIs) of *Per_Efficiency* and *Per_Utilization* of the cobot are obtained to evaluate the performance of the cobot in the Human–Robot Collaborative Workspace Experience. The *Per_Utilization* is calculated for each participant as

$$Per\_Utilization(participant) = \frac{\overline{Cycle\,Time} - \overline{Wait\,Time}}{\overline{Cycle\,Time}} \times 100 \qquad (5.4)$$

with $\overline{x}$ indicating the mean value of x.

The statistical analysis in Table 5.15, with a mean value of 83%, shows an *Per_Utilization* value higher than 80% in the use of cobot for the collaborative assembly task.

Table 5.15 Statistics of *Per_Utilization* for the cobot in HWRCE.

Mean Value	83%		
sd	0.03		
n	14		
Confidence Interval	Low	High	
	81%	85%	
Benchmark	80%	p-value	0.008

The percentage value of the efficiency, *Per_Efficiency*, is calculated considering the total time of a work cycle, in this case, it was set at 900 seconds:

$$Per\_Efficiency = \overline{Number\,Cycles\,Completed} \times \frac{\overline{Cycle\,Time}}{900} \times 100. \qquad (5.5)$$

The statistical analysis of *Per_Efficiency* in Table 5.16 shows a mean value of 84%, which is a value higher than 75%, with a p-value $= 0.03$, established as a reference in this experiment.

Table 5.16 Statistics *Per Efficiency* of cobot in HWRCE.

Mean Value	84%		
sd	0.13		
n	14		
Confidence Interval	Low	High	
	74%	96%	
Benchmark	75%	p-value	0.03

5.3.3 **Mental workload in HRCWE**

Now it is time to move for the measurement of the mental workload. Using the NASA-TLX questionnaire, results are shown in Table 5.17. In the first two columns, the used markers with adjectives that qualify the mental workload (MWL) (Hart and Staveland, 1988) are shown. Next, np TOH5 and np TOH5+CA represents the number of participants versus the observed qualitative mental workload.

Table 5.17 The interpretation % score for the NASA TLX index.

Mental Workload Range	Value	np TOH5	np TOH5+CA
Low	0–9	0	0
Medium	10–29	0	1
Somewhat High	30–49	5	2
High	50–79	12	13
Very High	80–100	1	2

5.3.3.1 Mental workload results

Descriptive statistics, *t*-test, and analysis of variance tests were used to analyze the effects of the experience in the participants. The statistical significance level was set at $p < 0.05$, and, in all the cases, the confidence level is 5%. Data collected from both scenarios were gathered and presented in the histogram in Fig. 5.10.

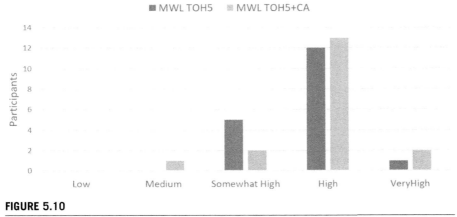

FIGURE 5.10

Histogram of participants' mental workload (MWL) for both scenarios.

The distribution of the data obtained is not symmetric, and they tend to accumulate in the areas with high mental workload. Twelve (13) out of eighteen (18) participants perceived that the mental workload of the task TOH5 was high or very high. Fifteen (15) of the total number of participants perceived that the mental workload of the joint main and secondary tasks TOH5+CA was high. Table 5.18 shows the obtained score for each scenario in terms of mean value and standard deviation. The mean values of the NASA TLX index score for both scenarios are very close, 59.11% and 60.17%, respectively. These scores are at the end of the first third of the range (High).

Table 5.18 Results of NASA TLX Index Score.

Statistics	TOH5	TOH5+CA
Mean value	59.11	60.17
sd	12.20	17.41
Nonblank	18	18
Interpretation Score	High	High

The hypothesis in this study is that when the operator performs the collaborative task with the robot (TOH5+CA, second scenario), the mental workload value is not very far from the mental workload when performing only the main task (TOH5, first scenario), that is, a very little increment δ is expected,

$$MWL_{TOH5+CA} \sim MWL_{TOH5} + \delta. \tag{5.6}$$

Moreover, both values would be in an intermediate comfort zone of mental workload; hence they are not saturating the operators' mental workload.

To test this hypothesis, a paired t-test was performed on the results obtained. The values in Table 5.19 show that there exists a p-value < 0.02 associated with the probability that the difference is greater than 10, so the null hypothesis is rejected, $\delta < 10$, and the alternative hypothesis is corroborated: certainly, there is only a small increase in mental workload (MWL) when the operator is moving from only one task to a dual task with a collaborative robot.

Table 5.19 Paired t-test.

Confidence Level	95		
Null Hypothesis	Diff > 10		
Descriptive Statistics	–	Average Difference	1.06
Mean Difference value	−1.10	Confidence Interval Low	−9.72
Median Difference value	−8.00	Confidence Interval High	7.61
sd	17.43	Margin Error	8.70
n (sample size)	18	p-value	0.02

The interpretation scores shown in Table 5.18 for the associated mental workload are in the low range of the label "High" (59.11 and 60.17) for both scenarios using the scale in Table 5.17. According to the cumulative frequency distributions of TLX Global Workload Scores by Task proposed by Grier (2015), a common experimental mental workload score is related to cognitive tasks with a value of 64.90 as the maximum and 54.66 as within 75% of the results obtained in experiments with the TLX-Index (see Table 5.20). Hence, since the results for scenarios TOH5 and TOH5+AC are in this range, they indicate that the proposed tasks are actually high cognitive tasks, but they are not saturating the set of regular experiments on cognitive tasks.

Table 5.20 Cumulative frequency distributions of mental workload scores by task.

	Min	25%	50%	75%	Max
Cognitive Tasks	13.08	38.00	46.00	54.66	64.90

Fig. 5.11 shows the distribution of the mean values of mental workload (MWL) for different subscales. The mental demand is the subscale with the highest values for both scenarios, which is in accordance with the working conditions established for this study.

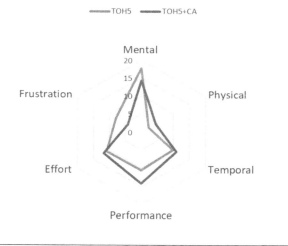

FIGURE 5.11

Mean values of subscales in the NASA TLX index on the experiment.

The results obtained for the subscales studied using the NASA TLX index are shown in Table 5.21. The physical subscale shows a p-value < 0.05, i.e., it is the only one showing significant statistical differences between both scenarios, whereas the other subscales do not. This is consistent with our hypothesis.

5.3.4 Task performance of the human–robot team

In this moment, usability and mental workload have been evaluated. Now it is time to consider the performance of the work developed by the human–robot team. The task performance is measured through *Effectiveness* and *Fluency*.

Table 5.21 Paired samples test for subscales of the NASA TLX index, TOH5 and TOH5+CA.

Subscale	Mean	St. Dev.	p-value
Mental	3.39	10.01	0.172
Physical	−2.11	2.66	**0.004**
Temporal	−1.15	10.03	0.633
Performance	−3.72	7.00	0.038
Effort	−1.07	8.39	0.594
Frustration	3.61	7.26	0.050

5.3.4.1 Effectiveness

This subsection shows the results for the effectiveness of the tasks developed in the Human–Robot Collaborative Workspace Experience. The variable *Task Completion Rate TCR* is considered. It is calculated as

$$TCR = \frac{N_{sucsess}}{N_{replay}} \times 100. \tag{5.7}$$

Table 5.22 shows the results for TCR when the Task TOH5 is solved in both scenarios, that is, only TOH5 or joint TOH5+CA. For the first scenario, a low effectiveness is obtained, with $TCR = 44.44\%$, whereas for the joint Scenario 2, there is a 22% of percent increase ($TCR = 66.67\%$) as a result of the experience gained from Scenario 1.

Table 5.22 TCR results for TOH5 in both scenarios.

	Scenario 1 (TOH5)	Scenario 2 (TOH5+CA)
Nsuccess	8	12
Nreplay	18	18
TCR	44.44%	66.67%
Difference	22.22%	

Table 5.23 shows the results for the effectiveness in the resolution of the TOH5 problem as well as in the collaboration in the assembly, CA. Results show that the collaboration is carried out effectively, with TCR = 94.44%.

5.3.4.2 Fluency

A measure able to evaluate the team's work is fluency. According to Hoffman (2019), fluency evaluation allows determining the performance as a team that the human–robot pair has. Metrics associated to fluency are percentage of concurrent activity $(C - ACT)$, human's idle time $(H - IDLE)$, robot's functional delay $(F - DEL)$, and robot's idle time $(R - IDLE)$. Since no functional delay is expected for the robot (it is not occupied in parallel tasks to assembly), the fluency values are calculated as

Table 5.23 TCR results for TOH5 and CA in Scenario 2.

	TOH5	CA
Nsuccess	12	17
Nreplay	18	18
TCR	66.67%	94.44%
Difference	27.77%	

follows:

$$C - ACT = \frac{Shared\_Time}{Time\,to\,Task}, \qquad (5.8)$$

$$H - IDLE = \frac{Cycle\_Time}{Time\,to\,Task}, \qquad (5.9)$$

$$R - IDLE = \frac{Idle\_Time}{Time\,to\,Task}, \qquad (5.10)$$

$$Time\,to\,Task = Cycle\_Time + Idle\_Time. \qquad (5.11)$$

To calculate the fluency, parameters shown in Table 5.24 were measured from the robot side. The obtained values are summarized in Table 5.25 in the form of mean values and standard deviation.

Table 5.24 Time parameters obtained from cobot.

Parameter	Description
Idle_Time	Sum Robot wait time
Cycle_Time	Sum Robot work time
Shared_Time	Sum Shared Time to resolve task

Table 5.25 Mean values of times obtained from cobot.

Statistics	Cycle_Time	Idle_Time	Shared_Time
Mean value	626	117	34
sd	176	38	8
n	18	–	–

Fig. 5.12 allows us to visualize the results of the calculation. We can see that the value for $H - IDLE$ is much higher than that for $R - IDLE$. Moreover, $C - ACT$ gets a low value.

5.4 Review questions

This chapter presents an effort to obtain experimental results and their analysis using various tools. It highlights the use of standardized usability questionnaires. These

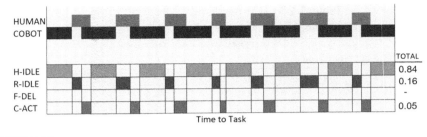

FIGURE 5.12

Objective fluency metrics in the Human–Robot Collaborative Workspace Experience.

standardized measures offer advantages: objectivity (all the practitioners using the same metrics), replicability (showing guidelines for experimental studies that may be useful to other researchers), and quantification (data statistics).

1. Read about *Software Usability Measurement Inventory (SUMI)* (Kirakowski and Corbett, 1993). Explain the main features of SUMI for software quality measurement from a user perspective.
2. Read about *Questionnaire for user interaction satisfaction (QUIS)* (Harper and Norman, 1993). Explain the main features of QUIS to assess users' subjective satisfaction with specific aspects of the human–computer interface.
3. *Technology Acceptance Model (TAM)*(Davis, 1989) was presented in this and previous chapters. Explain the main features of TAM paying attention to the factors that affect a user's intention to use a technology, perceived usefulness, and perceived ease of use.
4. Read about *Subjective Mental Effort Question (SMEQ)* compared with other post-task usability questionnaires (Sauro and Dumas, 2009). Explain the main features of SMEQ questionnaire, the rating scale, and the verbal labels (from "Not all hard to do" label to "Tremendously hard to do" label) to assess the mental effort.
5. *Subjective Workload Assessment Technique (SWAT)* was previously introduced by Rubio et al. (2004). Explain the main features of SWAT where a participant is required to perform a card sorting pretask procedure followed by a task (or event) scoring procedure for the assessment of mental workload.
6. There exists a vast literature about *Measuring mental workload using physiological measures* (Charles and Nixon, 2019). It explores the advantages and disadvantages of the use of physiological measures for measuring mental workload: heart rate, breath rate, pupil size of the eye, skin temperature measure, blood pressure, or brain measure.
7. Chapter 5 shows the detailed statistical results together with a conventional graphical representation in the form of a bar chart, for example. Find information to identify the functionality of the following charts: pie chart, polar area chart, and radar chart.

8. Propose a draft graphical dashboard related to human–robot performance. To do so, select some representative KPIs; arrange the KPIs in square or rectangular boxes; choose the graph that best shows the meaning of the KPI (pie chart, semi-circular gauge, bar charts, etc.).

Discussion, challenges, and lessons learned

6

Abstract

This chapter presents a discussion of the results obtained in the various stages of the applied methodology and usability testing. We will first present the design using the FRAM methodology and simulation from the experimentation in the HRCWE. We also discuss the usability, cognitive load, and performance of the human–robot team. From the general remarks obtained, we can refine the functionality of a cognitive assistant to act as a recommender system. The recommendations are presented in the form of an example in which high product quality is prioritized and the assignment of tasks for various operator profiles is recommended.

Experimental usability results, including mental workload and task performance of the human–robot teamwork, are then discussed with the aim of contributing to the redesign of experimental tasks in future studies.

Finally, a draft of a conceptual architecture for assistance is presented to show how the set of metrics provided in this book can help in the configuration of cognitive assistant functionality. The details of management, user interface design, and dialogue / interaction between cognitive assistant and human supervisor are beyond the scope of this chapter.

6.1 Introduction

We start this chapter by discussing the design principles and methodology for cognitive assistants in the domain of human–robot collaboration, extensively to Industry *4.0*. Certainly, there was a lack in the literature on realizations around this topic, which were initially based on commercial instruments like Google Home Apple's Siri, Amazon's Alexa, or IBM's Watson (Siddike et al., 2018; Maier et al., 2019). Only in the last years there appear some contributions dealing with the use of cognitive assistants in manufacturing, not expanding operator capabilities like using AR / VR but supporting the cognitive work of the operator.

Longo and Padovano (2020) considered that greater cognitive task load and a growing shortage of high-skilled labor are calling for new smart interactions between the cyber-physical production system (CPPS) and the Operator *4.0*. Hence they study the prospective adoption and acceptance of voice-enabled systems to assist the Operator *4.0* during industrial production processes within the Social Smart Factory. In Gong et al. (2021), future cyber-manufacturing is envisioned to be realized in a crowdsourcing environment, engaging a large population of manufacturers to collaborate with the cyber-platform on a shared understanding of the tasks for delivering manufacturing as a service (MaaS). In the review paper, the authors took into consideration that the cyber-platform and intelligent cognitive assistants will enhance MaaS fulfillment. Zitz et al. (2021) designed a system called "Reflect", which responds to critical user conditions by informing the user. It is found that, contrary to common belief, the use of cognitive assistance supporting workers or students in computer-oriented work is perceived positively by most participants and can be increased by emphasizing transparency and fair data processing.

As previously mentioned in the book, Bousdekis et al. (2022) proposed a framework for the evaluation of voice-enabled AI solutions in the Industry *5.0*, in particular, voice-enabled Digital Intelligent Assistants. Another previously mentioned contribution is Freire et al. (2023), where an AI cognitive assistant that provides on-the-job training to novices while acquiring and sharing (tacit) knowledge from experts is presented. Cognitive support is provided as dialectic recommendations for standard work instructions, decision-making, training material, and knowledge acquisition. They describe how the cognitive assistant is implemented, how it interacts with users, its usage scenarios, and the challenges and opportunities. This is January 2023!

Finally, there is no place where ChatGPT cannot arrive. Kernan Freire et al. (2023) offer cognitive assistants with Large Language Models (LLMs), like GPT-3.5, as a tool to bridge knowledge gaps and improve worker performance in manufacturing settings. Ye et al. (2023) introduced CLAICA, a Continuously Learning AI Cognitive Assistant, which supports workers in agile production lines. CLAICA learns from (experienced) workers, formalizes new knowledge, stores it in a knowledge base, along with contextual information, and shares it when relevant. A user study is conducted with 83 participants, who performed eight knowledge exchange tasks with CLAICA.

To start this discussion of the design principles and methodology for cognitive assistants in the domain of human–robot collaboration, the structure of the methodology resulting from the conception, design and evaluation of a *4.0* cognitive operator assistance system in a product assembly process is presented in Fig. 6.1. This methodology basically consists of five steps, the most relevant features of which are presented in this discussion.

1. Identify needs for the human-centered design. In our case the setup considers the Operator *4.0* within the production system CPS (Cyber-Physical System).
2. Understand and specify the context of use. During our work, the context of use is a human–robot collaborative workspace like a typical workstation in a manufacturing production line. Moreover, the CPS will be considered from a Joint Cognitive System framework, and tasks will be visualized from the cognive workload.
3. Specify the user and organizational requirements. A socio-technical system organization is considered, and a Value Sensitive Design approach will be taken into consideration.

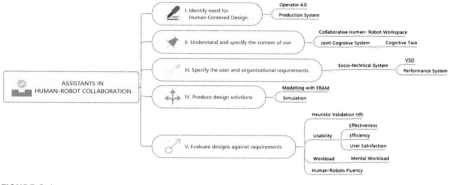

FIGURE 6.1

Methodology to follow in development of a cognitive assistant in the human–robot collaboration workspace.

4. **Produce design solutions.** To produce solutions as, for instance, the variability introduced by the humans in a collaborative setting, the FRAM modeling is considered. The initial solutions are developed in the form of simulations, akin to the concept of a digital twin.

5. **Evaluate designs against requirements.** The main metrics and measures under consideration in the last two chapters were the usability, mental workload, and human–robot fluency. Design of the H-R workplace followed a heuristic validation.

Another aspect to consider is the diversity of existing user profiles. At plant level, there are novice, standard, and expert operators. At management level the production supervisor is available, usually connected to a Manufacturing Execution System (MES) or Enterprise Resource Planning (ERP) system (Mantravadi and Møller, 2019). To these profiles, other ones like the customer or other stakeholders can be added (Cimini et al., 2023).

Besides, in terms of industrial scenarios, we have a range from scenarios in which manual tasks are performed to fully automated scenarios. In between, there are scenarios in which the H-R task is collaborative.

All these contributions in methodology, user profiles, and scenarios lead to a high diversity in design principles for assistants (Mark et al., 2021; Castañé et al., 2023). If the user is the supervisor or customer, then the assistant can adopt the role of system recommender: the assistant can recommend guidelines for increasing the performance of the productive system. In the other side, if the supervisory user is more concerned with the acquisition of skills by the plant operator, then the assistant can adopt the role of a cognitive assistant, that is, the assistant's help is focused on reducing the mental workload associated with the operator's task. The next sections show the integration of these approaches in manufacturing.

6.2 FRAM design and simulation

From the FRAM methodology, which allows us to define models, scenarios, and identification of variability and the simulation of the model that returns distribution functions and discrete event simulation, it has been quantitatively checked that variability in the output of the system is directly related to the performance of the type of operator in the workspace. Now it is time to convert these results into cognitive information, so the operator can organize her / his shift time, the supervisor can organize production, and so on. Eventually, according to this research, the robot can be equipped with an assistant-type module to be used as an assistant to recommend some strategy to the operator or supervisor in case some deviation happens in the actual production specifications.

For the analysis, the coefficient of variation CV, defined in Eq. (4.1) (page 85) as the ratio between standard deviation and mean, expressed as a percentage, is employed. This coefficient of variability is useful to compare the variability of different data from the scenarios, especially because these populations may have very different mean values. A higher CV value indicates greater relative variability compared to the mean value, whereas a lower CV value indicates lower variability relative to the mean value. The obtained value is used to quantify the human operator's variability, the one introducing variability in time. Hence CV_{TA} represents the variability that occurs due to differences in individual task performance within the scenario. For the experimentation, it is calculated and displayed in Table 6.1 in reference to the time variability in the five (5) activities to complete the product, as the mean value:

$$CV_{TA} = \frac{\overline{\sigma_t}}{\overline{mv_t}}. \tag{6.1}$$

As expected, it is observed that the variability coefficient of variation increases inversely to the expertness degree of the human operator. At the "Expert" experience level, the low mean value 2.34 is obtained with low standard deviation 0.07. It suggests that the measurements tend to be very close to the mean value. The variability coefficient 2.99 for "Expert" operators is a weighted measure of the variability in relation to the average value.

At the "Standard" level, the average value 2.70 is a little higher than at the "Expert" level, and the standard deviation 0.09 is also slightly larger, suggesting that

Table 6.1 Results for the overall activity (Manual Assembly). Values are the mean for each activity related to the task.

Operator (H)	$\overline{mv_t}(s)$	$\overline{\sigma_t}(s)$	CV_{TA}
Expert	2.34	0.07	2.99
Standard	2.70	0.09	3.33
Novice	2.99	0.10	3.34

the measurements have a slightly larger spread at this level. The variability coefficient 3.33 is accordingly increased.

Finally, at the "Novice" level, the mean value 2.99 is the highest of all levels with standard deviation 0.10 being also the highest one. This indicates a greater dispersion of measurements around the mean value at this level. The variability coefficient 3.34 is also the highest of all levels, but it is not so far from the value for the "Standard" operators.

In conclusion, as we progress from the "Expert" level to the "Novice" level, we observe a gradual increase in both the mean value and variability (measured by the standard deviation and variability coefficient). This fact indicates that, in general, as experience increases, the variability in measurements tends to decrease, and the mean value tends to be lower.

In Table 6.2, CV_{TT} represents the resulting variation in time for the total assembly of one product. The goal is to identify the source of variability in the process, which can help to take steps to optimize it. This may include machine adjustments, changes in operating conditions, or operator training to reduce variability and increase efficiency. The values for the mean and standard deviation are obtained from Table 5.4.

Table 6.2 Results for the overall time to task of manual assembly.

Operator (H)	$mv_t(s)$	$\sigma_t(s)$	CV_{TT}
Expert	11.87	0.43	3.62
Standard	13.77	0.57	4.14
Novice	15.20	0.81	5.33

At the "Expert" level of experience in manual assembly, we observe the following: the mean value 11.87 is relatively low, indicating that at this level, assemblies tend to have a lower variability. The standard deviation 0.43 is moderate, suggesting that there is some variability in assembly measurements, but it is not excessively high. The variability coefficient 3.62 is also moderately high, indicating variability relative to the mean value at this level, but it is not extremely high.

At the "Standard" level of manual assembly, the mean value 13.77 is higher than for the "Expert" level, suggesting that at this level, assemblies tend to have a higher average variability value. The standard deviation 0.57 is larger than at the "Expert" level, indicating that the assembly measurements have a greater spread. The variability coefficient 4.14 is also higher, indicating greater variability relative to the mean value at this level.

Finally, at the "Novice" level of manual assembly, the mean value 15.20 is the highest of all levels. The standard deviation 0.81 is the highest of all levels, suggesting that assembly measurements have the greatest dispersion at this level. The variability coefficient 5.33 is also the highest of all levels, indicating a very high variability relative to the mean value at this level. In conclusion, as we progress from the "Novice" to "Expert" level, a gradual decrease is observed in both the mean value and the variability (measured by the standard deviation and variability coefficient). Moreover, comparing both tables, difference in variability, measured using CV_{TA}, between "Novice" and "Standard" level is not so large for each activity, considered as a mean (3.33 vs 3.34). However, this variability spreads along the process, that is, the concatenation of activities, leading to an evident increase in variability for the overall process. Measured CV_{TT} values correspond to 4.14 for "Standard" operators and 5.33 for the "Novice" ones. This does not happen between "Expert" and "Standard" operators, with values for CV_{TT} not so far.

Next, for the *Time* variable, the percentage of variation from mean time in task and time in activity is obtained:

$$\%Var_t = \frac{CV_{TT}}{CV_{TA}}. \tag{6.2}$$

This percentage indicates the ratio between the variability of the specific task and the total variability of the activities performed by an operator. In Table 6.3, we show the results obtained for variability at each scenario.

A similar percentage of variation is calculated for *Quality*, also shown in Table 6.3. In this case, it is assumed that parts composing the assembly are introduced into the system with the same distribution, independently from the operator in the activities. The coefficient of quality in input, CV_{QI}, has the same value for all the cases, and the quality total of output is CV_{QT}, and hence we calculate

$$\%Var_Q = \frac{CV_{QT}}{CV_{QI}}. \tag{6.3}$$

Table 6.3 Relation of coefficient of variation for *Time* and *Quality*.

Scenario	Operator (H)	Operator (R)	CV_{TA}	CV_{TT}	$\%Var_t$	CV_{QI}	CV_{QT}	$\%Var_Q$
1	Expert		2.99	3.62	121.12	4.3	3.07	71.43
	Standard		3.33	4.14	124.18	4.3	3.79	97.93
	Novice		3.34	5.33	159.36	4.3	5.04	117.15
2		Optimized	0.0	0.0	0.0	4.3	3.97	92.43
		Basic	0.0	0.0	0.0	4.3	4.43	103.03
3	Expert	Optimized	2.99	2.28	76.46	4.3	3.13	72.85
	Standard		3.33	1.63	48.96	4.3	3.38	78.55
	Novice		3.34	3.47	103.92	4.3	4.34	100.97
3	Expert	Basic	2.99	1.63	54.56	4.3	3.02	70.24
	Standard		3.33	2.09	62.89	4.3	3.36	78.13
	Novice		3.34	4.02	120.31	4.3	4.29	99.79

6.2.1 **General remarks**

For the analysis of results displayed in Table 6.3, each scenario is revised according to the execution characteristics of the task based on the level of operators skills. Variables Time to Task and Percentage of Quality Products are considered for Time and Quality, respectively.

6.2.1.1 Scenario 1
6.2.1.1.1 Time to task

In this case, we consider a single operator, Human (H). In all three data sets, the level of experience varies from "Expert" to "Novice", allowing us to see how the variability relates to different levels of experience in the task or activity.

CV_{TA}: Task variability gradually increases from "Expert" (2.99) to "Standard" (3.33) and then to "Novice" operator (3.34). This indicates that, on average, task-specific measures show lower variability as the level of experience increases.

CV_{TT}: Similar to the task variability pattern, the total activity variability also increases from "Expert" (3.62) to "Standard" (4.14) and then to "Novice" (5.33). This suggests that, in general, measures of all the activities to complete the task show lower variability as the level of experience increases. Variability is amplified in a broader context.

$\%Var_t$: The ratio between task variability and total activity variability decreases as the level of experience increases. In other words, task variability represents an even smaller fraction of the total variability as experience decreases. This suggests that experience appears to be related to greater consistency in individual task performance compared to overall variability across activities.

In summary, this comparative analysis indicates that, in general, as the level of experience increases, both CV_{TA} and CV_{TT} tend to decrease, suggesting that skills experience can play an important role in the consistency and variability of performance on tasks and activities.

6.2.1.1.2 Quality of product

In all data sets, we observe that the quality variability measured with CV_{QI} is relatively high compared to the variability of the total activity, regardless of the level of experience.

CV_{QI} is similar across the "Expert", "Standard", and "Novice" data sets, suggesting that the quality of performance of the specific task can vary significantly across experience levels.

CV_{QT}, the measure including the multiple activities completing the task, increases slightly from "Standard" to "Novice", showing that other activities in the set may have higher variability in quality compared to the specific task.

$\%Var_Q$ is the lowest in the "Expert" data set (71.43) and highest in the "Standard" (97.93) and "Novice" (117.15) data sets, suggesting that the task represents a relatively larger fraction of the total variability in the "Standard" and "Novice" data sets.

In summary, this analysis highlights that variability in CV_{QI} is an important factor to be considered at all levels of experience but can also be influenced by other factors in the contexts of intermediate ("Standard") and low ("Novice") levels of experience.

6.2.1.2 Scenario 2

6.2.1.2.1 Quality of product

With a single operator, in this case a robot (R), we can conclude the following:

CV_{QI}: At both levels, optimized and basic robot, the variability in product quality is the same, with a value of 4.3. This means that, on average, the quality of the product executed by the cobot is equally variable in both cases.

CV_{QT}: At the "Optimized" level, the variability of the product is 3.97, whereas at the "Basic" level, it is slightly higher, with a value of 4.43. This result suggests that at the "Optimized" level, the total activity, which includes the task at hand along with other related activities, has slightly lower variability compared to the "Basic" level.

$\%Var_Q$: In the relationship between variability in the activities and variability in the total task, the "Basic" level has a greater ratio (103.3) compared to the "Optimized" level (92.43). This indicates that at the "Basic" level, variability in task quality has a relatively greater impact on the total variability of the robot activity compared to the "Optimized" level.

In summary, although CV_{QI} is the same at both levels, the "Optimized" level appears to achieve lower variability in CV_{QT} and a lower ratio. This suggests that, roughly speaking, the "Optimized" level can offer more consistent and higher quality execution of the total activity compared to the "Basic" level. However, it is important to consider other factors and additional data for a complete evaluation of the effectiveness and efficiency of each level.

6.2.1.3 Scenario 3

6.2.1.3.1 Time to task

With a human operator (H) and a robot (R), a comparative analysis of the results for the Human–Robot (H-R) teaming is performed at the three different experience levels: "Expert", "Standard", and "Novice".

At the expert experience level, CV_{TA} has a relatively high value compared to CV_{TT}. This suggests that even in teams with extensive human experience, differences in individual tasks can significantly affect the consistency in the duration of team activities. It is recommended to explore ways to standardize and improve efficiency in individual tasks.

At the "Standard" experience level, the results are similar to those of the "expert" team. This suggests that even at a level of experience considered "Standard", individual tasks can have a significant impact on CV_{TT}. It is suggested to look for ways to standardize and improve consistency in tasks.

At the "Novice" experience level, an extremely high ratio is observed between CV_{TA} and CV_{TT}. This indicates that differences in individual tasks have a very significant impact on the overall variability of H-R team work time. In "Novice" level teams, it is essential to address this high variability in individual tasks to improve consistency and efficiency in the execution of tasks and activities.

In summary, across all three experience levels, the importance of addressing variability in individual tasks is highlighted to improve consistency and efficiency in the work of the Human–Robot teamwork. As the level of experience increases, the variability may decrease but is still relevant. In all cases, it is recommended to consider the standardization of processes and the identification of factors that contribute to variability in tasks to achieve greater efficiency.

6.2.1.3.2 Product quality

The variable $\%Var_Q$ represents how much the total variability for the product process changes compared to the mean quality in each activity. The values in Scenario 3 are very similar; in fact, they are slightly better than those in Scenario 1, showing that the interaction between humans and robots improves, or at least does not decrease, the quality of the final product.

6.2.1.4 *Comparison of scenarios*

As we can see in Table 6.3, the input variability, measured with CV_{TA} and CV_{TT}, is amplified through the system due to the presence of human operators, with the highest values present in Scenario 1 (only manual task). Novice operators insert the greatest variation in comparison with standard and expert operators, and therefore there is the greatest amplification. Checking the values for $\%Var_t$, we observe that the overall variability of the total assembly CV_{TT} is larger than the mean variability for the five involved activities CV_{TA} leading to values larger than 100 for the aforementioned cases. This is not the case when the robot is introduced into the system and operator profile is expert or standard. In this case, variability introduced for humans in some of the activities is reduced due to the presence of the robot for the overall task. In these cases the values of $\%Var_t$ are lower than 100.

On the other hand, if the system activities are only executed by the robot (Scenario 2), then quality variability changes when moving from an optimized robot to a basic one, but not so much. This can be checked observing $\%Var_Q$ in Scenario 2.

The human–robot collaborative system (Scenario 3) presents less variability for time and quality with respect to a human only system, except for the extreme case of an expert operator when a basic cobot is introduced. Even in this case the values are very similar. Moreover, in Scenario 3, production is increased. The assignment of activities can be optimized based on the information of the activity times employed and the functions performed, so dynamic assignment of functions is possible. For the assignment of activities, a strategy is employed based on system operating conditions that are favorable to the operator and that maintain acceptable levels of efficiency within the work shift. The activity assigner can consider transitioning from a novice operator to an expert operator and modify the assignment to achieve maximum efficiency of the human–robot collaborative system.

6.2.2 Cognitive assistant as a recommender system

Let us suppose our customer is asking for a batch of products such that at least 85% are required to be of high quality. According to the variability study performed, a fully manual task (Scenario 1) with expert or standard operators provides for sure this result. It is impossible to get it for Scenario 2 only considering a fully automated task. Finally, in the collaborative Scenario 3, again expert or standard operators should be considered. Hence a first recommendation message is not to consider novice operators for this case. However, they could be considered in the case that the minimum asked high quality percentage were 75%. A fully automated scenario could be also considered.

Looking at the percentage of variation for *Quality*, $\%Var_Q$ is not spreading in Scenario 1 for expert and standard operators, so a standard one can be considered without risks. In the case that the percentage of high-quality products can be reduced to 75%, a novice operator is not a good choice for Scenario 1 because the variation is increased to 117.15%. However, it can be considered in case of Scenario 3. If a cognitive assistance module were implemented, then a recommendation from this module would be, in case only novice operators are available in this moment for this task, to work in a collaborative Scenario 3. In this case, for example, the supervisor can provide autonomy to the novice operator selecting the basic or the optimized version of the cobot, because the percentage and variation of high-quality products would be similar.

A similar study could be performed on the *Time* specification, depending on the customer specifications and the plant organization, to improve task effectiveness and productivity.

6.3 Usability on human–robot collaboration

The feasibility of extrapolating measures and theory from the usability experience in HCI toward (HRI) is clearly supported by the usability experimentation conducted in this study: the context of use, requirements, workspace design, task allocation between human and robot, experimental testing, and validation steps.

In the experimental study, with a *Task Completion rate* value of 78.6 in the effectiveness of Task 1 (TOH5), as we can check again in Table 5.8 (page 119), we can consider that the human operator can effectively solve Task 1 in the Human–Robot Collaborative Workspace Experience. In case of looking for increasing the effectiveness in this task, a first alternative is the incorporation of a training stage. Another alternative could be the use of an assistant that considers assisting the operator when the real-time value of the *Task Completion rate* is lower than a minimum set value. For the second task (collaborative assembly), the value of the *Task Completion rate* shows that the human–robot team effectively solves Task 2. However, a redesign of the physical architecture of the HRWCE, in which the human operator is closer to the work area, could improve the efficiency of the work team.

Efficiency in Task 1, measured through the variable *Time to Task* with mean values of 56.2 seconds for Task 1 and 108.09 seconds for Task 2, as reported in Table 5.10 (page 120), places the efficiency level into the range low to standard, with a higher accumulation toward the standard level. Hence we can consider that the human operator is able to efficiently solve the tasks in the HRCWE.

The SUS score shows that the collaborative workspace is perceived as "Acceptable" for working with humans (see Table 5.13 on page 122), and the star chart in Fig. 5.9 on page 123 proves that the performance of its components is balanced, as it was expected.

The evaluation carried out about HWRCE, through the KPIs, corroborate the capacity of the human–robot team with values higher than 80% of *Per_Utilization*, higher than 75% of *Per_Efficiency*, and higher than 80% of *Task Completion rate*. The variability analysis shows that the system is able to absorb the variability introduced by the human operator.

To improve the results obtained in task efficiency and effectiveness within the HWRCE, adding the real-time variable *Difficulty Task*, which considers the variables *Task Completion rate* and *Time to Task*, could be used to work with an assistant to guide a strategy for solving the tasks.

Overall, the usability benchmark additionally demonstrates the flexibility of the human operator to work in conjunction with a cobot operator in collaborative assembly tasks within the Human–Robot Collaborative Workspace Experience. This flexibility is needed initially in manual tasks in small- and medium-sized companies, where a proof of concept of the effectiveness of introducing a collaborative robot alongside the plant operator is required (Schnell, 2021; Álvarez and Væhrens, 2023).

6.4 Cognitive workload

The use of the NASA TLX index protocol has allowed us to perform a multidimensional assessment of the variation of the mental workload on the participant, in this case, in the role of human operator / collaborative robot. As established in the hypothesis of the study, it has been shown that there are no significant differences between the mental workload in the solution of the TOH5 problem and its solution when a not so demanding collaborative task with a robot is added in the same workspace. Moreover, as the results show, even though the level of mental workload found in both scenarios is high, this level is not overloading the operator. In the results, we can observe that no participant has indicated a level of underload in the mental workload, and according to the experience found with other experiments, the level of mental workload can be considered normal in cognitive tasks, such as the TOH5 of this study. It could be that a high level of mental workload is necessary to be alert and make decisions in time.

The TOH5 problem has allowed us to assess the mental workload of the operator in the task carried out experimentally. If there are continuous changes in the workspace, that is, changes in the tasks performed by the operator (new task, working next to the robot) or unforeseen events, then it is relevant to keep the change in mental workload limited. Adding this functionality to the cognitive assistant ensures that the operator continues to maintain adequate performance.

The NASA TLX index considers that the first three subscales (mental, physical, and temporal) correspond to the demands imposed on the operator. In this aspect, the results show that the mental demand is the largest subscale of the mental workload. However, no significant differences were found between the scenarios. The physical subscale is the least contributing subscale; however, the results show that there are significant differences in both scenarios, which is consistent with the differences in the physical characteristics of the scenarios.

The next three subscales (effort, frustration, and performance) refer to the interaction of the participant with the workspace. In this aspect, the results show that there are significant differences in performance between the scenarios, which is a result of the demand of attention that the cobot imposes on the participant. The frustration subscale, according to the results, does not show significant differences; however, it is an important subscale in the resolution of the problem when the operator begins his experience in the experiment. The use of descriptive adjectives and multidimensional graphs allows stakeholders to have a representative perspective of the results obtained.

6.5 Task performance of the human–robot team

In relation to the performance of the tasks, the results show that human operators can solve the task TOH5 effectively, with a value of $TCR = 66.67\%$. Additionally, the human–robot team working in the collaborative assembly task is also able of effectively solving the task ($TCR = 94.44\%$).

Following the results of the objective metrics and based on Hoffman (2019), some considerations can be presented. The measure *H-IDLE* relates the subjective perception of the human operator while waiting for the robot, e.g., wasting time or being bored. In this study, *H-IDLE* value remains at the same level, as shown in Fig. 5.12, when the human operator develops Task 1 while waiting for the robot's request for collaboration; hence we can say that the human operator is taking advantage of his/her time.

Moreover, Hoffman relates the *R-IDLE* measure with fluency, establishing two possible conditions: either the robot is physically inactive but is doing internal work on its processor, or it is inactive while waiting for an intervention from the human operator. In our use case the second condition is present: the robot starts its idle time by sending a message to the operators waiting for their collaboration and remains in this state until an operator informs it about the end of the collaboration. This collaboration time of the human operator is variable. In the subjective sense, this can be seen as either an inefficient use of the robot or an imbalance in the distribution of the task. In this study the *R-IDLE* value is much lower than the *H-IDLE value* (see Fig. 5.12), indicating that there is an efficient use of the robot. However, it could also indicate an imbalance in the distribution of the task.

Regarding *C-ACT*, Hoffman describes that a high value for this measure could indicate a subjective feeling of fluency when considering that the teams are well synchronized and that there is a similarity in the team members, perhaps a fair balance of work. In this study the value for *C-ACT* is low from a physical point of view (see Fig. 5.12). It could be considered an imbalance in the work. However, when considering a complete vision of the work capacities for each member, the distribution is fair in the sense that each member does what it does the best, i.e., the human operator undertakes more of the cognitive activity and the robot operator more of the physical activity.

For the measure *F-DEL*, it is established that a low level is related to the subjective perception of human–robot fluency, since it indicates an efficient use of the time of the team members. In this study, we can see that such *F-DEL* is not present (see Fig. 5.12). The human operator's sensation would be of efficient work; however, it should be taken into account that for this task, the level of collaboration is also low.

The human–robot fluency approach introduces a different perspective from the H-R team's workspace-sharing approach. In the temporal approach, there is a great inequality in the time in which the human operator performs the task with respect to the computational time, especially when the human operator is a novice and needs additional time in which to perfect his learning. In this sense, the assistant can use temporal fluctuations in human activity to improve recommendations associated with reducing the complexity of the task or showing a detailed step-by-step procedure with instructions, for example.

6.6 Conceptual architecture of the assistance system

The next step in the development of this book is to progress in cognitive computing to be applied in the case of assistance system. Cognitive computing for human–robot interaction uses computerized models to simulate the human thought process in Artificial Internet of Things environment with a certain level of uncertainty (Mittal et al., 2021; Manogaran et al., 2021).

Summarizing some of the ideas presented in the previous chapters and using the inspirational model created by Güell et al. (2020), Fig. 6.2 shows a conceptual architecture for a cognitive assistant in the form of a recommender system. The model is endowed with a set of layers, where the application layer allows the interaction with the user, and the bottom layer allows the integration of the methodology explained in this book. In the middle, we can use an interface that allows a dialogue between the human and the computerized model. Inside the computerized model, a client / server model is designed for the management of the request from the user, algorithms for classification of production scenarios, user profiles, natural language processing models, machine learning methods, etc. Güell et al. (2020) uses an ap-

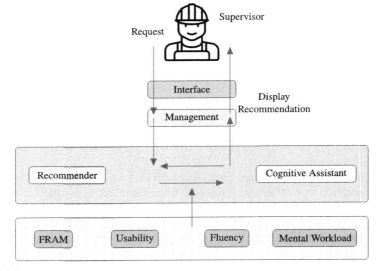

FIGURE 6.2

Conceptual architecture for a cognitive assistant in the form of a recommender system.

proach integrating a cognitive assistant within a critique-based recommender system. At the core of the critique-based recommender system, the computerized model is placed. This book does not develop the computerized model but provides guidelines for the design of a cognitive assistant and recommender system in the case study of human–robot collaboration. So Fig. 6.2 shows:

- *Top layer.* The supervisor makes a request about the benefits of a scenario, the operator, and the task. The system can ask questions related to the specific type of variation to be studied: either time or quality.
- *Medium layer.* This layer handles requests from the supervisor to the lower layer and manages the responses from the lower layer to the upper layer.
- *Lower layer.* This layer processes the features associated with variation, usability, and fluency mental workload to transform them into recommendation actions.

The main features of our human–robot collaborative system are assembly time and product quality. The supervisor requires help in determining the best performance of operator types and scenario based on the data obtained with the FRAM methodology in terms of quality variation.

In our case, a specific product assembly task has been considered. Generically, at an industrial level, the assembly of *n* different products could be considered in future research studies.

For a single product, a recommendation can be generated for each type of feature, one recommendation for quality and one recommendation for time.

Various user profiles have also been considered, in particular, novice, standard, or expert operators. In this section, it is the supervisor who requires help; in future extensions of the model, it could be the user who defines his/her own requests.

The main task of the management layer is to sort requests and assess whether they are better suited to the recommender system or cognitive assistant.

The cognitive part can be constituted as an internal part masked within the recommendation action. In the case where it is detected that the task being performed by the operator has a high mental workload, the recommendation to the supervisor is to limit the time or difficulty of the task being performed by the operator. It may be more understandable to a supervisor if the message conveyed is related to precise general objectives associated with the operator's task and not so much to objectives associated with cognitive psychology (time pressure, mental workload).

The internal model presented does not have to be visible to the supervisor. It is up to the system modeling experts to develop algorithms that automate the step from data to information gathering so that the cognitive assistant and the recommender system look like agents with whom a dialogue is taking place.

For future work, this conceptual architecture of the assistance system should be consistent with a cognitive architecture in the context of Industry 4.0 and human–agent interaction (Male and Martinez-Hernandez, 2023) (Jokinen, 2019).

6.7 **Review questions**

1. In a production environment, it has been decided to work with a collaborative robot, a novice operator, and an expert operator. The expert operator explains to the novice operator what kind of feature must be prioritized (assembly time or quality control). Using the FRAM Model Visualizer, define a FRAM model for this scenario.
2. Using the results from Table 6.3, develop a graphical dashboard. The aim of this dashboard is to improve the easiness of use and the usefulness and explainability of the results.
3. Following the cognitive assistant recommendations in Section 6.2.2, create a qualitative informative table with positive recommendations (recommend expert or standard operator for Scenario 3) and negative recommendations (avoid novice operator for Scenario 1). Insert colors in the table cells to enhance the meaning, red color as a negative recommendation and green color as a positive recommendation.
4. Beyond usability, look for useful metrics for measuring user experience in aspects of trust, acceptance, and emotional response.
5. The supervisor must automate a station where manual assembly is initially performed. The planning of a possible solution places a very high cognitive demand on her/him. The supervisor needs a cognitive assistant to show him/her several proofs of concept with some theoretical performance indicators. In the first proof of concept, a station with a human operator and a collaborative robot is designed.

In the second proof of concept, a station with a human operator and a mobile collaborative robot is designed. Model a sequential step planning to guide the supervisor in the selection of one or the other proof of concept, depending on possible theoretical performance results or on possible problems in actually implementing the proof of concept. The aim of this cognitive assistant is to facilitate the supervisor's decision-making.

Conclusions and future lines

7

Abstract

At the beginning of the book, we presented the main concepts related to Artificial Internet of Things and the research being carried out in the industrial context. Chapter 2 shows how a Human-centered Cyber-Physical System can be modeled as a Joint Cognitive System, which is one of the first times in the literature that this approach is employed. Chapters 3 and 4 deploy experimental methodology and show which parameters should be considered to design and evaluate the human–machine teamwork from a cognitive point of view. Chapter 5 shows how the introduction of new technology, a collaborative robot, affects the human–machine system performance in the workspace. Lastly, Chapter 6 presents the argumentation of the obtained results and the need to define the functionality of the cognitive assistant to support the human operator.

The approach followed in the book has allowed to show different aspects of cognitive assistants in the field of human–robot collaboration. All this contributes to answering the book questions posed at the beginning. Now this chapter presents the main conclusions and possible lines of future work.

7.1 Conclusions

A Human-centered Cyber-Physical System (HCPS) is a composite intelligent system comprising humans, cyber-systems, and physical systems to achieve specific manufacturing goals at an optimized level. Synergy combinations are required to support the development of smart and cognitive solutions. Understanding of Human-centered Cyber-Physical Systems from the area of socio-technical systems with the perspective of Joint Cognitive System (JCS) shows in the first place the current ability to provide the operators with functions and tools that allow them to amplify their abilities, in particular, the cognitive ones. For these skills, we can see that there are various cognitive tools, thanks to which cognitive solutions are capable of being applied.

In the main workstation considered in the book, human–robot collaboration, the underlying idea is to combine the strengths of robots and humans: the physical strength, precision, and endurance of robots with human problem-solving skills and the ability to cope with new and unexpected situations. This combination, together with a cognitive assistant, brings in the symbiotic relationship between human operators and technological operators. The assistance systems are developed to be integrated into manufacturing processes so that production is more efficient, safer, and more reliable.

The integration of various technologies in the Industry *4.0* context requires the operator to develop greater cognitive skills, so a cognitive assistant must, first of all, collaborate with the development of human values in the workspace; it must be integrated as an extension of the user, the system, even the industry itself, and the functions of the operator.

On the one hand, this book introduces the need to introduce human factors in the design of Industry *4.0* systems. It considers these concepts following the systematic approach of Neumann et al. (2021), an Industry *4.0* system as a socio-technical system. There human factors are considered at the early stages of the process / product design. Moreover, high work demands require keeping the mental workload under control. On the other hand, this book introduces a methodological and systematic guide for experimenting and evaluating experiments related to human–robot interaction in the assembly task workspace. Taking advantage of human–centered design, value-sensitive design, and usability in human–computer interaction, this experience has been expanded and adapted to the field of collaborative human–robot interaction to have a solid and well-founded basis for evaluating the collaborative workspace, where the human operator shares tasks with a robot. Reviewing and incorporating best practices from relations area can reduce the number of testing iterations required and save time and money developing and evaluating a process or system.

As it is suggested by Sheridan (2006), there is a positive relationship between the predictability of the system and the amount of mental work exerted on the user. One of the incentives of developing such an assistance system is to reduce the mental workload of the worker in the workspace. Achieving this goal can be challenging if the system exhibits high variability, or if the user may frequently find himself guessing, "What is the automation doing now?" The identification of sources of variability presented in this book, associated with performance metrics, is a first step in the design of a system that assists human in tasks allocation (human operator, collaborative robot), identification of optimal production scenarios, and gap reduction in the connectivity between plant and manufacturing execution systems, where it is important to analyze economical costs of possible production scenarios.

The previous chapter detailed the relationship between various human operators (expert, standard, novice) and the percentage of variation (time to task, quality) in an assembly system (manual task, fully automated task, H-R collaborative task). Next, the assembly task was modeled taking into account that it may be subject to variations in quality and fluctuations in productivity due to working styles and robot and operator expertise. The FRAM methodology was employed in this book as a first approach in this context.

The human–robot interaction, in particular, with a cobot, has the advantage of a high flexibility inherent in the human part and a high efficiency inherent in the technical part. In later stages, this mixed flexibility can be considered through indicators to reach an improved symbiosis within the human–robot collaborative system. In this symbiosis, an advanced topic is adding a principle of failure analysis. In the

FRAM methodology, it is necessary analyze how to maintain the same level of production when one part (human or robot) is working in abnormal situation, and it is necessary to increase the workload of the other part. Finally, it would be also possible to add another module inside the cognitive agent with recommendations in safety critical systems.

In the Industry *4.0* real scenarios, operators may be subject to task changes, task difficulty, task shared with a robot, and interruptions (for instance, noise) (Carvalho et al., 2020; Bläsing and Bornewasser, 2021). In these cases, understanding the cognitive load types (intrinsic, extraneous, germane) and the relationship with mental workload could be useful for the improvement of the human information processing system, human performance, and the effectiveness of the overall system (Galy et al., 2012; Orru and Longo, 2020). Understanding this human cognitive load will facilitate the design of smart assistant systems to aid and assist human operators in future cognitive manufacturing systems. Moreover, the vision of the performance of the human–robot team through fluency could be considered an additional component to improve the design of a help support system from the perspective of the human–robot team.

To ensure a high usability and performance, the assistance system must also be designed in accordance to human factor engineering principles, value-sensitive design, and human design centered to ensure the well-being of the operator *4.0*. The participants in the experimental session developed in this book show that it is possible to keep the mental workload under control while they are developing primary and secondary tasks. This feature could consider flexibility as an important parameter in the operator's condition.

In general, the operator's mental workload increases when the operator has to process the information presented in the workspace and make decisions based on it. Low-complexity highly integrated assistance systems could minimize operator distractions, i.e., the mental workload for the driver.

7.2 Future lines

The application and use of assistants alongside workers in the manufacturing industry can be an important and efficient strategy for companies to create added value in manufacturing and provide better employee welfare. Assistants can also be used by companies to increase the attractiveness of jobs in manufacturing production and thus become a socially sustainable factory. The field of worker assistance systems is therefore a research topic that can have a positive impact on the company itself and, above all, on the indispensable operator in manufacturing.

Assisting employees in acquiring the knowledge and skills necessary to use new services and technologies on the shop floor is critical for manufacturers to adapt to Industry *4.0* successfully. However, cognitive assistants as worker assistance systems in manufacturing production are only a recent research topic, and there are not so many studies available in the literature.

Let us mention the work in Li et al. (2023a), where they employ Learning, Training, Assistance-Formats, Issues, Tools (LTA-FIT) approach and propose a framework for a language-enabled virtual assistant (VA) to facilitate adaptation of operators. In this system the human–robot interaction is achieved through spoken natural language and a dashboard implemented as a web-based application. This type of interaction enables operators of all levels to control a collaborative robot intuitively in several industrial scenarios and use it as a complementary tool for developing their competencies. Through three different scenarios, the usability of the system is evaluated based on the system usability scale (SUS) and the cognitive effort required by the users based on the standardized NASA-TLX questionnaire.

Some research lines are proposed to expand our seminal work.

7.2.1 HCPS in intelligent manufacturing – AIoT

In terms of technology, the essence of intelligent manufacturing is to design, construct, and apply Human-centered Cyber-Physical Systems in various cases and at different levels. As defended by Zhou et al. (2019), advances in information technology have progressed intelligent manufacturing from the stages of digital manufacturing and digital-networked manufacturing toward new-generation intelligent manufacturing. The evolved situation is characterized by the in-depth integration of new-generation Artificial Intelligence technology with advanced manufacturing technology. This is what we defined in the book as Artificial Internet of Things (AIoT), the core driving force of the new industrial revolution. New studies about intelligent manufacturing from the perspective of HCPSs are needed, as well as a deep discussion of the implications, characteristics, technical frame, and key technologies of HCPSs for AIoT.

One of these novel studies related to AI extensions of AIoT is recently presented by Saad and Håkansson (2022). A combination of multiagent reinforcement learning with robustness analysis in introduced shaping a cyber-physical system infrastructure that reasons robustly in a dynamically changing environment. Robustness analysis identifies vulnerability issues when the system interacts within a dynamically changing environment. Based on this identification, when incorporated into the system, robustness analysis suggests robust solutions and actions rather than optimal ones provided by reinforcement learning alone.

Future research lines should be based on systemic methods helping to compare future proposals. In the same form that we are proposing Functional Resonance Analysis Method (FRAM) to analyze variability in production lines due to the human presence, in Adriaensen et al. (2022b) a socio-technical perspective is embraced to explore the potential of Joint Cognitive Systems to manage risk and safety in cobot applications. Three systemic safety analysis approaches are presented and tested with a demonstrator case study concerning their feasibility for cobot applications: System-Theoretic Accident Model and Processes (STAMP), Functional Resonance Analysis Method (FRAM), and Event Analysis of Systemic Teamwork (EAST). The power of systemic methods for safer and more efficient cobot operations lies in revealing the distributed and emergent result from joint actions and overcoming the reductionist view from individual failures or single agent responsibilities. This is a characteristic that we proved in our studies using FRAM. More studies are needed in various workplaces and other systemic analysis approaches like STAMP or EAST.

From the same research group, Adriaensen et al. (2023) also used the Functional Resonance Analysis Method and Interdependence Analysis in a collaborative robot framework. Both safety and efficiency are examined by selected case study highlights to gain an in-depth understanding of human operators' role as the central driver of human–machine (eco)systems in a warehouse distribution system, in which warehouse robot assistance is provided. The case study examples reveal the combined effects of the working system environment and the robot application and also demonstrate possible operational solutions to deal with socio-technical complexity.

Moreover, new definitions for Human-centered Cyber-Physical System are also expected. Zambrano-Rey and Pacaux-Lemoine (2022) focus on a new concept of Cyber-Physical Production and Human System (CPPHS) by proposing a common entity abstraction that can be instantiated to model human and artificial entities. Hence, using this entity model, cooperation becomes natural, because it is rooted in the entity's design and implementation. This work is inspired by the fact that in most of the literature reviewed on HCPS, there are few details on the design of digital entity representation and their functionalities, with an emphasis on cooperation between such heterogeneous human entities.

7.2.2 Shift from Industry *4.0* to Robotics *4.0*

In our book, the main workplace under study is a pick-and-place task completed through human–robot collaboration. Cobots are a main subject of study in Artificial Internet of Things and Industry *4.0*.

A roadmap and several case studies were provided by Gao et al. (2020) to demonstrate the current endeavor to achieve the idea of Robotics *4.0*. The authors revisit the roles of collaborative and intelligent robotic system and its enabling technologies including ROS and ROS2, integrated drive system, robotic sensors, horizontal integration of a robotic network, human–robot friendly and natural interaction, and deep learnt robots. In this form, it is established that in Robotics *4.0*, intelligences including motion, computing, perception, and cognition are expected to be seamlessly integrated to meet the diversified industrial and societal needs.

Since collaborative robots are an important key enabling technology of Industry *4.0*, the interaction between humans and robots should aim to improve system performance. To achieve this goal, it is necessary to investigate the effects of this close interaction on workers identifying individual factors involved and discerning which of them affect the introduction of HRC in a manufacturing system. For instance, the purpose of Simone et al. (2022) is to analyze the collaboration between humans and robots, identifying how the operator's work is affected by HRC. A valid taxonomy of key factors influencing the performance of collaborative operators should be identified in the future. Moreover, measures on trust, usability, and acceptance as key requirements for the successful introduction of HRC should be investigated.

In the same line, from the workers perspective, the study by Fournier et al. (2022) guides occupational health workers by identifying the potential gains (reduced perceived time demand, number of gestures, and number of errors) and concerns (the cobot takes a long time to perceive its environment, which leads to an increased completion time) associated with working with cobots. Similarly to our results, the collaboration between human and cobot during an assembly task did not negatively impact perceived cognitive load, increased completion time, and decreased perceived time demand. Thus performing the task in collaboration with a cobot improved the user's experience and performance, except for the increased completion time. This study opens future lines to investigate how to improve cobots to ensure the usability of the human–machine system at work.

7.2.2.1 Task allocation for human–robot collaboration

Over the past years, collaborative robots have been introduced as a new generation of industrial robotics working alongside humans to share the workload. These robots have the potential to enable human–robot collaboration (HRC) for flexible automation. However, the deployment of these robots in industrial environments, particularly in assembly, still comprises several challenges, of which one is skill-based task distribution between humans and robots. Hence one of the hot topics using cobots is the design of the HRC workplace and the preliminary assignment of human and robot tasks. Along the book, we propose a "common-sense" task allocation in our experimentation, but this is a research to be considered in the future.

The Human–Robot Collaborative workplace design and the automatic task allocation can significantly decrease the time of a new setup or a cell reconfiguration. In early times, Tsarouchi et al. (2016) proposed a method for an HRC workplace layout generation and a preliminary assignment of human and robot tasks. Later, Bruno and Antonelli (2018) proposed a decision-making framework for the location of all components in the available layout space to be decided upon.

In view of high cost pressure, resulting productivity requirements, and the trend toward human-centered automation in the context of Industry 5.0, a reasonable allocation of individual assembly tasks to humans or robots is of central importance. Malik and Bilberg (2019a) presented a methodology for task distribution between human and robot in assembly work by complexity-based task classification. There the assembly attributes affecting HRC automation are identified. The proposed methodology is presented for evaluating tasks for assigning to the robot and creating a workload balance forming a human–robot work team.

A more recent approach is introduced by Petzoldt et al. (2022) for dynamic task allocation, its integration into an intuitive block-based process planning framework, and its evaluation in comparison to both manual assembly and static task allocation. Fluency in the human–robot collaboration, as we proposed in our experiments, is also considered. Here good adaptation to process delays and reduction in the cycle time for assembly processes with sufficiently high degrees of parallelism are demonstrated. Conclusions can be drawn and results extended regarding assembly scenarios in which manual assembly or collaborative assembly with static or dynamic task allocation is most appropriate.

7.2.2.2 The cognitive human factor in human–robot collaboration

Although many manual operations have been replaced by automation in the manufacturing domain in various industries, skilled operators still carry out critical manual tasks such as final assembly, similarly to our experiment. The business case for automation in these areas is difficult to justify due to increased complexity and costs arising out of process variabilities associated with those tasks, as it was studied in the previous chapters. The lack of understanding process variability in automation design means that industrial automation often does not realize the full benefits. Goh et al. (2020) described a taxonomy of variability when considering the automation of manufacturing processes. Three industrial case studies were analyzed to develop the proposed taxonomy. Future research is still needed optimizing this first proposal.

Industry *4.0* is looking forward to developing interoperable and service-oriented systems with real time capabilities, leading to the installation of decentralized and reliable robotics cells with flexible cooperative capabilities. Smart operators' flexibility and robot productivity are mixed in cobots applications impacting on cognitive load. An agent-based model is presented by Fruggiero et al. (2020) with application in the automotive sector. The load of human in the collaborative work-cell is measured according with Functional states over different Behavioral Structures (FBS). The load of cognitive factors is quantified while reporting interaction analysis.

Taxonomies and ontologies are key research topics for further advancements. Olivares-Alarcos et al. (2022) proposed an Ontology for Collaborative Robotics and Adaptation (OCRA), which is built around two main notions, collaboration and plan adaptation. OCRA ensures reliable human–robot collaboration, since robots can formalize and reason about their plan adaptations and collaborations in unstructured collaborative robotic scenarios. The proposed formal model is validated by demonstrating that a robot may answer a set of competency questions using OCRA.

7.2.3 Metrics in human–robot collaboration

Further research is needed on how to design and evaluate system performance, usability, and user experience in the industrial environment due to its specific requirements. Criteria need to be developed for these new human–robot team contexts in production where safety and performance criteria are adapted. This is a problem that will have to be solved in the future, once production assistance systems are more consolidated.

Human–robot teaming receives an ever-increasing level of attention in research, development, and industry. Novel approaches to task sharing in hybrid teams range from optimized schedules to intelligent cobot assistants with a high degree of autonomy. These approaches must prove their usefulness and benefits compared to manual work or full automation – particularly when it comes to assessing their potential for productive industrial use. This leverages demand for standardized, repeatable benchmarks to compare approaches and measure improvements in a reproducible way. Designing such benchmarks is challenging as numerous aspects, from safety considerations to human factors and team performance, must be considered. Survey by Riedelbauch et al. (2023) seeks to contribute to the future development of benchmarks for the field of collaborative assembly, handling, and industrial cobot applications by giving a comprehensive overview of relevant metrics, evaluation strategies, and tasks for human–robot teams.

7.2.3.1 Usability

Several research studies in Information and Communication Technology (ICT) have shown that usability is an important goal for cyber-physical human systems to gain wider acceptance by their end-users. To evaluate the usability of a system under design, usability evaluation methods predominantly rely on subject matter experts or testers' assessments. However, integrating Artificial Intelligence (AI) technology and existing usability evaluation methods' processes can aid to evolve more effective user-centered designs. Gupta et al. (2023) conceptualized an AI-augmented usability evaluation framework (AIUEF) aiming at replacing "end-users" with "personas" to evaluate requirements involving human–computer interaction (HCI) for a given Software Requirements Specification (SRS). Authors present a blueprint of AIUEF establishing a theoretical basis for an automated usability evaluation of HCI requirements for a given SRS to improve the usability of a system under design.

Robotic systems are increasingly prevalent in different work domains and allow new forms of interaction between robot and worker. Usability plays an important role for the interaction quality. The development and validation process of a robot-specific usability questionnaire based on the DIN EN ISO 9241-110:2020-10 is presented by Heinold et al. (2022). Exploratory factor analysis showed a ten-factorial structure, closely representing the interaction principles. However, further research is needed to identify reasons for the deviating results of the confirmatory factor analysis.

7.2.3.2 Fluency

Advanced human–robot interaction becomes an essential resource in Industry 4.0. Specifically, the deployment of collaborative robots (cobots) has changed the game in modern smart factories. These robotic agents assist human operators, working with them side-by-side on joint task execution. Because cobots are designed to be more coworkers than tools, fluent interaction between the operators and their robotic counterparts is critical for employees' task accomplishment and thus high performance. Paliga (2022) investigates the relationships between four perspectives of human–robot interaction fluency (i.e., the human emotion-oriented, the human contribution-oriented, the robot-oriented, and the team-oriented fluency) and operators' subjective job performance. The analysis carried out on 190 male and female cobot operators working on the shop floor showed positive associations between human–robot interaction (HRI) fluency and job performance. The obtained results suggest that HRI fluency relates to employee job performance because of the positive affective–cognitive state experienced by the operator when cooperating with a cobot in a coordinated and well-synchronized manner.

7.2.3.3 Mental workload

Interest in the virtualization of human–robot interactions is increasing; however, the impact of collaborating with either virtual or physical robots on the mental state of the human operator is still insufficiently studied. Nenna et al. (2023) aimed to fill this gap by conducting a systematic assessment of a human–robot collaborative framework from a user-centric perspective. Mental workload was measured in participants working in synergistic cooperation with a physical and a virtual collaborative robot (cobot) under various levels of task demands. Performance and implicit and explicit workload were assessed as functions of pupil size variation and self-reporting questionnaires. In the face of a similar self-reported mental demand when maneuvering the virtual or physical cobot, operators showed shorter operation times and lower implicit workload when interacting with the virtual cobot compared to its physical counterpart. Furthermore, the benefits of collaborating with a virtual cobot most vividly manifested when the user had to position the robotic arm with higher precision. These results shed light on the feasibility and importance of relying on multidimensional assessments in real-life work settings, including implicit workload predictors such as pupillometric measures. From a broader perspective, authors findings suggest that virtual simulations have the potential to bring significant advantages for both the user's mental well-being and industrial production, particularly for highly complex and demanding tasks.

7.2.4 Human roles and behaviors

The complexity of production processes in Industry *4.0* is significantly increased. Within factories, humans communicate and cooperate with each other and with other smart resources of a production process. In that way, their role has dramatically changed. Specifying the human roles, capabilities, and competencies within production process modeling is a great challenge, as it has pointed out in this book. To deal with this problem, it is necessary to first identify and determine the human characteristics that are crucial in Industry *4.0*. A review of the literature describing the role of humans in Industry *4.0* is presented by Narandžić et al. (2021).

Modern workspaces are located within production systems, in which communication between different levels of the company is mandatory. In our research work, the workspace has been analyzed as an isolated system, considering the human as a mere operator. As a future work, communication with Manufacturing Execution System (MES type management systems) should be considered, toward a complete sociotechnical system. Moreover, by transforming the information obtained from data in a real-world process into knowledge it is possible to change the strategy of assignment of activities. A cognitive assistant could perfectly handle these strategies.

Following the same research line as digital twins, simulating the behavior of operators through a digital human model (DHM) is an intuitive way to reflect human factors in the workspace. Efficiency of digital human workspace simulation, the main bottleneck in the past restricting the application of DHMs in many workplaces, is now leading to realistic results with the development of Artificial Intelligence algorithms. In terms of human–robot collaborative assembly with DHMs, Yin and Li (2023) propose the difficulties and future development trends at the practical application.

7.2.5 Implementing cognitive assistants

Multiagent systems share common ground with CPSs and can empower them with a multitude of capabilities in their efforts to achieve complexity management, decentralization, intelligence, modularity, flexibility, robustness, adaptation, and responsiveness. Leitão et al. (2016) surveys and analyzes the current state of the industrial application of agent technology in CPSs and provides a vision on the way agents can effectively enable emerging CPS challenges.

Key factors such as design, technology, intelligence / algorithms, standardization, hardware, challenges, application, and cost are investigated by Karnouskos and Leitão (2017), who hypothesize that they are linked to the industrial agent acceptance. The results from empirical data acquired via a conducted survey indicate that all the factors are seen important issues that play a role toward deciding for or against an industrial agent solution. There are other works from that time on developing cognitive assistance frameworks for supporting human workers in industrial tasks (Haslgrubler et al., 2018).

These preliminary works on collaborative robots were developed because lightweight robots are especially suitable for small- and medium-sized enterprises. They offer new interaction opportunities and thereby pose new challenges with regard to technology acceptance. Despite acknowledging the importance of acceptance issues, small- and medium-sized enterprises often lack coherent strategies to identify barriers and foster acceptance. Therefore, in these papers, authors present a collection of crucial acceptance factors with regard to collaborative robot use at the industrial workplace. An evaluation with three German small- and medium-sized enterprises by Baumgartner et al. (2022) revealed that the tool's concept meets the demands of small- and medium-sized enterprises and is perceived as beneficial as it raises awareness and deepens knowledge on this topic. To realize economic potentials, further low-threshold usable tools are needed to transfer research findings into the daily practice of small- and medium-sized enterprises.

Another element under consideration is user experience for interface design. Human–Robot Collaboration (HRC) has become a strategic research field, considering the emergent need for common collaborative execution of manufacturing tasks, shared between humans and robots within the modern factories. However, beyond the research focusing on the technological aspects and enabling technologies, mainly directing to the robotic side, the human factors should not be neglected. This is the case in Prati et al. (2021), where the needs of the humans interacting with robots are integrated in the design in human–robot interaction. The research adopted the proposed method to an industrial case focused on assembly operations supported by collaborative robots and AGVs (Automated Guided Vehicles).

Tactile / haptic interactions are also possible future elements of interaction between operators and cobots. Standard ISO 9241-910:2011 provides a framework for understanding and communicating various aspects of such interactions. It does not address purely kinaesthetic interactions, such as gestures, although it might be useful for understanding such interactions (Iso, 2010).

Finally, as the demand for collaborative robots increases, the manufacturers have come to use touchpad-typed teaching devices, and human-friendly interfaces play a significant role in robot teaching. Accordingly, the need for development of a user-friendly intuitive interface is increasing. Dong et al. (2023) provide an easy robot teaching method for high-level hard tasks through a wizard that provides a step-by-step process without programming for the sophisticated teaching.

Documentation for participants

A.1 Participants selection

We need 30 participants in total. Each session lasts <25> minutes. We must have a candidate's completed screener at least one day in advance of the session, so we know which experimental group to assign him or her to.

- Introduction:

  This experiment is part of a research project related to Human–Robot Interaction (HRI). The basic objective is to determine the variation of mental load on the operator when a collaborative task with a robot is added.

- Selection questions:

  1. The participant is familiar with information and communication technologies.
  2. The participant is interested in the use of robotics and its applications.
  3. Participant feels confident working with a moving robot.
  4. Participant would like to help in this research.

- Exclusion questions:

  1. The participant is of legal age.
  2. The participant feels insecure working with automatic machines.

- Experience Questions

  1. Do you have experience in programming or using robots?
  2. Have you participated in projects related to mind uploading?
  3. Do you have experience playing the towers of Hanoi, in real physical format or in its digital version?

A.2 **Statement of informed consent. Consent form**

TITLE: Usability Test in the Human Robot Collaborative Workspace

PROTOCOL DIRECTOR: PhD student Alejandro Chacón.

DESCRIPTION: You have been invited to participate in a study that aims to improve the tasks performed by operators and cobots in workspaces within factories. The facilitator gives you the instruction (development of the game Hanoi's Tower and the collaboration with the robot in the assembly of the product).

TIME INVOLVEMENT: Your participation will take approximately 15 minutes.

RISKS AND BENEFITS: There are no risks in this study. The benefits are only for academic purposes. Your decision whether or not to participate in this study will not affect your grades in school.

PAYMENTS: You will not receive anything as payment for your participation. In fact, you will receive feedback about the experimental session.

SUBJECT'S RIGHTS: If you have read this form and have decided to participate in this project, then please understand that your participation is voluntary and you have the right to withdraw your consent or discontinue participation at any time without penalty or loss of benefits to which you are otherwise entitled. The alternative is to not participate. You have the right to refuse to answer particular questions. Your individual privacy will be maintained in all published and written data resulting from the study.

CONTACT INFORMATION:
Questions: If you have any questions, concerns, or complaints about this research, its procedures, risks, and benefits, contact the Protocol Director Alejandro Chacón, luis.alejandro.chacon@upc.edu.
I give consent for my identity to be revealed in written materials resulting from this study only inside the class with my teacher and colleagues.
Please initial: _Yes _ No

The extra copy of this consent form is for you to keep.

SIGNATURE   DATE

Experimental scenario

B

B.1 Case study

Two different tasks are defined in this scenario, with different conditions and operating characteristics, as shown in Table B.1. Each participant participates in two tasks, with Task 1 always being the first one. One iteration of scenario is performed for each operator for 15 minutes.

Table B.1 Experimental scenario.

	Task	Performance	Time
1	TOH5	Maximum number of TOH5 game replays with 31 moves	
2	CA	At least 7 Cycles Work completed	15 minutes

The objective for the participant in the TOH5 task is to perform as many repetitions as possible. The number of movements and the time of each repetition are recorded by the participant in the data Table B.2.

The second task, Assembly, is related with responding to requests for collaboration from the robot, which are indicated by the green light of the beacon in the area of assembly. Both time that human takes to place caps, defined as Wait Time, and Cycle time are recorded in the data Table B.2, jointly with figures for Task 1 when the operator is in Scenario 2. In the assembly task, the activities of the participant are:

- performing quality control of the assembly process,
- place the caps on the subassembly zone,
- refill the base and bearing warehouses.

Table B.2 Scenario. Task 1 & Task 2: Resolve TOH5 & Collaborate with cobot (CA).

Operator			Cobot		
Replay	N_moves	Time to Task (sec)	Cycle	Wait Time (sec)	Cycle Time (sec)
1			1		
. . .			. . .		

At the end of the experiment the participant answers the System Usability Scale (SUS) as a satisfaction questionnaire.

B.2 **Demonstrations**

The main facilitator shows the participant the two areas and how the tasks are performed, in particular, highlighting the activities that the operator must perform.

B.2.1 **TOH5**

Using the app's built-in functions, the facilitator demonstrates once how to solve the game with the least number of moves; see Fig. B.1.

FIGURE B.1

TOH5 – Solver.

B.2.2 **Assembly**

The facilitator shows a complete work cycle, indicating the activities that the operator must perform: place the caps, click on the teach pendant, and reload stores, as well as the meaning of the lights on the indicator tower; see Fig. B.2.

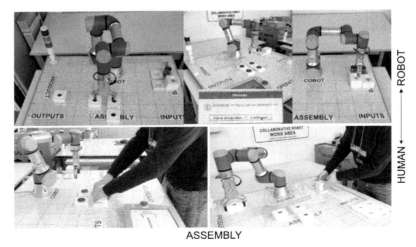

FIGURE B.2

Demonstration Assembly Cycle Work Human–Robot.

Bibliography

Adli, H.K., Remli, M.A., Wan Salihin Wong, K.N.S., Ismail, N.A., González-Briones, A., Corchado, J.M., Mohamad, M.S., 2023. Recent advancements and challenges of aiot application in smart agriculture: a review. Sensors 23. https://doi.org/10.3390/s23073752. https://www.mdpi.com/1424-8220/23/7/3752, 2023.

Adriaensen, A., Berx, N., Pintelon, L., Costantino, F., Di Gravio, G., Patriarca, R., 2022a. Interdependence analysis in collaborative robot applications from a joint cognitive functional perspective. International Journal of Industrial Ergonomics 90, 103320. https://doi.org/10.1016/j.ergon.2022.103320.

Adriaensen, A., Costantino, F., Di Gravio, G., Patriarca, R., 2022b. Teaming with industrial cobots: a socio-technical perspective on safety analysis. Human Factors and Ergonomics in Manufacturing & Service Industries 32, 173–198. https://doi.org/10.1002/hfm.20939. https://onlinelibrary.wiley.com/doi/abs/10.1002/hfm.20939.

Adriaensen, A., Patriarca, R., Smoker, A., Bergström, J., 2019. A socio-technical analysis of functional properties in a joint cognitive system: a case study in an aircraft cockpit. Ergonomics, 1–19. https://doi.org/10.1080/00140139.2019.1661527.

Adriaensen, A., Pintelon, L., Costantino, F., Di Gravio, G., Patriarca, R., 2023. Systems-theoretic interdependence analysis in robot-assisted warehouse management. Safety Science 168, 106294. https://doi.org/10.1016/j.ssci.2023.106294.

Al-Turjman, F., Nayyar, A., Devi, A., Shukla, P., 2021. Intelligence of Things: AI-IoT Based Critical-Applications and Innovations. Springer International Publishing. https://books.google.es/books?id=BXR_zwEACAAJ.

Alshamrani, M., 2022. Iot and artificial intelligence implementations for remote healthcare monitoring systems: a survey. Journal of King Saud University: Computer and Information Sciences 34, 4687–4701. https://doi.org/10.1016/j.jksuci.2021.06.005.

Álvarez, D.D., Værhens, L., 2023. The future of smart production for smes: a methodological and practical approach towards digitalization in smes. In: Madsen, O., Berger, U., Møller, C., Heidemann Lassen, A., Vejrum Waehrens, B., Schou, C. (Eds.), Collaborative Robots for Smart Production in SMEs. Springer International Publishing, Cham, pp. 363–369. https://doi.org/10.1007/978-3-031-15428-7_33.

Angulo, C., 2022. Cognitive human factors in the artificial intelligence of things. In: 2022 IEEE International Conference on Services Computing (SCC). IEEE Computer Society, Los Alamitos, CA, USA, pp. 351–352. https://doi.org/10.1109/SCC55611.2022.00058. https://doi.ieeecomputersociety.org/10.1109/SCC55611.2022.00058.

Angulo, C., Chacón, A., Ponsa, P., 2023. Towards a cognitive assistant supporting human operators in the artificial intelligence of things. Internet of Things 21, 100673. https://doi.org/10.1016/j.iot.2022.100673.

Ansar, S.A., Arya, S., Aggrawal, S., Saxena, S., Kushwaha, A., Pathak, P.C., 2023. Security in iot layers: emerging challenges with countermeasures. In: Shukla, P.K., Singh, K.P., Tripathi, A.K., Engelbrecht, A. (Eds.), Computer Vision and Robotics. Springer Nature Singapore, Singapore, pp. 551–563.

Arai, T., Kato, R., Fujita, M., 2010. Assessment of operator stress induced by robot collaboration in assembly. CIRP Annals 59, 5–8. https://doi.org/10.1016/j.cirp.2010.03.043.

Aslam, F., Aimin, W., Li, M., Ur Rehman, K., 2020. Innovation in the era of iot and industry 5.0: absolute innovation management (aim) framework. Information 11. https://doi.org/10.3390/info11020124. https://www.mdpi.com/2078-2489/11/2/124.

Atzori, L., Iera, A., Morabito, G., 2010. The internet of things: a survey. Computer Networks 54, 2787–2805. https://doi.org/10.1016/j.comnet.2010.05.010.

Bajcsy, A., Losey, D.P., O'Malley, M.K., Dragan, A.D., 2017. Learning robot objectives from physical human interaction. In: Levine, S., Vanhoucke, V., Goldberg, K. (Eds.), Proceedings of the 1st Annual Conference on Robot Learning. PMLR, pp. 217–226. http://proceedings.mlr.press/v78/bajcsy17a.html.

Baker, S., Xiang, W., 2023. Artificial intelligence of things for smarter healthcare: a survey of advancements, challenges, and opportunities. IEEE Communications Surveys and Tutorials 25, 1261–1293. https://doi.org/10.1109/COMST.2023.3256323.

Bakir, A., Dahlan, M., 2023. Higher education leadership and curricular design in industry 5.0 environment: a cursory glance. Development and Learning in Organizations: An International Journal 37, 15–17. https://doi.org/10.1108/DLO-08-2022-0166.

Bances, E., Schneider, U., Siegert, J., Bauernhansl, T., 2020. Exoskeletons towards industrie 4.0: benefits and challenges of the iot communication architecture. Procedia Manufacturing 42, 49–56. https://doi.org/10.1016/j.promfg.2020.02.087. International Conference on Industry 4.0 and Smart Manufacturing (ISM 2019).

Bangor, A., Kortum, P.T., Miller, J.T., 2008. An empirical evaluation of the system usability scale. International Journal of Human-Computer Interaction 24, 574–594. https://doi.org/10.1080/10447310802205776.

Banholzer, V.M., 2022. From "Industry 4.0" to "Society 5.0" and "Industry 5.0": Value- and Mission-Oriented Policies. Technical Report 2022,2. Technische Hochschule Nürnberg.

Baratta, A., Cimino, A., Gnoni, M.G., Longo, F., 2023. Human robot collaboration in industry 4.0: a literature review. Procedia Computer Science 217, 1887–1895. https://doi.org/10.1016/j.procs.2022.12.389. 4th International Conference on Industry 4.0 and Smart Manufacturing.

Barnawi, A., Chhikara, P., Tekchandani, R., Kumar, N., Alzahrani, B., 2021. Artificial intelligence-enabled internet of things-based system for covid-19 screening using aerial thermal imaging. Future Generation Computer Systems 124, 119–132. https://doi.org/10.1016/j.future.2021.05.019.

Barnum, C.M., 2011. 4 – Understanding users and their goals. In: Barnum, C.M. (Ed.), Usability Testing Essentials. Morgan Kaufmann, Boston, pp. 83–103. https://doi.org/10.1016/B978-0-12-375092-1.00004-0.

Baumgartner, M., Kopp, T., Kinkel, S., 2022. Analysing factory workers' acceptance of collaborative robots: a web-based tool for company representatives. Electronics 11. https://doi.org/10.3390/electronics11010145. https://www.mdpi.com/2079-9292/11/1/145.

Baxter, G., Sommerville, I., 2010. Socio-technical systems: from design methods to systems engineering. Interacting with Computers 23, 4–17. https://doi.org/10.1016/j.intcom.2010.07.003. https://academic.oup.com/iwc/article-pdf/23/1/4/2038336/iwc23-0004.pdf.

Bejarano, R., Ferrer, B.R., Mohammed, W.M., Martinez Lastra, J.L., 2019. Implementing a human–robot collaborative assembly workstation. In: 2019 IEEE 17th International Conference on Industrial Informatics (INDIN), pp. 557–564. https://doi.org/10.1109/INDIN41052.2019.8972158.

Belkadi, F., Dhuieb, M.A., Aguado, J.V., Laroche, F., Bernard, A., Chinesta, F., 2019. Intelligent assistant system as a context-aware decision-making support for the workers of the future. Computers & Industrial Engineering, 105732. https://doi.org/10.1016/j.cie.2019.02.046.

Bellini, E., Coconea, L., Nesi, P., 2020. A functional resonance analysis method driven resilience quantification for socio-technical systems. IEEE Systems Journal 14, 1234–1244. https://doi.org/10.1109/JSYST.2019.2905713.

Bennett, K.B., Edman, C., Cravens, D., Jackson, N., 2023. Decision support for flexible manufacturing systems: application of the cognitive systems engineering and ecological interface design approach. Journal of Cognitive Engineering and Decision Making 17, 99–119. https://doi.org/10.1177/15553434221118976.

Bhargava, A., Bester, M., Bolton, L., 2021. Employees' perceptions of the implementation of robotics, artificial intelligence, and automation (raia) on job satisfaction, job security, and employability. Journal of Technology in Behavioral Science 6, 106–113. https://doi.org/10.1007/s41347-020-00153-8.

Blandino, G., 2023. How to measure stress in smart and intelligent manufacturing systems: a systematic review. Systems 11. https://doi.org/10.3390/systems11040167. https://www.mdpi.com/2079-8954/11/4/167.

Bläsing, D., Bornewasser, M., 2021. Influence of increasing task complexity and use of informational assistance systems on mental workload. Brain Sciences 11. https://doi.org/10.3390/brainsci11010102. https://www.mdpi.com/2076-3425/11/1/102.

Bocklisch, F., Paczkowski, G., Zimmermann, S., Lampke, T., 2022. Integrating human cognition in cyber-physical systems: a multidimensional fuzzy pattern model with application to thermal spraying. Journal of Manufacturing Systems 63, 162–176. https://doi.org/10.1016/j.jmsy.2022.03.005.

Bogataj, D., Battini, D., Calzavara, M., Persona, A., 2019. The ageing workforce challenge: investments in collaborative robots or contribution to pension schemes, from the multi-echelon perspective. International Journal of Production Economics 210, 97–106. https://doi.org/10.1016/j.ijpe.2018.12.016.

Bouchard, S., 2017. Lean robotics: a guide to making robots work in your factory. Robotics: Second Edition, 222.

Bousdekis, A., Mentzas, G., Apostolou, D., Wellsandt, S., 2022. Evaluation of AI-based digital assistants in smart manufacturing. In: Kim, D.Y., von Cieminski, G., Romero, D. (Eds.), Advances in Production Management Systems. Smart Manufacturing and Logistics Systems: Turning Ideas into Action. Springer Nature, Switzerland, Cham, pp. 503–510.

Boyes, H., Hallaq, B., Cunningham, J., Watson, T., 2018. The industrial internet of things (iiot): an analysis framework. Computers in Industry 101, 1–12. https://doi.org/10.1016/j.compind.2018.04.015.

Brooke, J., 1996. SUS – a quick and dirty usability scale. In: Usability Evaluation in Industry. CRC Press. ISBN 9780748404605. https://www.crcpress.com/product/isbn/9780748404605.

Brooke, J., 2013. Sus: a retrospective. Journal of Usability Studies 8, 29–40.

Bruno, G., Antonelli, D., 2018. Dynamic task classification and assignment for the management of human–robot collaborative teams in workcells. The International Journal of Advanced Manufacturing Technology 98, 2415–2427.

Buerkle, A., Eaton, W., Al-Yacoub, A., Zimmer, M., Kinnell, P., Henshaw, M., Coombes, M., Chen, W.H., Lohse, N., 2023. Towards industrial robots as a service (iraas): flexibility, usability, safety and business models. Robotics and Computer-Integrated Manufacturing 81, 102484. https://doi.org/10.1016/j.rcim.2022.102484.

Bunte, A., Fischbach, A., Strohschein, J., Bartz-Beielstein, T., Faeskorn-Woyke, H., Niggemann, O., 2019. Evaluation of cognitive architectures for cyber-physical production systems. Computing Research Repository (CoRR). arXiv:1902.08448 [abs].

Cangelosi, A., Asada, M., 2022. Cognitive Robotics. Massachusetts Institute of Technology. https://doi.org/10.7551/mitpress/13780.001.0001. https://direct.mit.edu/books/oa-edited-volume/5331/Cognitive-Robotics.

Caputo, F., Greco, A., Fera, M., Macchiaroli, R., 2019. Digital twins to enhance the integration of ergonomics in the workplace design. International Journal of Industrial Ergonomics 71, 20–31. https://doi.org/10.1016/j.ergon.2019.02.001.

Carayannis, E.G., Morawska-Jancelewicz, J., 2022. The futures of Europe: society 5.0 and industry 5.0 as driving forces of future universities. Journal of the Knowledge Economy 13, 3445–3471. https://doi.org/10.1007/s13132-021-00854-2.

Carvalho, A.V., Chouchene, A., Lima, T.M., Charrua-Santos, F., 2020. Cognitive manufacturing in industry 4.0 toward cognitive load reduction: a conceptual framework. Applied System Innovation 3. https://doi.org/10.3390/asi3040055. https://www.mdpi.com/2571-5577/3/4/55, 2020.

Castañé, G., Dolgui, A., Kousi, N., Meyers, B., Thevenin, S., Vyhmeister, E., Östberg, P.O., 2023. The assistant project: AI for high level decisions in manufacturing. International Journal of Production Research 61, 2288–2306. https://doi.org/10.1080/00207543.2022.2069525.

Chacón, A., Angulo, C., Ponsa, P., 2020a. Developing cognitive advisor agents for operators in industry 4.0. In: Martínez, L.R., Rios, R.A.O., Prieto, M.D. (Eds.), New Trends in the Use of Artificial Intelligence for the Industry 4.0. IntechOpen, Rijeka. https://doi.org/10.5772/intechopen.90211. Chapter 7 (online).

Chacón, A., Ponsa, P., Angulo, C., 2020b. On cognitive assistant robots for reducing variability in industrial human–robot activities. Applied Sciences 10. https://doi.org/10.3390/app10155137. https://www.mdpi.com/2076-3417/10/15/5137.

Chacón, A., Ponsa, P., Angulo, C., 2021a. Cognitive interaction analysis in human–robot collaboration using an assembly task. Electronics. https://doi.org/10.3390/electronics10111317. https://www.mdpi.com/2079-9292/10/11/1317.

Chacón, A., Ponsa, P., Angulo, C., 2021b. Usability study through a human–robot collaborative workspace experience. Designs 5. https://doi.org/10.3390/designs5020035. https://www.mdpi.com/2411-9660/5/2/35.

Chacón, L.A., 2022. A Socio-Technical Approach for Assistants in Human–Robot Collaboration in Industry 4.0. Ph.D. thesis. Automatic Control Department, Barcelona, Spain.

Chang, C.K., 2016. Situation analytics: a foundation for a new software engineering paradigm. Computer 49, 24–33. https://doi.org/10.1109/MC.2016.21.

Charles, R.L., Nixon, J., 2019. Measuring mental workload using physiological measures: a systematic review. Applied Ergonomics 74, 221–232. https://doi.org/10.1016/j.apergo.2018.08.028.

Chen, D., He, J., Chen, G., Yu, X., He, M., Yang, Y., Li, J., Zhou, X., 2020. Human–robot skill transfer systems for mobile robot based on multi sensor fusion. In: 2020 29th IEEE International Conference on Robot and Human Interactive Communication (RO-MAN), pp. 1354–1359. https://doi.org/10.1109/RO-MAN47096.2020.9223440.

Cherubini, A., Passama, R., Crosnier, A., Lasnier, A., Fraisse, P., 2016. Collaborative manufacturing with physical human–robot interaction. Robotics and Computer-Integrated Manufacturing 40, 1–13. https://doi.org/10.1016/j.rcim.2015.12.007.

Choi, T.M., Kumar, S., Yue, X., Chan, H.L., 2022. Disruptive technologies and operations management in the industry 4.0 era and beyond. Production and Operations Management 31, 9–31. https://doi.org/10.1111/poms.13622. https://onlinelibrary.wiley.com/doi/abs/10.1111/poms.13622. https://onlinelibrary.wiley.com/doi/pdf/10.1111/poms.13622.

Chowdhury, A., Ahtinen, A., Pieters, R., Vaananen, K., 2020. User experience goals for designing industrial human–cobot collaboration: a case study of Franka Panda robot. In: Proceedings of the 11th Nordic Conference on Human–Computer Interaction: Shaping Experiences. Shaping Society, Association for Computing Machinery, New York, NY, USA, pp. 83:1–83:13. https://doi.org/10.1145/3419249.3420161.

Chu, C.H., Liu, Y.L., 2023. Augmented reality user interface design and experimental evaluation for human–robot collaborative assembly. Journal of Manufacturing Systems 68, 313–324. https://doi.org/10.1016/j.jmsy.2023.04.007.

Cialdini, R.B., Goldstein, N.J., 2004. Social influence: compliance and conformity. Annual Review of Psychology 55, 591–621. https://doi.org/10.1146/annurev.psych.55.090902.142015. pMID: 14744228.

Cimini, C., Romero, D., Pinto, R., Cavalieri, S., 2023. Task classification framework and job-task analysis method for understanding the impact of smart and digital technologies on the operators 4.0 job profiles. Sustainability 15. https://doi.org/10.3390/su15053899. https://www.mdpi.com/2071-1050/15/5/3899, 2023.

Cimino, A., Elbasheer, M., Longo, F., Nicoletti, L., Padovano, A., 2023. Empowering field operators in manufacturing: a prospective towards industry 5.0. Procedia Computer Science 217, 1948–1953. https://doi.org/10.1016/j.procs.2022.12.395. 4th International Conference on Industry 4.0 and Smart Manufacturing.

Clarkson, E., Arkin, R.C., 2006. Applying Heuristic Evaluation to Human–Robot Interaction Systems. Technical Report. Georgia Tech.

Coelho, P., Bessa, C., Landeck, J., Silva, C., 2023. Industry 5.0: the arising of a concept. Procedia Computer Science 217, 1137–1144. https://doi.org/10.1016/j.procs.2022.12.312. 4th International Conference on Industry 4.0 and Smart Manufacturing.

Corbett, A.T., Koedinger, K.R., Anderson, J.R., 1997. Chapter 37 – Intelligent tutoring systems. In: Helander, M.G., Landauer, T.K., Prabhu, P.V. (Eds.), Handbook of Human–Computer Interaction, second edition. North-Holland, Amsterdam, pp. 849–874. https://doi.org/10.1016/B978-044481862-1.50103-5.

Coronado, E., Kiyokawa, T., Ricardez, G.A.G., Ramirez-Alpizar, I.G., Venture, G., Yamanobe, N., 2022. Evaluating quality in human-robot interaction: a systematic search and classification of performance and human-centered factors, measures and metrics towards an industry 5.0. Journal of Manufacturing Systems 63, 392–410. https://doi.org/10.1016/j.jmsy.2022.04.007.

Cowley, A.W., 2006. IUPS – a retrospective. The Physiologist 49, 171–173.

Cunha, L., Silva, D., Maggioli, S., 2022. Exploring the status of the human operator in industry 4.0: a systematic review. Frontiers in Psychology 13. https://doi.org/10.3389/fpsyg.2022.889129. https://www.frontiersin.org/articles/10.3389/fpsyg.2022.889129, 2022.

Davis, F.D., 1989. Perceived usefulness, perceived ease of use, and user acceptance of information technology. MIS Quarterly 13, 319–340. http://www.jstor.org/stable/249008.

De Nicola, A., Villani, M.L., Sujan, M., Watt, J., Costantino, F., Falegnami, A., Patriarca, R., 2023. Development and measurement of a resilience indicator for cyber-socio-technical systems: the allostatic load. Journal of Industrial Information Integration 35, 100489. https://doi.org/10.1016/j.jii.2023.100489.

De Santis, A., Siciliano, B., De Luca, A., Bicchi, A., 2008. An atlas of physical human–robot interaction. Mechanism and Machine Theory 43, 253–270. https://doi.org/10.1016/j.mechmachtheory.2007.03.003.

de Vries, G.J., Gentile, E., Miroudot, S., Wacker, K.M., 2020. The rise of robots and the fall of routine jobs. Labour Economics 66, 101885. https://doi.org/10.1016/j.labeco.2020.101885.

Debauche, O., Mahmoudi, S., Mahmoudi, S.A., Manneback, P., Lebeau, F., 2020. A new edge architecture for ai-iot services deployment. Procedia Computer Science 175, 10–19. https://doi.org/10.1016/j.procs.2020.07.006. The 17th International Conference on Mobile Systems and Pervasive Computing (MobiSPC), The 15th International Conference on Future Networks and Communications (FNC), The 10th International Conference on Sustainable Energy Information Technology.

Deguchi, A., Hirai, C., Matsuoka, H., Nakano, T., Oshima, K., Tai, M., Tani, S., 2020. What is Society 5.0?. In: Society 5.0: A People-Centric Super-Smart Society. Springer Singapore, Singapore, pp. 1–23. https://doi.org/10.1007/978-981-15-2989-4_1.

Dekker, S.W.A., Woods, D.D., 2002. Maba-Maba or abracadabra? Progress on human–automation co-ordination. Cognition Technology & Work 4, 240–244. https://doi.org/10.1007/s101110200022.

Demir, K.A., Döven, G., Sezen, B., 2019. Industry 5.0 and human–robot co-working. Procedia Computer Science 158, 688–695. https://doi.org/10.1016/j.procs.2019.09.104. 3rd World Conference on Technology, Innovation and Entrepreneurship "Industry 4.0 Focused Innovation, Technology, Entrepreneurship and Manufacture" June 21–23, 2019.

Di Nuovo, A., Varrasi, S., Conti, D., Bamsforth, J., Lucas, A., Soranzo, A., McNamara, J., 2019. Usability evaluation of a robotic system for cognitive testing. In: Proceedings of the 14th ACM/IEEE International Conference on Human–Robot Interaction. IEEE Press, pp. 588–589.

Dillenbourg, P., Baker, M., 1996. Negotiation spaces in human–computer collaborative learning. In: Proceedings of COOP'96, Second International Conference on Design of Cooperative Systems. INRIA, pp. 187–206.

Dong, J., Kang, D., Nam, S.W., 2023. Development of interactive teaching device for difficult teaching of collaborative robot. In: Stephanidis, C., Antona, M., Ntoa, S., Salvendy, G. (Eds.), HCI International 2023 Posters. Springer Nature Switzerland, Cham, pp. 54–59.

Ebraheem, A., Ivanov, I., 2022. Iot standardization: an overview of organizations and standards. In: 2022 Moscow Workshop on Electronic and Networking Technologies (MWENT), pp. 1–5. https://doi.org/10.1109/MWENT55238.2022.9802373.

Emmanouilidis, C., Pistofidis, P., Bertoncelj, L., Katsouros, V., Fournaris, A., Koulamas, C., Ruiz-Carcel, C., 2019. Enabling the human in the loop: linked data and knowledge in industrial cyber-physical systems. Annual Reviews in Control 47, 249–265. https://doi.org/10.1016/j.arcontrol.2019.03.004.

Enang, E., Bashiri, M., Jarvis, D., 2023. Exploring the transition from techno centric industry 4.0 towards value centric industry 5.0: a systematic literature review. International Journal of Production Research, 1–37. https://doi.org/10.1080/00207543.2023.2221344.

Muñoz-de Escalona, E., Cañas, J.J., Morales-Guaman, J.F., 2020. Fundamental frequency as an alternative method for assessing mental fatigue. In: Longo, L., Leva, M.C. (Eds.), Human Mental Workload: Models and Applications. Springer International Publishing, Cham, pp. 58–75.

Estrada-Jimenez, L.A., Pulikottil, T., Peres, R.S., Nikghadam-Hojjati, S., Barata, J., 2021. Complexity theory and self-organization in cyber-physical production systems. Procedia CIRP 104, 1831–1836. https://doi.org/10.1016/j.procir.2021.11.309. 54th CIRP CMS 2021 – Towards Digitalized Manufacturing 4.0.

Eswaran, M., Bahubalendruni, M.V.A.R., 2022. Challenges and opportunities on ar/vr technologies for manufacturing systems in the context of industry 4.0: a state of the art review. Journal of Manufacturing Systems 65, 260–278. https://doi.org/10.1016/j.jmsy.2022.09.016.

ETSI, 2000. ETSI Guide: Human Factors (HF); Usability evaluation for the design of telecommunication systems, services and terminals. Standard ETSI EG 201472 2000. European Telecommunications Standards Institute, Sophia Antipolis. https://www.etsi.org/deliver/etsi_eg/201400_201499/201472/01.01.01_60/eg_201472v010101p.pdf.

EUnited, 2021. Good work charter of the European Robotics Industry. Technical Report. European Engineering Industries Association. https://www.eu-nited.net/cms/upload/pdf/2020-01_28_EUnited_Press_Release_Charter_Final_with_Infograph.pdf, 2021.

European Commission, Directorate-General for Research and Innovation, Breque, M., De Nul, L., Petridis, A., 2021. Industry 5.0 – Towards a Sustainable, Human-Centric and Resilient European Industry. Publications Office of the European Union.

Evjemo, L.D., Gjerstad, T., Grøtli, E.I., Sziebig, G., 2020. Trends in smart manufacturing: role of humans and industrial robots in smart factories. Current Robotics Reports 1, 35–41. https://doi.org/10.1007/s43154-020-00006-5.

Fallaha, M., 2019. Operator 4.0 and Cognitive Ergonomics. Master's thesis. Eastern Mediterranean University, Cyprus.

Fantini, P., Pinzone, M., Taisch, M., 2020. Placing the operator at the centre of industry 4.0 design: modelling and assessing human activities within cyber-physical systems. Computers & Industrial Engineering 139, 105058. https://doi.org/10.1016/j.cie.2018.01.025.

Fasth-Berglund, A., Stahre, J., 2013. Cognitive automation strategy for reconfigurable and sustainable assembly systems. Assembly Automation 33, 294–303. https://doi.org/10.1108/AA-12-2013-036.

Fiore, S.M., Wiltshire, T.J., 2016. Technology as teammate: examining the role of external cognition in support of team cognitive processes. Frontiers in Psychology 7. https://doi.org/10.3389/fpsyg.2016.01531.

Fischbach, A., Strohschein, J., Bunte, A., Stork, J., Faeskorn-Woyke, H., Moriz, N., Bartz-Beielstein, T., 2020. CAAI – a cognitive architecture to introduce artificial intelligence in cyber-physical production systems. The International Journal of Advanced Manufacturing Technology, 609–626.

Fletcher, S., Johnson, T., Adlon, T., Larreina, J., Casla, P., Parigot, L., Alfaro, P.J., del Mar Otero, M., 2019. Adaptive automation assembly: identifying system requirements for technical efficiency and worker satisfaction. Computers & Industrial Engineering. https://doi.org/10.1016/j.cie.2019.03.036.

Fournier, E., Kilgus, D., Landry, A., Hmedan, B., Pellier, D., Fiorino, H., Jeoffrion, C., 2022. The impacts of human-cobot collaboration on perceived cognitive load and usability during an industrial task: an exploratory experiment. IISE Transactions on Occupational Ergonomics and Human Factors 10, 83–90. https://doi.org/10.1080/24725838.2022.2072021. pMID: 35485174.

Frank, A.G., Dalenogare, L.S., Ayala, N.F., 2019. Industry 4.0 technologies: implementation patterns in manufacturing companies. International Journal of Production Economics 210, 15–26. https://doi.org/10.1016/j.ijpe.2019.01.004.

Freire, S.K., Panicker, S.S., Ruiz-Arenas, S., Rusák, Z., Niforatos, E., 2023. A cognitive assistant for operators: AI-powered knowledge sharing on complex systems. IEEE Pervasive Computing 22, 50–58. https://doi.org/10.1109/MPRV.2022.3218600.

Fruggiero, F., Lambiase, A., Panagou, S., Sabattini, L., 2020. Cognitive human modeling in collaborative robotics. Procedia Manufacturing 51, 584–591. https://doi.org/10.1016/j.promfg.2020.10.082. 30th International Conference on Flexible Automation and Intelligent Manufacturing (FAIM2021).

Gallo, T., Santolamazza, A., 2021. Industry 4.0 and human factor: how is technology changing the role of the maintenance operator? Procedia Computer Science 180, 388–393. https://

doi.org/10.1016/j.procs.2021.01.364. Proceedings of the 2nd International Conference on Industry 4.0 and Smart Manufacturing (ISM 2020).

Galy, E., Cariou, M., Mélan, C., 2012. What is the relationship between mental workload factors and cognitive load types? International Journal of Psychophysiology 83, 269–275. https://doi.org/10.1016/j.ijpsycho.2011.09.023.

Gambao, E., 2023. Analysis exploring risks and opportunities linked to the use of collaborative industrial robots in Europe. Study PE 740.259. Panel for the Future of Science and Technology European Parliamentary Research Services (EPRS), Brussels, BE. https://www.europarl.europa.eu/RegData/etudes/STUD/2023/740259/EPRS_STU(2023)740259_EN.pdf.

Gao, Y., Li, H., Xiong, G., Song, H., 2023. Aiot-informed digital twin communication for bridge maintenance. Automation in Construction 150, 104835. https://doi.org/10.1016/j.autcon.2023.104835.

Gao, Z., Wanyama, T., Singh, I., Gadhrri, A., Schmidt, R., 2020. From industry 4.0 to robotics 4.0 – a conceptual framework for collaborative and intelligent robotic systems. Procedia Manufacturing 46, 591–599. https://doi.org/10.1016/j.promfg.2020.03.085. 13th International Conference Interdisciplinarity in Engineering, INTER-ENG 2019, 3–4 October 2019, Targu Mures, Romania.

Garbev, A., Atanassov, A., 2020. Comparative analysis of robodk and robot operating system for solving diagnostics tasks in off-line programming. In: 2020 International Conference Automatics and Informatics (ICAI), pp. 1–5. https://doi.org/10.1109/ICAI50593.2020.9311332.

Garcia, M.A.R., Rojas, R., Gualtieri, L., Rauch, E., Matt, D., 2019. A human-in-the-loop cyber-physical system for collaborative assembly in smart manufacturing. Procedia CIRP 81, 600–605. https://doi.org/10.1016/j.procir.2019.03.162. 52nd CIRP Conference on Manufacturing Systems (CMS), Ljubljana, Slovenia, June 12–14, 2019.

Garg, K., Goswami, C., Chhatrawat, R., Kumar Dhakar, S., Kumar, G., 2022. Internet of things in manufacturing: a review. Materials Today: Proceedings 51, 286–288. https://doi.org/10.1016/j.matpr.2021.05.321. cMAE'21.

Gazzaneo, L., Padovano, A., Umbrello, S., 2020. Designing smart operator 4.0 for human values: a value sensitive design approach. Procedia Manufacturing 42, 219–226. https://doi.org/10.1016/j.promfg.2020.02.073.

Gazzotti, S., Ferlay, F., Meunier, L., Viudes, P., Huc, K., Derkazarian, A., Friconneau, J.P., Peluso, B., Martins, J.P., 2021. Virtual and augmented reality use cases for fusion design engineering. Fusion Engineering and Design 172, 112780. https://doi.org/10.1016/j.fusengdes.2021.112780.

Gelenbe, E., Guennouni, H., 1991. Flexsim: a flexible manufacturing system simulator. European Journal of Operational Research 53, 149–165. https://doi.org/10.1016/0377-2217(91)90131-E.

Gely, C., Trentesaux, D., Sénéchal, O., Pacaux-Lemoine, M.P., 2020. Human–machine cooperation with autonomous CPS in the context of industry 4.0: a literature review. In: SOHOMA 2020: Service Oriented, Holonic and Multi-Agent Manufacturing Systems for Industry of the Future. Springer, Paris, France, pp. 327–342. https://doi.org/10.1007/978-3-030-69373-2_23. https://uphf.hal.science/hal-03529700.

Gervasi, R., Mastrogiacomo, L., Franceschini, F., 2020. A conceptual framework to evaluate human–robot collaboration. International Journal of Advanced Manufacturing Technology 108, 841–865. https://doi.org/10.1007/s00170-020-05363-1.

Gladysz, B., Tran, T., Romero, D., van Erp, T., Abonyi, J., Ruppert, T., 2023. Current development on the operator 4.0 and transition towards the operator 5.0: a systematic literature review in light of industry 5.0. Journal of Manufacturing Systems 70, 160–185. https://doi.org/10.1016/j.jmsy.2023.07.008.

Goh, Y.M., Micheler, S., Sanchez-Salas, A., Case, K., Bumblauskas, D., Monfared, R., 2020. A variability taxonomy to support automation decision-making for manufacturing processes. Production Planning & Control 31, 383–399. https://doi.org/10.1080/09537287.2019.1639840.

Golovianko, M., Terziyan, V., Branytskyi, V., Malyk, D., 2023. Industry 4.0 vs. industry 5.0: co-existence, transition, or a hybrid. Procedia Computer Science 217, 102–113. https://doi.org/10.1016/j.procs.2022.12.206. 4th International Conference on Industry 4.0 and Smart Manufacturing.

Gong, X., Jiao, R., Jariwala, A., Morkos, B., 2021. Crowdsourced manufacturing cyber platform and intelligent cognitive assistants for delivery of manufacturing as a service: fundamental issues and outlook. The International Journal of Advanced Manufacturing Technology 117, 1997–2007. https://doi.org/10.1007/s00170-021-07789-7.

Gorecky, D., Schmitt, M., Loskyll, M., Zühlke, D., 2014. Human–machine-interaction in the industry 4.0 era. In: Proceedings – 2014 12th IEEE International Conference on Industrial Informatics, INDIN 2014, pp. 289–294. https://doi.org/10.1109/INDIN.2014.6945523.

Granell, C., Kamilaris, A., Kotsev, A., Ostermann, F.O., Trilles, S., 2020. Internet of things. In: Guo, H., Goodchild, M.F., Annoni, A. (Eds.), Manual of Digital Earth. Springer Singapore, Singapore, pp. 387–423. https://doi.org/10.1007/978-981-32-9915-3_11.

Gray, R., Gaska, J., Winterbottom, M., 2016. Relationship between sustained, orientated, divided, and selective attention and simulated aviation performance: training & pressure effects. Journal of Applied Research in Memory and Cognition 5, 34–42. https://doi.org/10.1016/j.jarmac.2015.11.005.

Greer, C., Burns, M., Wollman, D., Griffor, E., 2019. Cyber-Physical Systems and Internet of Things. Technical Report. National Institute of Standards and Technology. https://doi.org/10.6028/NIST.SP.1900-202.

Grier, R.A., 2015. How high is high? A meta-analysis of NASA-TLX global workload scores. Proceedings of the Human Factors and Ergonomics Society 2015-January, 1727–1731. https://doi.org/10.1177/1541931215591373.

Griffor, E., Greer, C., Wollman, D., Burns, M., 2017. Framework for cyber-physical systems: Volume 1, overview. https://doi.org/10.6028/NIST.SP.1500-201.

Groover, M.P., Weiss, M., Nagel, R.N., Odrey, N.G., 1986. Industrial Robotics: Technology, Programming, and Applications. McGraw–Hill, New York.

Gualtieri, L., Fraboni, F., De Marchi, M., Rauch, E., 2022. Development and evaluation of design guidelines for cognitive ergonomics in human–robot collaborative assembly systems. Applied Ergonomics 104, 103807. https://doi.org/10.1016/j.apergo.2022.103807.

Gualtieri, L., Rauch, E., Vidoni, R., 2021. Emerging research fields in safety and ergonomics in industrial collaborative robotics: a systematic literature review. Robotics and Computer-Integrated Manufacturing 67, 101998. https://doi.org/10.1016/j.rcim.2020.101998.

Gualtieri, L., Rojas, R.A., Ruiz Garcia, M.A., Rauch, E., Vidoni, R., 2020. Implementation of a laboratory case study for intuitive collaboration between man and machine in sme assembly. In: Matt, D.T., Modrák, V., Zsifkovits, H. (Eds.), Industry 4.0 for SMEs: Challenges, Opportunities and Requirements. Springer International Publishing, Cham, pp. 335–382. https://doi.org/10.1007/978-3-030-25425-4_12.

Gubbi, J., Buyya, R., Marusic, S., Palaniswami, M., 2013. Internet of things (iot): a vision, architectural elements, and future directions. Future Generation Computer Systems 29, 1645–1660. https://doi.org/10.1016/j.future.2013.01.010. Including Special sections: Cyber-enabled Distributed Computing for Ubiquitous Cloud and Network Services

& Cloud Computing and Scientific Applications — Big Data, Scalable Analytics, and Beyond.

Gupta, S., Epiphaniou, G., Maple, C., 2023. Ai-augmented usability evaluation framework for software requirements specification in cyber physical human systems. Internet of Things 23, 100841. https://doi.org/10.1016/j.iot.2023.100841.

Güell, M., Salamó, M., Contreras, D., Boratto, L., 2020. Integrating a cognitive assistant within a critique-based recommender system. Cognitive Systems Research 64, 1–14. https://doi.org/10.1016/j.cogsys.2020.07.003.

Gürdür Broo, D., Kaynak, O., Sait, S.M., 2022. Rethinking engineering education at the age of industry 5.0. Journal of Industrial Information Integration 25, 100311. https://doi.org/10.1016/j.jii.2021.100311.

Hansen, E.B., Bøgh, S., 2021. Artificial intelligence and internet of things in small and medium-sized enterprises: a survey. Journal of Manufacturing Systems 58, 362–372. https://doi.org/10.1016/j.jmsy.2020.08.009. Digital Twin towards Smart Manufacturing and Industry 4.0.

Hardy, D.J., Wright, M.J., 2018. Assessing workload in neuropsychology: an illustration with the Tower of Hanoi test. Journal of Clinical and Experimental Neuropsychology 40, 1022–1029. https://doi.org/10.1080/13803395.2018.1473343.

Hariyanto, D., Nugraha, A.C., Asmara, A., Liu, H., 2019. An asynchronous serial communication learning media: usability evaluation. Journal of Physics. Conference Series 1413, 012018. https://doi.org/10.1088/1742-6596/1413/1/012018.

Harper, P., Norman, K.L., 1993. Improving user satisfaction: the questionnaire for user interaction satisfaction version 5. In: Proceedings of the 1st Annual Mid-Atlantic Human Factors Conference, pp. 224–228. https://api.semanticscholar.org/CorpusID:60950368.

Harriott, C.E., Buford, G.L., Adams, J.A., Zhang, T., 2015. Mental workload and task performance in peer-based human–robot teams. Journal of Human–Robot Interaction 4, 61–96.

Harriott, C.E., Buford, G.L., Zhang, T., Adams, J.A., 2012. Assessing workload in human–robot peer-based teams. In: 2012 7th ACM/IEEE International Conference on Human–Robot Interaction (HRI), pp. 141–142. https://doi.org/10.1145/2157689.2157725.

Hart, S.G., Staveland, L.E., 1988. Development of nasa-tlx (task load index): results of empirical and theoretical research. In: Hancock, P.A., Meshkati, N. (Eds.), Human Mental Workload. In: Advances in Psychology, vol. 52. North-Holland, pp. 139–183. https://doi.org/10.1016/S0166-4115(08)62386-9.

Haslgrubler, M., Gollan, B., Ferscha, A., 2018. A cognitive assistance framework for supporting human workers in industrial tasks. IT Professional 20, 48–56. https://doi.org/10.1109/MITP.2018.053891337.

Havlíček, J., Lališ, A., Vokáč, R., 2020. Functional resonance of the airport passengers security check. In: 2020 New Trends in Civil Aviation (NTCA), pp. 89–94. https://doi.org/10.23919/NTCA50409.2020.9290934.

Havur, G., Haspalamutgil, K., Palaz, C., Erdem, E., Patoglu, V., 2013. A case study on the tower of Hanoi challenge: representation, reasoning and execution. In: 2013 IEEE International Conference on Robotics and Automation (ICRA), pp. 4552–4559.

Hazbar, T., Kumar, S., Sahin, F., 2019. Cyber-physical testbed for human–robot collaborative task planning and execution. arXiv:1905.00199 [abs].

Heard, J., Heald, R., Harriott, C.E., Adams, J.A., 2019. A diagnostic human workload assessment algorithm for collaborative and supervisory human–robot teams. Journal of Human–Robot Interaction 8. https://doi.org/10.1145/3314387.

Hehenberger, P., Vogel-Heuser, B., Bradley, D., Eynard, B., Tomiyama, T., Achiche, S., 2016. Design, modelling, simulation and integration of cyber physical systems: methods and applications. Computers in Industry 82, 273–289. https://doi.org/10.1016/j.compind.2016.05.006.

Heinold, E., Rosen, P.H., Wischniewski, S., 2022. Validation of a usability questionnaire for summative evaluation of robotic systems. In: 2022 31st IEEE International Conference on Robot and Human Interactive Communication (RO-MAN), pp. 109–114. https://doi.org/10.1109/RO-MAN53752.2022.9900612.

Hentout, A., Aouache, M., Maoudj, A., Akli, I., 2019. Human–robot interaction in industrial collaborative robotics: a literature review of the decade 2008–2017. Advanced Robotics 33, 764–799. https://doi.org/10.1080/01691864.2019.1636714.

Herterich, M.M., Uebernickel, F., Brenner, W., 2015. The impact of cyber-physical systems on industrial services in manufacturing. Procedia CIRP 30, 323–328. 7th Industrial Product-Service Systems Conference – PSS, industry transformation for sustainability and business.

Hiatt, L.M., Harrison, A.M., Trafton, J.G., 2011. Accommodating human variability in human–robot teams through theory of mind. In: Twenty-Second International Joint Conference on Artificial Intelligence, pp. 2066–2071.

Hinds, P.J., Roberts, T.L., Jones, H., 2004. Whose job is it anyway? A study of human–robot interaction in a collaborative task. Human-Computer Interaction 19, 151–181. https://doi.org/10.1080/07370024.2004.9667343. https://www.tandfonline.com/doi/abs/10.1080/07370024.2004.9667343. https://www.tandfonline.com/doi/pdf/10.1080/07370024.2004.9667343.

Hoffman, G., 2019. Evaluating fluency in human–robot collaboration. IEEE Transactions on Human-Machine Systems 49, 209–218. https://doi.org/10.1109/THMS.2019.2904558.

Hoffman, G., Breazeal, C., 2007. Cost-based anticipatory action selection for human–robot fluency. IEEE Transactions on Robotics 23, 952–961.

Hollan, J., Hutchins, E., Kirsh, D., 2000. Distributed cognition: toward a new foundation for human–computer interaction research. ACM Transactions on Computer-Human Interaction 7, 174–196. https://doi.org/10.1145/353485.353487.

Hollnagel, E., 2009. The Etto Principle: Why Things That Go Right Sometimes Go Wrong. Ashgate, Farnham, UK.

Hollnagel, E., 2010. Prolegomenon to cognitive task design. In: Handbook of Cognitive Task Design, pp. 3–15. https://doi.org/10.1201/9781410607775.pt1.

Hollnagel, E., 2012. FRAM: The Functional Resonance Analysis Method: Modelling Complex Socio-Technical Systems. Ashgate. https://doi.org/10.3357/asem.3712.2013.

Hollnagel, E., 2013. An Application of the Functional Resonance Analysis Method (FRAM) to Risk Assessment of Organisational Change. Report 2013:09. Swedish Radiation Safety Authority, Stockholm, Sweden. https://www.stralsakerhetsmyndigheten.se/, 2013.

Hollnagel, E., 2017. FRAM: The Functional Resonance Analysis Method: Modelling Complex Socio-Technical Systems. CRC Press.

Hollnagel, E., Woods, D.D., 2005. Joint Cognitive Systems: Foundations of Cognitive Systems Engineering, 1st ed. CRC Press, Boca Raton. https://doi.org/10.1201/9781420038194.

Holroyd, C., 2022. Technological innovation and building a 'super smart' society: Japan's vision of society 5.0. Journal of Asian Public Policy 15, 18–31. https://doi.org/10.1080/17516234.2020.1749340.

Hopko, S., Wang, J., Mehta, R., 2022. Human factors considerations and metrics in shared space human-robot collaboration: a systematic review. Frontiers in Robotics and AI 9. https://doi.org/10.3389/frobt.2022.799522. https://www.frontiersin.org/articles/10.3389/frobt.2022.799522.

Hu, L., Xie, N., Kuang, Z., Zhao, K., 2012. Review of cyber-physical system architecture. In: 2012 IEEE 15th International Symposium on Object/Component/Service-Oriented Real-Time Distributed Computing Workshops. IEEE, pp. 25–30.

Hu, Q., Lu, Y., Pan, Z., Gong, Y., Yang, Z., 2021. Can ai artifacts influence human cognition? The effects of artificial autonomy in intelligent personal assistants. International Journal of Information Management 56, 102250. https://doi.org/10.1016/j.ijinfomgt.2020.102250.

Huang, S., Wang, B., Li, X., Zheng, P., Mourtzis, D., Wang, L., 2022. Industry 5.0 and society 5.0—comparison, complementation and co-evolution. Journal of Manufacturing Systems 64, 424–428. https://doi.org/10.1016/j.jmsy.2022.07.010.

IFR, 2020. Next Generation Skills – Enabling today's and tomorrow's workforce to benefit from automation. Positioning Paper. International Federation of Robotics, Frankfurt, Germany. https://ifr.org/papers/next-generation-skills, 2020.

Illankoon, P., Tretten, P., Kumar, U., 2019. Modelling human cognition of abnormal machine behaviour. Human-Intelligent Systems Integration 1, 3–26. https://doi.org/10.1007/s42454-019-00002-x.

International Federation of Robotics, 2018. The Impact of Robots on Productivity, Employment and Jobs. Positioning Paper. International Federation of Robotics, Frankfurt, Germany. https://ifr.org/downloads/papers/IFR_The_Impact_of_Robots_on_Employment_Positioning_Paper_updated_version_2018.pdf.

Iso, 2010. Ergonomics of human–system interaction. The Japanese Journal of Ergonomics 30, 1. https://doi.org/10.5100/jje.30.1.

ISO Central Secretary, 2011. Ergonomics of human–system interaction – Part 420: Selection of physical input devices. Standard ISO 9241-420:2011. International Organization for Standardization, Geneva, CH. https://www.iso.org/standard/52938.html.

ISO Central Secretary, 2016a. Ergonomics principles in the design of work systems. Standard ISO 6385:2016. International Organization for Standardization, Geneva, CH. https://www.iso.org/standard/63785.htmll, 2016.

ISO Central Secretary, 2016b. ISO/TS 15066:2016 Robots and robotic devices — Collaborative robots. Standard. International Organization for Standardization, Geneva, CH. https://www.iso.org/standard/52938.html, 2016.

ISO Central Secretary, 2018a. Ergonomics of human-system interaction — Part 11: usability: definitions and concepts. Standard ISO 9241-11:2018. International Organization for Standardization, Geneva, CH. https://www.iso.org/standard/63500.html.

ISO Central Secretary, 2018b. ISO 10218-1:2011 Robots and robotic devices — Safety requirements for industrial robots — Part 1: Robots. Standard. International Organization for Standardization, Geneva, CH. https://www.iso.org/standard/51330.html.

ISO Central Secretary, 2018c. ISO 10218-2:2011 Robots and Robotic Devices – Safety Requirements for Industrial Robots – Part 2: Robot Systems and Integration. Standard. International Organization for Standardization, Geneva, CH. https://www.iso.org/standard/41571.html.

ISO Central Secretary, 2022a. Framework for Artificial Intelligence (AI) Systems Using Machine Learning (ML). Standard ISO 23053:2022. International Organization for Standardization, Geneva, CH. https://www.iso.org/standard/74438.html, 2022.

ISO Central Secretary, 2022b. Information Technology – Artificial Intelligence – Artificial Intelligence Concepts and Terminology. Standard ISO 22989:2022. International Organization for Standardization, Geneva, CH. https://www.iso.org/standard/74296.html, 2022.

ISO Central Secretary, 2022c. Internet of Things (IoT) — Compatibility requirements and model for devices within industrial IoT systems. Standard ISO 30162:2022. International Organization for Standardization, Geneva, CH. https://www.iso.org/standard/53282.html.

Izsak, K., Romanainen, J., Stamenov, B., 2021. Advanced Technologies for Industry, Policy Brief – Industrial Recovery and Technology Policy. Publications Office of the European Union, Luxembourg. https://www.cde.ual.es/wp-content/uploads/2021/10/EA0921339ENN.en_.pdf.

Jacob, F., Grosse, E.H., Morana, S., König, C.J., 2023. Picking with a robot colleague: a systematic literature review and evaluation of technology acceptance in human–robot collaborative warehouses. Computers & Industrial Engineering 180, 109262. https://doi.org/10.1016/j.cie.2023.109262.

Jan, Z., Ahamed, F., Mayer, W., Patel, N., Grossmann, G., Stumptner, M., Kuusk, A., 2023. Artificial intelligence for industry 4.0: systematic review of applications, challenges, and opportunities. Expert Systems with Applications 216, 119456. https://doi.org/10.1016/j.eswa.2022.119456.

Jesse, N., 2016. Internet of things and big data – the disruption of the value chain and the rise of new software ecosystems. IFAC-PapersOnLine 49, 275–282. https://doi.org/10.1016/j.ifacol.2016.11.079. 17th IFAC Conference on International Stability, Technology and Culture TECIS 2016.

Jia, W., Wang, S., Xie, Y., Chen, Z., Gong, K., 2022. Disruptive technology identification of intelligent logistics robots in aiot industry: based on attributes and functions analysis. Systems Research and Behavioral Science 39, 557–568. https://doi.org/10.1002/sres.2859. https://onlinelibrary.wiley.com/doi/abs/10.1002/sres.2859. https://onlinelibrary.wiley.com/doi/pdf/10.1002/sres.2859.

Jocelyn, S., Ledoux, Élise, Armas Marrero, I., Burlet-Vienney, D., Chinniah, Y., Bonev, I.A., Ben Mosbah, A., Berger, I., 2023. Classification of collaborative applications and key variability factors to support the first step of risk assessment when integrating cobots. Safety Science 166, 106219. https://doi.org/10.1016/j.ssci.2023.106219.

Jokinen, K., 2019. Constructing human–robot interaction with standard cognitive architecture. In: Cangelosi, A., Lieto, A. (Eds.), Proceedings of the 7th International Workshop on Artificial Intelligence and Cognition. Manchester, UK, September 10–11, 2019. CEUR-WS.org, pp. 1–9. https://ceur-ws.org/Vol-2483/paper1.pdf.

Jones, A.T., Romero, D., Wuest, T., 2018. Modeling agents as joint cognitive systems in smart manufacturing systems. Manufacturing Letters 17, 6–8. https://doi.org/10.1016/j.mfglet.2018.06.002.

Jordan, P.W., Thomas, B., McClelland, I.L., Weerdmeester, B., 1996. Usability Evaluation in Industry. Taylor & Francis. https://doi.org/10.1201/9781498710411.

Kaasinen, E., Anttila, A.H., Heikkilä, P., Laarni, J., Koskinen, H., Väätänen, A., 2022. Smooth and resilient human–machine teamwork as an industry 5.0 design challenge. Sustainability 14. https://doi.org/10.3390/su14052773. https://www.mdpi.com/2071-1050/14/5/2773.

Kaasinen, E., Schmalfuß, F., Özturk, C., Aromaa, S., Boubekeur, M., Heilala, J., Heikkilä, P., Kuula, T., Liinasuo, M., Mach, S., Mehta, R., Petäjä, E., Walter, T., 2020. Empowering and engaging industrial workers with Operator 4.0 solutions. Computers & Industrial Engineering 139, 105678. https://doi.org/10.1016/j.cie.2019.01.052.

Kadir, B.A., Broberg, O., 2020. Human well-being and system performance in the transition to industry 4.0. International Journal of Industrial Ergonomics 76, 102936. https://doi.org/10.1016/j.ergon.2020.102936.

Kagermann, H., Helbig, J., Hellinger, A., Wahlster, W., 2013. Recommendations for implementing the strategic initiative INDUSTRIE 4.0: Securing the future of German manufacturing industry; final report of the Industrie 4.0 Working Group. Forschungsunion.

Kalmbach, S., Bargmann, D., Lindblom, J., Wang, W., Wang, V., 2018. Symbiotic human–robot collaboration for safe and dynamic multimodal manufacturing systems. Technical Report 2018-06-21. Rob.

Karakikes, M., Nathanael, D., 2023. The effect of cognitive workload on decision authority assignment in human–robot collaboration. Cognition, Technology & Work 25, 31–43. https://doi.org/10.1007/s10111-022-00719-x.

Karnouskos, S., Leitão, P., 2017. Key contributing factors to the acceptance of agents in industrial environments. IEEE Transactions on Industrial Informatics 13, 696–703. https://doi.org/10.1109/TII.2016.2607148.

Karnouskos, S., Ribeiro, L., Leitao, P., Luder, A., Vogel-Heuser, B., 2019. Key directions for industrial agent based cyber-physical production systems. In: 2019 IEEE International Conference on Industrial Cyber Physical Systems (ICPS), pp. 17–22. https://doi.org/10.1109/ICPHYS.2019.8780360.

Karre, H., Hammer, M., Kleindienst, M., Ramsauer, C., 2017. Transition towards an industry 4.0 state of the leanlab at Graz University of Technology. Procedia Manufacturing 9, 206–213. https://doi.org/10.1016/j.promfg.2017.04.006. 7th Conference on Learning Factories, CLF 2017.

Kasinathan, P., Pugazhendhi, R., Elavarasan, R.M., Ramachandaramurthy, V.K., Ramanathan, V., Subramanian, S., Kumar, S., Nandhagopal, K., Raghavan, R.R.V., Rangasamy, S., Devendiran, R., Alsharif, M.H., 2022. Realization of sustainable development goals with disruptive technologies by integrating industry 5.0, society 5.0, smart cities and villages. Sustainability 14. https://doi.org/10.3390/su142215258. https://www.mdpi.com/2071-1050/14/22/15258.

Kebria, P.M., Al-wais, S., Abdi, H., Nahavandi, S., 2016. Kinematic and dynamic modelling of ur5 manipulator. In: 2016 IEEE International Conference on Systems, Man, and Cybernetics (SMC), pp. 004229–004234. https://doi.org/10.1109/SMC.2016.7844896.

Kernan Freire, S., Foosherian, M., Wang, C., Niforatos, E., 2023. Harnessing large language models for cognitive assistants in factories. In: Proceedings of the 5th International Conference on Conversational User Interfaces. Association for Computing Machinery, New York, NY, USA, pp. 1–6. https://doi.org/10.1145/3571884.3604313.

Keshvarparast, A., Battini, D., Battaia, O., Pirayesh, A., 2023. Collaborative robots in manufacturing and assembly systems: literature review and future research agenda. Journal of Intelligent Manufacturing. https://doi.org/10.1007/s10845-023-02137-w.

Kim, Y.C., Yoon, W.C., Kwon, H.T., Yoon, Y.S., Kim, H.J., 2007. A cognitive approach to enhancing human–robot interaction for service robots. In: Smith, M.J., Salvendy, G. (Eds.), Human Interface and the Management of Information. Methods, Techniques and Tools in Information Design. Springer Berlin Heidelberg, Berlin, Heidelberg, pp. 858–867.

Kimble, K., Van Wyk, K., Falco, J., Messina, E., Sun, Y., Shibata, M., Uemura, W., Yokokohji, Y., 2020. Benchmarking protocols for evaluating small parts robotic assembly systems. IEEE Robotics and Automation Letters 5, 883–889.

Kirakowski, J., Corbett, M., 1993. Sumi: the software usability measurement inventory. British Journal of Educational Technology 24, 210–212. https://doi.org/10.1111/j.1467-8535.1993.tb00076.x. https://bera-journals.onlinelibrary.wiley.com/doi/abs/10.1111/j.1467-8535.1993.tb00076.x. https://bera-journals.onlinelibrary.wiley.com/doi/pdf/10.1111/j.1467-8535.1993.tb00076.x.

Kolbeinsson, A., Lagerstedt, E., Lindblom, J., 2019. Foundation for a classification of collaboration levels for human–robot cooperation in manufacturing. Production & Manufacturing Research 7, 448–471. https://doi.org/10.1080/21693277.2019.1645628.

Kolberg, D., Zühlke, D., 2015. Lean automation enabled by industry 4.0 technologies. IFAC-PapersOnLine 48, 1870–1875. https://doi.org/10.1016/j.ifacol.2015.06.359. 15th IFAC Symposium on Information Control Problems in Manufacturing.

Kragic, D., Gustafson, J., Karaoğuz, H., Jensfelt, P., Krug, R., 2018. Interactive, collaborative robots: challenges and opportunities. In: IJCAI International Joint Conference on Artificial Intelligence. International Joint Conferences on Artificial Intelligence, pp. 18–25. https://doi.org/10.24963/ijcai.2018/3. Part of proceedings, ISBN 978-0-9992411-2-7QC 20190402.

Krause, P.J., Bokinala, V., 2023. A tutorial on data mining for Bayesian networks, with a specific focus on iot for agriculture. Internet of Things 22, 100738. https://doi.org/10.1016/j.iot.2023.100738.

Krugh, M., Mears, L., 2018. A complementary Cyber-Human Systems framework for Industry 4.0 Cyber-Physical Systems. Manufacturing Letters 15, 89–92. https://doi.org/10.1016/j.mfglet.2018.01.003.

Krüger, J., Lien, T.K., Verl, A., 2009. Cooperation of human and machines in assembly lines. CIRP Annals – Manufacturing Technology 58, 628–646. https://doi.org/10.1016/j.cirp.2009.09.009.

Kuo, Y.H., Wu, E.H.K., 2023. Advanced, innovative aiot and edge computing for unmanned vehicle systems in factories. Electronics 12. https://doi.org/10.3390/electronics12081843. https://www.mdpi.com/2079-9292/12/8/1843.

Kuschan, J., Krüger, J., 2021. Fatigue recognition in overhead assembly based on a soft robotic exosuit for worker assistance. CIRP Annals 70, 9–12. https://doi.org/10.1016/j.cirp.2021.04.034.

Lasi, H., Fettke, P., Kemper, H.G., Feld, T., Hoffmann, M., 2014. Industry 4.0. Business & Information Systems Engineering 6, 239–242. https://doi.org/10.1007/s12599-014-0334-4.

Lasota, P.A., Rossano, G.F., Shah, J.A., 2014. Toward safe close-proximity human–robot interaction with standard industrial robots. In: 2014 IEEE International Conference on Automation Science and Engineering (CASE), pp. 339–344.

Leitão, P., Karnouskos, S., Ribeiro, L., Lee, J., Strasser, T., Colombo, A.W., 2016. Smart agents in industrial cyber-physical systems. Proceedings of the IEEE 104, 1086–1101. https://doi.org/10.1109/JPROC.2016.2521931. https://core.ac.uk/download/pdf/153416645.pdf.

Lemaignan, S., Warnier, M., Sisbot, E.A., Clodic, A., Alami, R., 2017. Artificial cognition for social human–robot interaction: an implementation. Artificial Intelligence 247, 45–69. Special Issue on AI and Robotics.

Leng, J., Sha, W., Wang, B., Zheng, P., Zhuang, C., Liu, Q., Wuest, T., Mourtzis, D., Wang, L., 2022. Industry 5.0: prospect and retrospect. Journal of Manufacturing Systems 65, 279–295. https://doi.org/10.1016/j.jmsy.2022.09.017.

Leveson, N.G., 2012. Engineering a Safer World: Systems Thinking Applied to Safety. The MIT Press. https://doi.org/10.7551/mitpress/8179.001.0001. https://direct.mit.edu/book-pdf/2091815/book_9780262298247.pdf.

Lewis, J.R., 2006. Usability testing. In: Handbook of Human Factors and Ergonomics. John Wiley, Hoboken, NJ, pp. 1275–1316.

Li, C., Chrysostomou, D., Pinto, D., Hansen, A.K., Bøgh, S., Madsen, O., 2023a. Hey max, can you help me? An intuitive virtual assistant for industrial robots. Applied Sciences 13. https://doi.org/10.3390/app13010205. https://www.mdpi.com/2076-3417/13/1/205.

Li, L., 2018. China's manufacturing locus in 2025: with a comparison of "made-in-China 2025" and "industry 4.0". Technological Forecasting & Social Change 135, 66–74. https://doi.org/10.1016/j.techfore.2017.05.028.

Li, P., Bastone, A., Mohamad, T.A., Schiavone, F., 2023b. How does artificial intelligence impact human resources performance. Evidence from a healthcare institution in the United Arab Emirates. Journal of Innovation & Knowledge 8. https://doi.org/10.1016/j.jik.2023.100340. https://www.elsevier.es/en-revista-journal-innovation-knowledge-376-articulo-how-does-artificial-intelligence-impact-S2444569X23000367.

Li, S., Zheng, P., Liu, S., Wang, Z., Wang, X.V., Zheng, L., Wang, L., 2023c. Proactive human–robot collaboration: mutual-cognitive, predictable, and self-organising perspectives. Robotics and Computer-Integrated Manufacturing 81, 102510. https://doi.org/10.1016/j.rcim.2022.102510.

Li, X., Liu, H., Wang, W., Zheng, Y., Lv, H., Lv, Z., 2022. Big data analysis of the internet of things in the digital twins of smart city based on deep learning. Future Generation Computer Systems 128, 167–177. https://doi.org/10.1016/j.future.2021.10.006.

Liau, Y.Y., Ryu, K., 2020. Task allocation in human–robot collaboration (hrc) based on task characteristics and agent capability for mold assembly. Procedia Manufacturing 51, 179–186. https://doi.org/10.1016/j.promfg.2020.10.026. 30th International Conference on Flexible Automation and Intelligent Manufacturing (FAIM2021).

Lin, C.J., Lukodono, R.P., 2022. Classification of mental workload in human–robot collaboration using machine learning based on physiological feedback. Journal of Manufacturing Systems 65, 673–685. https://doi.org/10.1016/j.jmsy.2022.10.017.

Lin, Y.S., Chen, S.Y., Tsai, C.W., Lai, Y.H., 2021. Exploring computational thinking skills training through augmented reality and aiot learning. Frontiers in Psychology 12. https://doi.org/10.3389/fpsyg.2021.640115. https://www.frontiersin.org/articles/10.3389/fpsyg.2021.640115.

Liu, L., Guo, F., Zou, Z., Duffy, V.G., 2022. Application, development and future opportunities of collaborative robots (cobots) in manufacturing: a literature review. International Journal of Human-Computer Interaction, 1–18. https://doi.org/10.1080/10447318.2022.2041907.

Longo, F., Nicoletti, L., Padovano, A., 2017. Smart operators in industry 4.0: a human-centered approach to enhance operators' capabilities and competencies within the new smart factory context. Computers & Industrial Engineering 113, 144–159. https://doi.org/10.1016/j.cie.2017.09.016.

Longo, F., Padovano, A., 2020. Voice-enabled assistants of the operator 4.0 in the social smart factory: prospective role and challenges for an advanced human–machine interaction. Manufacturing Letters 26, 12–16. https://doi.org/10.1016/j.mfglet.2020.09.001.

Longo, F., Padovano, A., Umbrello, S., 2020. Value-oriented and ethical technology engineering in industry 5.0: a human-centric perspective for the design of the factory of the future. Applied Sciences (Switzerland) 10, 1–25. https://doi.org/10.3390/APP10124182.

Lu, L., Xie, Z., Wang, H., Li, L., Xu, X., 2022a. Mental stress and safety awareness during human–robot collaboration – review. Applied Ergonomics 105, 103832. https://doi.org/10.1016/j.apergo.2022.103832.

Lu, Y., 2017. Industry 4.0: a survey on technologies, applications and open research issues. Journal of Industrial Information Integration 6, 1–10. https://doi.org/10.1016/j.jii.2017.04.005.

Lu, Y., Xu, X., Wang, L., 2020. Smart manufacturing process and system automation – a critical review of the standards and envisioned scenarios. Journal of Manufacturing Systems 56, 312–325. https://doi.org/10.1016/j.jmsy.2020.06.010.

Lu, Y., Zheng, H., Chand, S., Xia, W., Liu, Z., Xu, X., Wang, L., Qin, Z., Bao, J., 2022b. Outlook on human-centric manufacturing towards industry 5.0. Journal of Manufacturing Systems 62, 612–627. https://doi.org/10.1016/j.jmsy.2022.02.001.

Lv, Z., 2023. Digital twins in industry 5.0. Research 6, 0071. https://doi.org/10.34133/research.0071. https://spj.science.org/doi/abs/10.34133/research.0071. https://spj.science.org/doi/pdf/10.34133/research.0071.

Maddikunta, P.K.R., Pham, Q.V., B, P., et al., 2022. Industry 5.0: a survey on enabling technologies and potential applications. Journal of Industrial Information Integration 26, 100257. https://doi.org/10.1016/j.jii.2021.100257.

Madni, A.M., Sievers, M., 2018. Model-based systems engineering: motivation, current status, and research opportunities. Systems Engineering 21, 172–190. https://doi.org/10.1002/sys.21438.

Maier, T., Donghia, V., Chen, C., Menold, J., McComb, C., 2019. Assessing the impact of cognitive assistants on mental workload in simple tasks. In: ASME 2019 International Design Engineering Technical Conferences and Computers and Information in Engineering Conference, pp. 1–10. https://doi.org/10.1115/DETC2019-97543.

Male, J., Martinez-Hernandez, U., 2023. Deep learning based robot cognitive architecture for collaborative assembly tasks. Robotics and Computer-Integrated Manufacturing 83. https://doi.org/10.1016/j.rcim.2023.102572.

Malik, A.A., Bilberg, A., 2018. Digital twins of human robot collaboration in a production setting. Procedia Manufacturing 17, 278–285. https://doi.org/10.1016/j.promfg.2018.10.047. 28th International Conference on Flexible Automation and Intelligent Manufacturing (FAIM2018), June 11–14, 2018, Columbus, OH, USA Global Integration of Intelligent Manufacturing and Smart Industry for Good of Humanity.

Malik, A.A., Bilberg, A., 2019a. Complexity-based task allocation in human–robot collaborative assembly. Industrial Robot 46, 471–480. https://doi.org/10.1108/IR-11-2018-0231.

Malik, A.A., Bilberg, A., 2019b. Developing a reference model for human–robot interaction. International Journal on Interactive Design and Manufacturing 13, 1541–1547. https://doi.org/10.1007/s12008-019-00591-6.

Malik, P.K., Sharma, R., Singh, R., Gehlot, A., Satapathy, S.C., Alnumay, W.S., Pelusi, D., Ghosh, U., Nayak, J., 2021. Industrial internet of things and its applications in industry 4.0: state of the art. Computer Communications 166, 125–139. https://doi.org/10.1016/j.comcom.2020.11.016.

Manogaran, G., Qudrat-Ullah, H., Xin, Q., 2021. Editorial on "cognitive computing for human–robot interaction". Complex & Intelligent Systems 7, 1709–1710. https://doi.org/10.1007/s40747-021-00468-w.

Mantravadi, S., Møller, C., 2019. An overview of next-generation manufacturing execution systems: how important is mes for industry 4.0? Procedia Manufacturing 30, 588–595. Digital Manufacturing Transforming Industry Towards Sustainable Growth.

Marco, J., 2022. Panel: software development methods in the IoT-laden, AI/ML-driven era. In: 2022 IEEE International Conference on Services Computing (SCC), pp. 349–350. https://doi.org/10.1109/SCC55611.2022.00057.

Maretto, L., Faccio, M., Battini, D., 2023. The adoption of digital technologies in the manufacturing world and their evaluation: a systematic review of real-life case studies and future research agenda. Journal of Manufacturing Systems 68, 576–600. https://doi.org/10.1016/j.jmsy.2023.05.009.

Margherita, E.G., Braccini, A.M., 2021. Socio-technical perspectives in the Fourth Industrial Revolution – analysing the three main visions: Industry 4.0, the socially sustainable factory of Operator 4.0 and Industry 5.0. In: 7th International Workshop on Socio-Technical Perspective in IS Development (STPIS 2021). Trento, Italy, pp. 74–82. https://hal.science/hal-03442406.

Mark, B.G., Rauch, E., Matt, D.T., 2021. Worker assistance systems in manufacturing: a review of the state of the art and future directions. Journal of Manufacturing Systems 59, 228–250. https://doi.org/10.1016/j.jmsy.2021.02.017.

Martín-Gómez, A., Ávila Gutiérrez, M.J., Aguayo-González, F., 2021. Holonic reengineering to foster sustainable cyber-physical systems design in cognitive manufacturing. Applied Sciences 11. https://doi.org/10.3390/app11072941. https://www.mdpi.com/2076-3417/11/7/2941.

Marvel, J.A., 2013. Performance metrics of speed and separation monitoring in shared workspaces. IEEE Transactions on Automation Science and Engineering 10, 405–414. https://doi.org/10.1109/TASE.2013.2237904.

Marvel, J.A., Bagchi, S., Zimmerman, M., Aksu, M., Antonishek, B., Wang, Y., Mead, R., Fong, T., Ben Amor, H., 2019. Test methods and metrics for effective hri in collaborative human–robot teams. In: 2019 14th ACM/IEEE International Conference on Human–Robot Interaction (HRI), pp. 696–697. https://doi.org/10.1109/HRI.2019.8673149.

Marvel, J.A., Bagchi, S., Zimmerman, M., Antonishek, B., 2020. Towards effective interface designs for collaborative hri in manufacturing: metrics and measures. Journal of Human-Robot Interaction 9. https://doi.org/10.1145/3385009.

Marvel, J.A., Falco, J., Marstio, I., 2015. Characterizing task-based human–robot collaboration safety in manufacturing. IEEE Transactions on Systems, Man, and Cybernetics: Systems 45, 260–275.

Masó, B., Ponsa, P., Tornil, S., 2020. Diseño de tareas persona-robot en el ámbito académico. Interacción, Revista digital de AIPO 2, 26–38.

Matin, A., Islam, M.R., Wang, X., Huo, H., Xu, G., 2023. Aiot for sustainable manufacturing: overview, challenges, and opportunities. Internet of Things, 100901. https://doi.org/10.1016/j.iot.2023.100901.

Messeri, C., Bicchi, A., Zanchettin, A.M., Rocco, P., 2022. A dynamic task allocation strategy to mitigate the human physical fatigue in collaborative robotics. IEEE Robotics and Automation Letters 7, 2178–2185. https://doi.org/10.1109/LRA.2022.3143520.

Mihelj, M., Bajd, T., Ude, A., Lenarčič, J., Stanovnik, A., Munih, M., Rejc, J., Šlajpah, S., 2019. Collaborative robots. In: Robotics. Springer International Publishing, Cham, pp. 173–187. https://doi.org/10.1007/978-3-319-72911-4_12.

Miller, B., 2021. Is technology value-neutral? Science, Technology, & Human Values 46, 53–80. https://doi.org/10.1177/0162243919900965.

Mittal, M., Shah, R.R., Roy, S. (Eds.), 2021. Cognitive Computing for Human–Robot Interaction. Principles and Practices. Cognitive Data Science in Sustainable Computing. Academic Press. https://doi.org/10.1016/B978-0-323-85769-7.00018-5. https://www.sciencedirect.com/book/9780323857697/cognitive-computing-for-human-robot-interaction.

Mizanoor Rahman, S.M., 2019. Cognitive cyber-physical system (c-cps) for human–robot collaborative manufacturing. In: 2019 14th Annual Conference System of Systems Engineering (SoSE), pp. 125–130. https://doi.org/10.1109/SYSOSE.2019.8753835.

Mohamudally, N., 2022. Paving the way towards collective intelligence at the iot edge. Procedia Computer Science 203, 8–15. https://doi.org/10.1016/j.procs.2022.07.004. 17th International Conference on Future Networks and Communications / 19th International Conference on Mobile Systems and Pervasive Computing / 12th International Conference on Sustainable Energy Information Technology (FNC/MobiSPC/SEIT 2022), August 9-11, 2022, Niagara Falls, Ontario, Canada.

Moniz, A.B., Krings, B.J., 2016. Robots working with humans or humans working with robots? Searching for social dimensions in new human–robot interaction in industry. Societies 6. https://doi.org/10.3390/soc6030023. https://www.mdpi.com/2075-4698/6/3/23.

Mourtzis, D., Angelopoulos, J., Panopoulos, N., 2022. A literature review of the challenges and opportunities of the transition from industry 4.0 to society 5.0. Energies 15. https://doi.org/10.3390/en15176276. https://www.mdpi.com/1996-1073/15/17/6276.

Mourtzis, D., Tsoubou, S., Angelopoulos, J., 2023. Robotic cell reliability optimization based on digital twin and predictive maintenance. Electronics 12. https://doi.org/10.3390/electronics12091999. https://www.mdpi.com/2079-9292/12/9/1999.

Mukherjee, D., Gupta, K., Chang, L.H., Najjaran, H., 2022. A survey of robot learning strategies for human-robot collaboration in industrial settings. Robotics and Computer-Integrated Manufacturing 73, 102231. https://doi.org/10.1016/j.rcim.2021.102231.

Müller, R., Oehm, L., 2019. Process industries versus discrete processing: how system characteristics affect operator tasks. Cognition Technology & Work 21, 337–356. https://doi.org/10.1007/s10111-018-0511-1.

Munirathinam, S., 2020. Chapter six – industry 4.0: industrial internet of things (iiot). In: Raj, P., Evangeline, P. (Eds.), The Digital Twin Paradigm for Smarter Systems and Environments: The Industry Use Cases. In: Advances in Computers, vol. 117(1). Elsevier, pp. 129–164. https://doi.org/10.1016/bs.adcom.2019.10.010.

Murashov, V., Hearl, F., Howard, J., 2016. Working safely with robot workers: recommendations for the new workplace. Journal of Occupational and Environmental Hygiene 13, D61–D71. https://doi.org/10.1080/15459624.2015.1116700. https://www.ncbi.nlm.nih.gov/pubmed/26554511. pMC4779796.

Murphy, R.R., Schreckenghost, D., 2013. Survey of metrics for human–robot interaction. In: 2013 8th ACM/IEEE International Conference on Human–Robot Interaction (HRI), pp. 197–198.

Murugesan, U., Subramanian, P., Srivastava, S., Dwivedi, A., 2023. A study of artificial intelligence impacts on human resource digitalization in industry 4.0. Decision Analytics Journal 7, 100249. https://doi.org/10.1016/j.dajour.2023.100249.

Muslikhin, M., Horng, J.R., Yang, S.Y., Wang, M.S., Awaluddin, B.A., 2021. An artificial intelligence of things-based picking algorithm for online shop in the society 5.0's context. Sensors 21. https://doi.org/10.3390/s21082813. https://www.mdpi.com/1424-8220/21/8/2813.

Mutlu, B., Roy, N., Šabanović, S., 2016. Cognitive human–robot interaction. In: Siciliano, B., Khatib, O. (Eds.), Springer Handbook of Robotics. Springer International Publishing, Cham, pp. 1907–1934. https://doi.org/10.1007/978-3-319-32552-1_71.

Müller, R., Vette, M., Geenen, A., 2017. Skill-based dynamic task allocation in human–robot-cooperation with the example of welding application. In: 27th International Conference on Flexible Automation and Intelligent Manufacturing, FAIM2017. Modena, Italy, 27–30 June 2017. In: Procedia Manufacturing, vol. 11, pp. 13–21. https://doi.org/10.1016/j.promfg.2017.07.113.

Naeini, A.M., Nadeau, S., 2022. Application of fram to perform risk analysis of the introduction of a data glove to assembly tasks. Robotics and Computer-Integrated Manufacturing 74, 102285. https://doi.org/10.1016/j.rcim.2021.102285.

Nagalingam, S.V., Lin, G.C., 2008. Cim—still the solution for manufacturing industry. Robotics and Computer-Integrated Manufacturing 24, 332–344. https://doi.org/10.1016/j.rcim.2007.01.002.

Nahavandi, S., 2019. Industry 5.0 – a human-centric solution. Sustainability 11. https://doi.org/10.3390/su11164371. https://www.mdpi.com/2071-1050/11/16/4371.

Nair, M.M., Tyagi, A.K., Sreenath, N., 2021. The future with industry 4.0 at the core of society 5.0: open issues, future opportunities and challenges. In: 2021 International Conference on Computer Communication and Informatics (ICCCI), pp. 1–7. https://doi.org/10.1109/ICCCI50826.2021.9402498.

Narandžić, D., Spasojević, I., Lolić, T., Stefanović, D., Ristić, S., 2021. Human roles, competencies and skills in industry 4.0: systematic literature review. https://www.proquest.com/conference-papers-proceedings/human-roles-competencies-skills-industry-4-0/docview/2604879779/se-2. Copyright – © 2021. This work is published under http://archive.ceciis.foi.hr/app/index.php/ceciis/archive (the "License"). Notwithstanding the ProQuest Terms and Conditions. You may use this content in accordance with the terms of the License; Last updated – 2023-03-28.

Nardo, M., Forino, D., Murino, T., 2020. The evolution of man–machine interaction: the role of human in industry 4.0 paradigm. Production & Manufacturing Research 8, 20–34. https://doi.org/10.1080/21693277.2020.1737592.

Narvaez Rojas, C., Alomia Peñafiel, G.A., Loaiza Buitrago, D.F., Tavera Romero, C.A., 2021. Society 5.0: a Japanese concept for a superintelligent society. Sustainability 13. https://doi.org/10.3390/su13126567. https://www.mdpi.com/2071-1050/13/12/6567.

Nelles, J., Kuz, S., Mertens, A., Schlick, C.M., 2016. Human-centered design of assistance systems for production planning and control. In: Proceedings 2016 IEEE International Conference on Industrial Technology (Icit), pp. 2099–2104.

Nemeth, C., 2013. Erik Hollnagel: Fram: The functional resonance analysis method, modeling complex socio-technical systems. Cognition Technology & Work 15, 117–118. https://doi.org/10.1007/s10111-012-0246-3.

Nenna, F., Orso, V., Zanardi, D., Gamberini, L., 2023. The virtualization of human–robot interactions: a user-centric workload assessment. Virtual Reality 27, 553–571. https://doi.org/10.1007/s10055-022-00667-x.

Neumann, W.P., Winkelhaus, S., Grosse, E.H., Glock, C.H., 2021. Industry 4.0 and the human factor – a systems framework and analysis methodology for successful development. International Journal of Production Economics 233, 107992. https://doi.org/10.1016/j.ijpe.2020.107992.

Nguyen, T.H., Bundas, M., Son, T.C., Balduccini, M., Garwood, K.C., Griffor, E.R., 2022. Specifying and reasoning about cps through the lens of the nist cps framework. arXiv:2201.05710.

Nordgren, W.B., 2002. Flexsim: Flexsim simulation environment. In: Proceedings of the 34th Conference on Winter Simulation: Exploring New Frontiers, Winter Simulation Conference, pp. 250–252.

Nozari, H., Tavakkoli-Moghaddam, R., Ghahremani-Nahr, J., Najafi, E., 2023. Chapter 8 – a conceptual framework for artificial intelligence of medical things (aiomt). In: Maleh, Y., El-Latif, A.A.A., Curran, K., Siarry, P., Dey, N., Ashour, A., Fong, S.J. (Eds.), Advances in Ubiquitous Sensing Applications for Healthcare. In: Computational Intelligence for Medical Internet of Things (MIoT) Applications, vol. 14. Academic Press, pp. 175–189. https://doi.org/10.1016/B978-0-323-99421-7.00007-6. https://www.sciencedirect.com/science/article/pii/B9780323994217000076.

Nwanya, S., Achebe, C., Ajayi, O., Mgbemene, C., 2016. Process variability analysis in make-to-order production systems. Cogent Engineering 3. https://doi.org/10.1080/23311916.2016.1269382.

Olivares-Alarcos, A., Foix, S., Borgo, S., Alenyà, Guillem, 2022. Ocra – an ontology for collaborative robotics and adaptation. Computers in Industry 138, 103627. https://doi.org/10.1016/j.compind.2022.103627.

de Oliveira, C.S., Sanin, C., Szczerbicki, E., 2019. Visual content representation and retrieval for cognitive cyber physical systems. Procedia Computer Science 159, 2249–2257. Knowledge-Based and Intelligent Information & Engineering Systems: Proceedings of the 23rd International Conference KES2019.

Oosthuizen, R.M., 2022. The fourth industrial revolution – smart technology, artificial intelligence, robotics and algorithms: industrial psychologists in future workplaces. Frontiers in Artificial Intelligence 5. https://doi.org/10.3389/frai.2022.913168. https://www.frontiersin.org/articles/10.3389/frai.2022.913168.

Orru, G., Longo, L., 2020. Direct and constructivist instructional design: a comparison of efficiency using mental workload and task performance. In: Longo, L., Leva, M.C. (Eds.), Human Mental Workload: Models and Applications. Springer International Publishing, Cham, pp. 99–123.

Osterrieder, P., Budde, L., Friedli, T., 2020. The smart factory as a key construct of industry 4.0: a systematic literature review. International Journal of Production Economics 221, 107476. https://doi.org/10.1016/j.ijpe.2019.08.011.

Othman, U., Yang, E., 2023. Human & robot collaborations in smart manufacturing environments: review and outlook. Sensors 23. https://doi.org/10.3390/s23125663. https://www.mdpi.com/1424-8220/23/12/5663.

Pacaux-Lemoine, M.P., Berdal, Q., Guérin, C., Rauffet, P., Chauvin, C., Trentesaux, D., 2022. Designing human–system cooperation in industry 4.0 with cognitive work analysis: a first evaluation. Cognition Technology & Work 24, 93–111. https://doi.org/10.1007/s10111-021-00667-y.

Pairet, E., Ardón, P., Liu, X., Lopes, J., Hastie, H., Lohan, K.S., 2019. A digital twin for human–robot interaction. In: 2019 14th ACM/IEEE International Conference on Human–Robot Interaction (HRI), p. 372. https://doi.org/10.1109/HRI.2019.8673015.

Paliga, M., 2022. Human–cobot interaction fluency and cobot operators' job performance. The mediating role of work engagement: a survey. Robotics and Autonomous Systems 155, 104191. https://doi.org/10.1016/j.robot.2022.104191.

Palmiter, S.L., Elkerton, J., 1987. Evaluation metrics and a tool for control panel design. Proceedings of the Human Factors Society Annual Meeting 31, 1123–1127. https://doi.org/10.1177/154193128703101011.

Pan, Z., Polden, J., Larkin, N., Van Duin, S., Norrish, J., 2012. Recent progress on programming methods for industrial robots. Robotics and Computer-Integrated Manufacturing 28, 87–94. https://doi.org/10.1016/j.rcim.2011.08.004.

Parihar, V., Malik, A., Bhawna, Bhushan B., Chaganti, R., 2023. Ai models for blockchain-based intelligent networks in iot systems: concepts, methodologies, tools, and applications. In: Bhushan, B., Sangaiah, A.K., Nguyen, T.N. (Eds.), From Smart Devices to Smarter Systems: The Evolution of Artificial Intelligence of Things (AIoT) with Characteristics, Architecture, Use Cases and Challenges. Springer International Publishing, Cham, pp. 1–28. https://doi.org/10.1007/978-3-031-31952-5_1.

Patriarca, R., Chatzimichailidou, M., Karanikas, N., Di Gravio, G., 2022. The past and present of system-theoretic accident model and processes (stamp) and its associated techniques: a scoping review. Safety Science 146, 105566. https://doi.org/10.1016/j.ssci.2021.105566.

Patriarca, R., Di Gravio, G., Costantino, F., 2017. A Monte Carlo evolution of the functional resonance analysis method (fram) to assess performance variability in complex systems. Safety Science 91, 49–60. https://doi.org/10.1016/j.ssci.2016.07.016.

Pereira, A., Oertel, C., Fermoselle, L., Mendelson, J., Gustafson, J., 2019. Responsive joint attention in human–robot interaction. In: 2019 IEEE/RSJ International Conference on Intelligent Robots and Systems (IROS), pp. 1080–1087. https://doi.org/10.1109/IROS40897.2019.8968130.

Pervez, A., Ryu, J., 2011. Safe physical human robot interaction – past, present and future. Journal of Mechanical Science and Technology 22, 469–483. https://doi.org/10.1007/s12206-007-1109-3.

Petzoldt, C., Niermann, D., Maack, E., Sontopski, M., Vur, B., Freitag, M., 2022. Implementation and evaluation of dynamic task allocation for human–robot collaboration in assembly. Applied Sciences 12. https://doi.org/10.3390/app122412645. https://www.mdpi.com/2076-3417/12/24/12645.

Pfeiffer, S., 2016. Robots, industry 4.0 and humans, or why assembly work is more than routine work. Societies 6. https://doi.org/10.3390/soc6020016. https://www.mdpi.com/2075-4698/6/2/16.

Phuyal, S., Bista, D., Bista, R., 2020. Challenges, opportunities and future directions of smart manufacturing: a state of art review. Sustainable Futures 2, 100023. https://doi.org/10.1016/j.sftr.2020.100023.

Piera, M.À., 2004. Modelado y simulación. Aplicación a procesos logísticos de fabricación y servicios. Universitat Politècnica de Catalunya. Iniciativa Digital Politècnica.

Pise, A., Yoon, B., Singh, S., 2023. Enabling ambient intelligence of things (aiot) healthcare system architectures. Computer Communications 198, 186–194. https://doi.org/10.1016/j.comcom.2022.10.029.

Pivoto, D.G., de Almeida, L.F., da Rosa Righi, R., Rodrigues, J.J., Lugli, A.B., Alberti, A.M., 2021. Cyber-physical systems architectures for industrial internet of things applications in industry 4.0: a literature review. Journal of Manufacturing Systems 58, 176–192. https://doi.org/10.1016/j.jmsy.2020.11.017.

Pizoń, J., Gola, A., 2023. Human–machine relationship: perspective and future roadmap for industry 5.0 solutions. Machines 11. https://doi.org/10.3390/machines11020203. https://www.mdpi.com/2075-1702/11/2/203.

Pizzagalli, S.L., Kuts, V., Otto, T., 2021. User-centered design for human–robot collaboration systems. IOP Conference Series: Materials Science and Engineering 1140, 012011. https://doi.org/10.1088/1757-899X/1140/1/012011.

Poláková, M., Suleimanová, J.H., Madzík, P., Copuš, L., Molnárová, I., Polednová, J., 2023. Soft skills and their importance in the labour market under the conditions of industry 5.0. Heliyon 9, e18670. https://doi.org/10.1016/j.heliyon.2023.e18670.

Prabha, C., Mittal, P., Sharma, A., Singh, J., 2022. Aiot emerging technologies, use cases, and its challenges in implementing smart cities. In: 2022 IEEE North Karnataka Subsection Flagship International Conference (NKCon), pp. 1–5. https://doi.org/10.1109/NKCon56289.2022.10126917.

Prati, E., Peruzzini, M., Pellicciari, M., Raffaeli, R., 2021. How to include user experience in the design of human-robot interaction. Robotics and Computer-Integrated Manufacturing 68, 102072. https://doi.org/10.1016/j.rcim.2020.102072.

Prinz, C., Kreimeier, D., Kuhlenkötter, B., 2017. Implementation of a learning environment for an industrie 4.0 assistance system to improve the overall equipment effectiveness. Procedia Manufacturing 9, 159–166. https://doi.org/10.1016/j.promfg.2017.04.004. 7th Conference on Learning Factories, CLF 2017.

Păvăloaia, V.D., Necula, S.C., 2023. Artificial intelligence as a disruptive technolo – a systematic literature review. Electronics 12. https://doi.org/10.3390/electronics12051102. https://www.mdpi.com/2079-9292/12/5/1102.

Rabby, K.M., Khan, M., Karimoddini, A., Jiang, S.X., 2019. An effective model for human cognitive performance within a human–robot collaboration framework. In: 2019 IEEE International Conference on Systems, Man and Cybernetics (SMC), pp. 3872–3877. https://doi.org/10.1109/SMC.2019.8914536.

Rajanen, M., Rajanen, D., 2020. Usability: a cybernetics perspective. CEUR Workshop Proceedings 2789, 28–33.

Ranz, F., Komenda, T., Reisinger, G., Hold, P., Hummel, V., Sihn, W., 2018. A morphology of human robot collaboration systems for industrial assembly. Procedia CIRP 72, 99–104. https://doi.org/10.1016/j.procir.2018.03.011. 51st CIRP Conference on Manufacturing Systems.

Rauch, E., Linder, C., Dallasega, P., 2020. Anthropocentric perspective of production before and within Industry 4.0. Computers & Industrial Engineering 139, 105644. https://doi.org/10.1016/j.cie.2019.01.018.

Rauffet, P., Chauvin, C., Morel, G., Berruet, P., 2015. Designing sociotechnical systems: a CWA-based method for dynamic function allocation. ACM International Conference Proceeding Series 01-03-Jul-2015. https://doi.org/10.1145/2788412.2788433.

Read, G.J., Salmon, P.M., Lenné, M.G., Stanton, N.A., 2015. Designing sociotechnical systems with cognitive work analysis: putting theory back into practice. Ergonomics 58, 822–851. https://doi.org/10.1080/00140139.2014.980335.

Reid, G.B., Nygren, T.E., 1988. The subjective workload assessment technique: a scaling procedure for measuring mental workload. In: Hancock, P.A., Meshkati, N. (Eds.), Advances in Psychology. In: Human Mental Workload, vol. 52. North-Holland, pp. 185–218. https://doi.org/10.1016/S0166-4115(08)62387-0.

Reischauer, G., 2018. Industry 4.0 as policy-driven discourse to institutionalize innovation systems in manufacturing. Technological Forecasting & Social Change 132, 26–33. https://doi.org/10.1016/j.techfore.2018.02.012.

Richards, D., 2017a. Escape from the factory of the robot monsters: agents of change. Team Performance Management: An International Journal 23, 96–108. https://doi.org/10.1108/TPM-10-2015-0052.

Richards, D., 2017b. Robot wars: advances in robot technology throws up questions about how to integrate them into human–robot teams. Human Resource Management International Digest 25, 13–14. https://doi.org/10.1108/HRMID-05-2017-0089.

Riedelbauch, D., Höllerich, N., Henrich, D., 2023. Benchmarking teamwork of humans and cobots—an overview of metrics, strategies, and tasks. IEEE Access 11, 43648–43674. https://doi.org/10.1109/ACCESS.2023.3271602.

Rizwan, A., Ahmad, R., Khan, A.N., Xu, R., Kim, D.H., 2023. Intelligent digital twin for federated learning in aiot networks. Internet of Things 22, 100698. https://doi.org/10.1016/j.iot.2023.100698.

Robinson, S.J., Brewer, G., 2016. Performance on the traditional and the touch screen, tablet versions of the corsi block and the tower of Hanoi tasks. Computers in Human Behavior 60, 29–34. https://doi.org/10.1016/j.chb.2016.02.047.

Romero, D., Bernus, P., Noran, O., Stahre, J., Fast-Berglund, A., 2016a. The operator 4.0: human cyber-physical systems & adaptive automation towards human-automation symbiosis work systems. In: Nääs, I., Vendrametto, O., Mendes Reis, J., Gonçalves, R.F., Silva, M.T., von Cieminski, G., Kiritsis, D. (Eds.), Advances in Production Management Systems. Initiatives for a Sustainable World. Springer International Publishing, Cham, pp. 677–686.

Romero, D., Noran, O., Stahre, J., Bernus, P., Fast-Berglund, A., 2015. Towards a human-centred reference architecture for next generation balanced automation systems: human-automation symbiosis. IFIP Advances in Information and Communication Technology 460, 556–566. https://doi.org/10.1007/978-3-319-22759-7_64.

Romero, D., Stahre, J., Wuest, T., Noran, O., Bernus, P., Fasth Fast-Berglund, A., Gorecky, D., 2016b. Towards an operator 4.0 typology: a human-centric perspective on the fourth industrial revolution technologies. In: Conference: International Conference on Computers & Industrial Engineering (CIE46), pp. 1–11.

Rubio, S., Díaz, E., Martín, J., Puente, J.M., 2004. Evaluation of subjective mental workload: a comparison of SWAT, NASA-TLX, and workload profile methods. Applied Psychology 53, 61–86. https://doi.org/10.1111/j.1464-0597.2004.00161.x.

Ruppert, T., Jaskó, S., Holczinger, T., Abonyi, J., 2018. Enabling technologies for operator 4.0: a survey. Applied Sciences 8, 1650. https://doi.org/10.3390/app8091650.

Rüßmann, M., Lorenz, M., de Sousa Gerbert, P., Waldner, M., Justus, J., Engel, P., Harnisch, M.J., 2015. Industry 4.0: the future of productivity and growth in manufacturing industries. https://web-assets.bcg.com/img-src/Industry_40_Future_of_Productivity_April_2015_tcm9-61694.pdf. The Boston Consulting Group.

Saad, A., Håkansson, A., 2022. Ramarl: robustness analysis with multi-agent reinforcement learning – robust reasoning in autonomous cyber-physical systems. Procedia Computer Science 207, 3662–3671. https://doi.org/10.1016/j.procs.2022.09.426. Knowledge-Based and Intelligent Information & Engineering Systems: Proceedings of the 26th International Conference KES2022.

Sadeghi-Niaraki, A., 2023. Internet of thing (iot) review of review: bibliometric overview since its foundation. Future Generation Computer Systems 143, 361–377. https://doi.org/10.1016/j.future.2023.01.016.

Sadri, A.A., Rahmani, A.M., Saberikamarposhti, M., Hosseinzadeh, M., 2022. Data reduction in fog computing and internet of things: a systematic literature survey. Internet of Things 20, 100629. https://doi.org/10.1016/j.iot.2022.100629.

Sahoo, S., Lo, C.Y., 2022. Smart manufacturing powered by recent technological advancements: a review. Journal of Manufacturing Systems 64, 236–250. https://doi.org/10.1016/j.jmsy.2022.06.008,

Salehi, V., Smith, D., Veitch, B., Hanson, N., 2021a. A dynamic version of the fram for capturing variability in complex operations. MethodsX 8, 101333. https://doi.org/10.1016/j.mex.2021.101333.

Salehi, V., Veitch, B., Smith, D., 2021b. Modeling complex socio-technical systems using the fram: a literature review. Human Factors and Ergonomics in Manufacturing & Service Industries 31, 118–142. https://doi.org/10.1002/hfm.20874. https://onlinelibrary.wiley.com/doi/abs/10.1002/hfm.20874. https://onlinelibrary.wiley.com/doi/pdf/10.1002/hfm.20874.

Salmon, P.M., Stanton, N.A., Walker, G.H., Hulme, A., Goode, N., Thompson, J., Read, G.J., 2022. Handbook of Systems Thinking Methods. CRC Press.

Sanchez-Salas, A., Goh, Y., Case, K., 2017. Identifying variability key characteristics for automation design – a case study of finishing process. In: Proceedings of the 21st International Conference on Engineering Design (ICED 17), pp. 21–30. https://pdfs.semanticscholar.org/cb81/3433a2a5baf2d96e71d850904c11e544c10f.pdf.

Sandner, P., Gross, J., Richter, R., 2020. Convergence of blockchain, iot, and ai. Frontiers in Blockchain 3. https://doi.org/10.3389/fbloc.2020.522600. https://www.frontiersin.org/articles/10.3389/fbloc.2020.522600.

Saranya, T., Deisy, C., Sridevi, S., Anbananthen, K.S.M., 2023. A comparative study of deep learning and internet of things for precision agriculture. Engineering Applications of Artificial Intelligence 122, 106034. https://doi.org/10.1016/j.engappai.2023.106034.

Sauro, J., 2011. A Practical Guide to the System Usability Scale: Background, Benchmarks & Best Practices. http://books.google.com/books/about/A_Practical_Guide_to_the_System_Usabilit.html?id=BL0kKQEACAAJ&pgis=1.

Sauro, J., Dumas, J.S., 2009. Comparison of three one-question, post-task usability questionnaires. In: Proceedings of the SIGCHI Conference on Human Factors in Computing Systems. Association for Computing Machinery, New York, NY, USA, pp. 1599–1608. https://doi.org/10.1145/1518701.1518946.

Sauro, J., Lewis, J.R., 2010. Average task times in usability tests: what to report? In: Proceedings of the SIGCHI Conference on Human Factors in Computing Systems. Association for Computing Machinery, New York, NY, USA, pp. 2347–2350. https://doi.org/10.1145/1753326.1753679.

Sauro, J., Lewis, J.R., 2016. Quantifying the User Experience. Practical Statistics for User Research. MK Morgan Kaufmann.

Scalera, L., Giusti, A., Vidoni, R., Di Cosmo, V., Matt, D.T., Riedl, M., 2020. Application of dynamically scaled safety zones based on the ISO/TS 15066:2016 for collaborative robotics. International Journal of Mechanics and Control 21, 41–49.

Schnell, M., 2021. Challenges when introducing collaborative robots in sme manufacturing industry.

Scholtz, J., 2003. Theory and evaluation of human robot interactions. In: Proceedings of the 36th Annual Hawaii International Conference on System Sciences, HICSS. https://doi.org/10.1109/HICSS.2003.1174284, 2003.

Schou, C., Andersen, R.S., Chrysostomou, D., Bøgh, S., Madsen, O., 2018. Skill-based instruction of collaborative robots in industrial settings. Robotics and Computer-Integrated Manufacturing 53, 72–80. https://doi.org/10.1016/j.rcim.2018.03.008.

Schrum, M., Ghuy, M., Hedlund-botti, E., Natarajan, M., Johnson, M., Gombolay, M., 2023. Concerning trends in Likert scale usage in human-robot interaction: towards improving best practices. Journal on Human-Robot Interaction 12. https://doi.org/10.1145/3572784.

Schrum, M.L., Johnson, M., Ghuy, M., Gombolay, M.C., 2020. Four years in review: statistical practices of Likert scales in human-robot interaction studies. In: Companion of the 2020 ACM/IEEE International Conference on Human-Robot Interaction. Association for Computing Machinery, New York, NY, USA, pp. 43–52. https://doi.org/10.1145/3371382.3380739.

Schumacher, R.M., 2010. Chapter 1 – foundations and definition. In: Schumacher, R.M. (Ed.), Handbook of Global User Research. Morgan Kaufmann, Boston, pp. 1–20. https://doi.org/10.1016/B978-0-12-374852-2.00001-X.

Schömig, N., Metz, B., 2013. Three levels of situation awareness in driving with secondary tasks. Safety Science 56, 44–51. https://doi.org/10.1016/j.ssci.2012.05.029. Situation Awareness and Safety.

Secretary I.C., 2011. Ergonomics – General approach, principles and concepts. Standard ISO 26800:2011. International Organization for Standardization, Geneva, CH. https://www.iso.org/standard/42885.html.

Álvaro Segura, Diez H.V., Barandiaran, I., Arbelaiz, A., Álvarez, H., Simões, B., Posada, J., García-Alonso, A., Ugarte, R., 2020. Visual computing technologies to support the operator 4.0. Computers & Industrial Engineering 139, 105550. https://doi.org/10.1016/j.cie.2018.11.060.

Segura, P., Lobato-Calleros, O., Ramírez-Serrano, A., Soria, I., 2021. Human-robot collaborative systems: structural components for current manufacturing applications. Advances in Industrial and Manufacturing Engineering 3, 100060. https://doi.org/10.1016/j.aime.2021.100060.

Seidita, V., Chella, A., Lanza, F., Chella, A., Seidita, V., 2019. A cognitive architecture for human–robot teaming interaction. In: AIC 2018 Artificial Intelligence and Cognition 2018 Proceedings of the 6th International Workshop on Artificial Intelligence and Cognition, pp. 82–89.

Semeraro, F., Griffiths, A., Cangelosi, A., 2023. Human–robot collaboration and machine learning: a systematic review of recent research. Robotics and Computer-Integrated Manufacturing 79, 102432. https://doi.org/10.1016/j.rcim.2022.102432.

Shang, X., Tan, L., Yu, K., Zhang, J., Kaur, K., Hassan, M.M., 2021. Newton-interpolation-based zk-snark for artificial internet of things. Ad Hoc Networks 123, 102656. https://doi.org/10.1016/j.adhoc.2021.102656.

Shen, L., Wang, F., Zhang, M., Liu, J., Liu, G., Fan, X., 2023a. Aiot-empowered smart grid energy management with distributed control and non-intrusive load monitoring. In: 2023 IEEE/ACM 31st International Symposium on Quality of Service (IWQoS), pp. 1–10. https://doi.org/10.1109/IWQoS57198.2023.10188781.

Shen, M., Gu, A., Kang, J., Tang, X., Lin, X., Zhu, L., Niyato, D., 2023b. Blockchains for artificial intelligence of things: a comprehensive survey. IEEE Internet of Things Journal 10, 14483–14506. https://doi.org/10.1109/JIOT.2023.3268705.

Sheridan, T., 2000. Function allocation: algorithm, alchemy or apostasy? International Journal of Human-Computer Studies 52, 203–216. https://doi.org/10.1006/ijhc.1999.0285.

Sheridan, T.B., 1992. Telerobotics, Automation, and Human Supervisory Control. MIT Press.

Sheridan, T.B., 2006. Supervisory Control. John Wiley & Sons, Ltd., pp. 1025–1052. https://doi.org/10.1002/0470048204.ch38. Chapter 38. https://onlinelibrary.wiley.com/doi/abs/10.1002/0470048204.ch38. https://onlinelibrary.wiley.com/doi/pdf/10.1002/0470048204.ch38.

Shi, Y., Shen, W., Wang, L., Longo, F., Nicoletti, L., Padovano, A., 2022. A cognitive digital twins framework for human–robot collaboration. Procedia Computer Science 200, 1867–1874. https://doi.org/10.1016/j.procs.2022.01.387. 3rd International Conference on Industry 4.0 and Smart Manufacturing.

Shojaeinasab, A., Charter, T., Jalayer, M., Khadivi, M., Ogunfowora, O., Raiyani, N., Yaghoubi, M., Najjaran, H., 2022. Intelligent manufacturing execution systems: a systematic review. Journal of Manufacturing Systems 62, 503–522. https://doi.org/10.1016/j.jmsy.2022.01.004.

Siddike, M.A.K., Spohrer, J., Demirkan, H., Kohda, Y., 2018. A framework of enhanced performance: people's interactions with cognitive assistants. International Journal of Systems and Service-Oriented Engineering (IJSSOE) 8, 1–17. https://EconPapers.repec.org/RePEc:igg:jssoe0:v:8:y:2018:i:3:p:1-17.

Simone, V.D., Pasquale, V.D., Giubileo, V., Miranda, S., 2022. Human–robot collaboration: an analysis of worker's performance. Procedia Computer Science 200, 1540–1549. https://doi.org/10.1016/j.procs.2022.01.355. 3rd International Conference on Industry 4.0 and Smart Manufacturing.

Simões, A.C., Pinto, A., Santos, J., Pinheiro, S., Romero, D., 2022. Designing human–robot collaboration (hrc) workspaces in industrial settings: a systematic literature review. Journal of Manufacturing Systems 62, 28–43. https://doi.org/10.1016/j.jmsy.2021.11.007.

Singh, S., Sharma, P.K., Yoon, B., Shojafar, M., Cho, G.H., Ra, I.H., 2020. Convergence of blockchain and artificial intelligence in iot network for the sustainable smart city. Sustainable Cities and Society 63, 102364. https://doi.org/10.1016/j.scs.2020.102364.

Skobelev, P.O., Borovik, S.Y., 2017. On the way from industry 4.0 to industry 5.0: from digital manufacturing to digital society. Industry 4.0 2, 307–311.

Slama, D., 2023. Digital equipment operator. In: Slama, D., Rückert, T., Thrun, S., Homann, U., Lasi, H. (Eds.), The Digital Playbook: A Practitioner's Guide to Smart, Connected Products and Solutions with AIoT. Springer International Publishing, Cham, pp. 83–90. https://doi.org/10.1007/978-3-030-88221-1_8.

Sony, M., Naik, S., 2020. Industry 4.0 integration with socio-technical systems theory: a systematic review and proposed theoretical model. Technology in Society 61, 101248. https://doi.org/10.1016/j.techsoc.2020.101248.

Soori, M., Arezoo, B., Dastres, R., 2023. Artificial intelligence, machine learning and deep learning in advanced robotics, a review. Cognitive Robotics 3, 54–70. https://doi.org/10.1016/j.cogr.2023.04.001.

Soria-Oliver, M., López, J.S., Torrano, F., 2018. Relations between mental workload and decision-making in an organizational setting. Psicologia: Reflexão e Crítica 30, 7. https://doi.org/10.1186/s41155-017-0061-0.

Sorri, K., Mustafee, N., Seppänen, M., 2022. Revisiting iot definitions: a framework towards comprehensive use. Technological Forecasting and Social Change 179, 121623. https://doi.org/10.1016/j.techfore.2022.121623.

Sotirios, P., Fabio, F., Francesco, M., 2023. A methodological framework to assess mental fatigue in assembly lines with a collaborative robot. In: Kim, K.Y., Monplaisir, L., Rickli, J. (Eds.), Flexible Automation and Intelligent Manufacturing: The Human-Data-Technology Nexus. Springer International Publishing, Cham, pp. 297–306.

Sparrow, D.E., Kruger, K., Basson, A.H., 2022. An architecture to facilitate the integration of human workers in industry 4.0 environments. International Journal of Production Research 60, 4778–4796. https://doi.org/10.1080/00207543.2021.1937747.

Stanton, N.A.D., 2018. Systems Thinking in Practice: Applications of the Event Analysis of Systemic Teamwork Method. Transportation Human Factors, first edition. CRC Press, Boca Raton, FL.

Steinfeld, A., Fong, T.W., Kaber, D., Scholtz, J., Schultz, A.C., Goodrich, M., 2006. Common metrics for human–robot interaction. In: First ACM/IEEE International Conference on Human–Robot Interaction. ACM, Salt Lake City, pp. 23–40.

Stern, H., Becker, T., 2017. Development of a model for the integration of human factors in cyber-physical production systems. Procedia Manufacturing 9, 151–158. https://doi.org/10.1016/j.promfg.2017.04.030. 7th Conference on Learning Factories, CLF 2017.

Sujan, M., Pickup, L., de Vos, M., Patriarca, R., Konwinski, L., Ross, A., McCulloch, P., 2023. Operationalising fram in healthcare: a critical reflection on practice. Safety Science 158, 105994. https://doi.org/10.1016/j.ssci.2022.105994.

Sung, T.K., 2018. Industry 4.0: a Korea perspective. Technological Forecasting and Social Change 132, 40–45. https://doi.org/10.1016/j.techfore.2017.11.005.

Szegedy, M., 1999. In how many steps the k peg version of the towers of Hanoi game can be solved. Lecture Notes in Computer Science (including subseries Lecture Notes in Artificial Intelligence and Lecture Notes in Bioinformatics) 1563, 356–361. https://doi.org/10.1007/3-540-49116-3_33.

Tao, F., Qi, Q., Wang, L., Nee, A., 2019. Digital twins and cyber–physical systems toward smart manufacturing and industry 4.0: correlation and comparison. Engineering 5, 653–661. https://doi.org/10.1016/j.eng.2019.01.014.

Tecuci, G., Marcu, D., Boicu, M., Schum, D., 2016. Knowledge Engineering: Building Cognitive Assistants for Evidence-Based Reasoning. Cambridge University Press. https://www.cambridge.org/us/universitypress/subjects/computer-science/artificial-intelligence-and-natural-language-processing/knowledge-engineering-building-cognitive-assistants-evidence-based-reasoning?format=HB&isbn=9781107122567.

Tekniker, Pilz, ZEMA, 2017. Definition and guidelines for collaborative workspaces. Technical Report GA number 637095. FourByThree.

Teo, G., Matthews, G., Reinerman-Jones, L., Barber, D., 2019. Adaptive aiding with an individualized workload model based on psychophysiological measures. Human-Intelligent Systems Integration. https://doi.org/10.1007/s42454-019-00005-8.

Terziyan, V., Gryshko, S., Golovianko, M., 2018. Patented intelligence: cloning human decision models for industry 4.0. Journal of Manufacturing Systems 48, 204–217. https://doi.org/10.1016/j.jmsy.2018.04.019. special Issue on Smart Manufacturing.

Thorvald, P., Fasth Fast-Berglund, A., Romero, D., 2021. The cognitive operator 4.0. In: Shafik, M., Case, K. (Eds.), 18th International Conference on Manufacturing Research, pp. 3–8. https://doi.org/10.3233/ATDE210003.

Tian, W., Caponecchia, C., 2020. Using the functional resonance analysis method (fram) in aviation safety: a systematic review. Journal of Advanced Transportation 2020, 8898903. https://doi.org/10.1155/2020/8898903.

Tsai, C.C., Cheng, Y.M., Tsai, Y.S., Lou, S.J., 2021. Impacts of aiot implementation course on the learning outcomes of senior high school students. Education Sciences 11. https://doi.org/10.3390/educsci11020082. https://www.mdpi.com/2227-7102/11/2/82.

Tsai, Y.T., Lee, C.H., Liu, T.Y., Chang, T.J., Wang, C.S., Pawar, S., Huang, P.H., Huang, J.H., 2020. Utilization of a reinforcement learning algorithm for the accurate alignment of a robotic arm in a complete soft fabric shoe tongues automation process. Journal of Manufacturing Systems 56, 501–513. https://doi.org/10.1016/j.jmsy.2020.07.001.

Tsang, P.S., Velazquez, V.L., 1996. Diagnosticity and multidimensional subjective workload ratings. Ergonomics 39, 358–381. https://doi.org/10.1080/00140139608964470. pMID: 8849491.

Tsarouchi, P., Matthaiakis, A.S., Makris, S., Chryssolouris, G., 2017. On a human–robot collaboration in an assembly cell. International Journal of Computer Integrated Manufacturing 30, 580–589. https://doi.org/10.1080/0951192X.2016.1187297.

Tsarouchi, P., Spiliotopoulos, J., Michalos, G., Koukas, S., Athanasatos, A., Makris, S., Chryssolouris, G., 2016. A decision making framework for human robot collaborative workplace generation. Procedia CIRP 44. https://doi.org/10.1016/j.procir.2016.02.103.

Tzafestas, S.G., 2018. Roboethics: fundamental concepts and future prospects. Information 9. https://doi.org/10.3390/info9060148. https://www.mdpi.com/2078-2489/9/6/148.

Ubina, N.A., Lan, H.Y., Cheng, S.C., Chang, C.C., Lin, S.S., Zhang, K.X., Lu, H.Y., Cheng, C.Y., Hsieh, Y.Z., 2023. Digital twin-based intelligent fish farming with artificial intelligence Internet of things (aiot). Smart Agricultural Technology 5, 100285. https://doi.org/10.1016/j.atech.2023.100285.

Ullah, W., Ullah, A., Hussain, T., Muhammad, K., Heidari, A.A., Del Ser, J., Baik, S.W., De Albuquerque, V.H.C., 2022. Artificial intelligence of things-assisted two-stream neural network for anomaly detection in surveillance big video data. Future Generation Computer Systems 129, 286–297. https://doi.org/10.1016/j.future.2021.10.033.

Universal Robots, 2015. User Manual UR3/CB3, Version 3.

Ustunel, Z., Gunduz, T., 2017. Human–robot collaboration on an assembly work with extended cognition approach. Journal of Advanced Mechanical Design, Systems, and Manufacturing 11, 1–11. https://doi.org/10.1299/jamdsm.2017jamdsm0057.

Vaidya, S., Ambad, P., Bhosle, S., 2018. Industry 4.0 – a glimpse. In: 2nd International Conference on Materials, Manufacturing and Design Engineering (iCMMD2017), 11–12 December 2017. In: Procedia Manufacturing, vol. 20. MIT, Aurangabad, Maharashtra, India, pp. 233–238. https://doi.org/10.1016/j.promfg.2018.02.034.

Valentina, D.P., Valentina, D.S., Salvatore, M., Stefano, R., 2021. Smart operators: how industry 4.0 is affecting the worker's performance in manufacturing contexts. Procedia Computer Science 180, 958–967. https://doi.org/10.1016/j.procs.2021.01.347. Proceedings of the 2nd International Conference on Industry 4.0 and Smart Manufacturing (ISM 2020).

Valette, E., El-Haouzi, H.B., Demesure, G., 2023. Industry 5.0 and its technologies: a systematic literature review upon the human place into iot- and cps-based industrial systems. Computers & Industrial Engineering, 109426. https://doi.org/10.1016/j.cie.2023.109426.

Vernim, S., Bauer, H., Rauch, E., Ziegler, M.T., Umbrello, S., 2022. A value sensitive design approach for designing ai-based worker assistance systems in manufacturing. Procedia Computer Science 200, 505–516. https://doi.org/10.1016/j.procs.2022.01.248. 3rd International Conference on Industry 4.0 and Smart Manufacturing.

Vernon, D., 2014. Artificial Cognitive Systems. Massachusetts Institute of Technology. http://www.vernon.eu/ACS.htm.

Veruggio, G., Operto, F., 2008. Roboethics: social and ethical implications of robotics. In: Siciliano, B., Khatib, O. (Eds.), Springer Handbook of Robotics. Springer Berlin Heidelberg, Berlin, Heidelberg, pp. 1499–1524. https://doi.org/10.1007/978-3-540-30301-5_65.

Villani, V., Pini, F., Leali, F., Secchi, C., 2018. Survey on human–robot collaboration in industrial settings: safety, intuitive interfaces and applications. Mechatronics 55, 248–266. https://doi.org/10.1016/j.mechatronics.2018.02.009.

Villarreal-Lozano, C., Vijayan, K.K., 2020. Literature review on cyber physical systems design. Procedia Manufacturing 45, 295–300. https://doi.org/10.1016/j.promfg.2020.04.020. Learning Factories across the value chain – from innovation to service – the 10th Conference on Learning Factories 2020.

Walker, G.H., Stanton, N.A., Salmon, P.M., Jenkins, D.P., 2008. A review of sociotechnical systems theory: a classic concept for new command and control paradigms. Theoretical Issues in Ergonomics Science 9, 479–499.

Wang, B., Peng, T., Wang, X.V., Wuest, T., Romero, D., Wang, L., 2023. Human-centric smart manufacturing. Journal of Manufacturing Systems 69, 18–19. https://doi.org/10.1016/j.jmsy.2023.06.001.

Wang, B., Xue, Y., Yan, J., Yang, X., Zhou, Y., 2020. Human-centered intelligent manufacturing: overview and perspectives. Strategic Study of Chinese Academy of Engineering 22, 139. https://doi.org/10.15302/J-SSCAE-2020.04.020. https://journal.hep.com.cn/sscae/EN/abstract/article_28132.shtml.

Wang, B., Zheng, P., Yin, Y., Shih, A., Wang, L., 2022. Toward human-centric smart manufacturing: a human-cyber-physical systems (hcps) perspective. Journal of Manufacturing Systems 63, 471–490. https://doi.org/10.1016/j.jmsy.2022.05.005.

Wang, L., 2019. From intelligence science to intelligent manufacturing. Engineering 5, 615–618. https://doi.org/10.1016/j.eng.2019.04.011.

Wang, L., 2022. A futuristic perspective on human-centric assembly. Journal of Manufacturing Systems 62, 199–201. https://doi.org/10.1016/j.jmsy.2021.11.001.

Wang, L., Gao, R., Váncza, J., Krüger, J., Wang, X., Makris, S., Chryssolouris, G., 2019a. Symbiotic human–robot collaborative assembly. CIRP Annals 68, 701–726. https://doi.org/10.1016/j.cirp.2019.05.002.

Wang, L., Liu, S., Cooper, C., Wang, X.V., Gao, R.X., 2021. Function block-based human–robot collaborative assembly driven by brainwaves. CIRP Annals 70, 5–8. https://doi.org/10.1016/j.cirp.2021.04.091.

Wang, W., Chen, Y., Li, R., Jia, Y., 2019b. Learning and comfort in human–robot interaction: a review. Applied Sciences 9. https://doi.org/10.3390/app9235152. https://www.mdpi.com/2076-3417/9/23/5152.

Warrol, C., Stahre, J., 2015. Manufacturing research, innovation, and phd education on a national level – produktion2030, a Swedish example. In: Umeda, S., Nakano, M., Mizuyama,

H., Hibino, H., Kiritsis, D., von Cieminski, G. (Eds.), Advances in Production Management Systems: Innovative Production Management Towards Sustainable Growth. Springer International Publishing, Cham, pp. 101–109.

Waschull, S., Bokhorst, J., Wortmann, J., Molleman, E., 2022. The redesign of blue- and white-collar work triggered by digitalization: collar matters. Computers & Industrial Engineering 165, 107910. https://doi.org/10.1016/j.cie.2021.107910.

Weiss, A., Bernhaupt, R., Lankes, M., Tscheligi, M., 2009. The usus evaluation framework for human–robot interaction. In: Dautenhahn, K., Saunders, J. (Eds.), Proceedings of the 23rd Convention on Artificial Intelligence and Simulated Behavior (AISB2009) – New Frontiers in Human–Robot Interaction. In: Advances in Interaction Studies. John Benjamins Publishing Company, pp. 89–110.

Welfare, K.S., Hallowell, M.R., Shah, J.A., Riek, L.D., 2019. Consider the human work experience when integrating robotics in the workplace. In: 2019 14th ACM/IEEE International Conference on Human–Robot Interaction (HRI), pp. 75–84. https://doi.org/10.1109/HRI. 2019.8673139.

Weyer, S., Schmitt, M., Ohmer, M., Gorecky, D., 2015. Towards industry 4.0 – standardization as the crucial challenge for highly modular, multi-vendor production systems. IFAC-PapersOnLine 48, 579–584. https://doi.org/10.1016/j.ifacol.2015.06.143. 15th IFAC Symposium on Information Control Problems in Manufacturing.

Wickens, C.D., 1987. 2. Attention. In: Hancock, P.A. (Ed.), Advances in Psychology. In: Human Factors Psychology, vol. 47. North-Holland, pp. 29–80. https://doi.org/10.1016/S0166-4115(08)62306-7.

Wilcock, A.A., 1998. An Occupational Perspective of Health. Slack.

Wittenberg, C., 2016. Human-cps interaction – requirements and human-machine interaction methods for the industry 4.0. IFAC-PapersOnLine 49, 420–425. 13th IFAC Symposium on Analysis, Design, and Evaluation of Human-Machine Systems HMS 2016.

Wolfartsberger, J., Zenisek, J., Wild, N., 2020. Supporting teamwork in industrial virtual reality applications. Procedia Manufacturing 42, 2–7. https://doi.org/10.1016/j.promfg.2020. 02.016. International Conference on Industry 4.0 and Smart Manufacturing (ISM 2019).

Wong, C.Y., Seet, G., 2017. Workload, awareness and automation in multiple-robot supervision. International Journal of Advanced Robotic Systems 14, 1729881417710463. https://doi.org/10.1177/1729881417710463.

Xhafa, F., 2023. Towards artificial intelligence internet of things (aiot) and intelligent edge: the intelligent edge is where action is!: Editorial preface. Internet of Things 22, 100752. https://doi.org/10.1016/j.iot.2023.100752.

Xia, X., Zhu, W., 2016. Evaluation for the stability variation of the manufacturing process based on fuzzy norm method. In: 2016 12th International Conference on Natural Computation, Fuzzy Systems and Knowledge Discovery (ICNC-FSKD), pp. 1057–1064.

Xifan, Y., Nanfeng, M., Cunji, Z., Jiajun, Z., 2022. Human-centric smart manufacturing: evolution and outlook. Journal of Mechanical Engineering 58, 2–15. https://doi.org/10.3901/JME.2022.18.002. http://qikan.cmes.org/jxgcxb/EN/10.3901/JME.2022.18.002.

Xu, J., Gu, B., Tian, G., 2022a. Review of Agricultural Iot Technology. Artificial Intelligence in Agriculture, vol. 6, pp. 10–22. https://doi.org/10.1016/j.aiia.2022.01.001.

Xu, J., Kovatsch, M., Mattern, D., Mazza, F., Harasic, M., Paschke, A., Lucia, S., 2022b. A review on ai for smart manufacturing: deep learning challenges and solutions. Applied Sciences 12. https://doi.org/10.3390/app12168239. https://www.mdpi.com/2076-3417/12/16/8239.

Xu, X., Lu, Y., Vogel-Heuser, B., Wang, L., 2021. Industry 4.0 and industry 5.0—inception, conception and perception. Journal of Manufacturing Systems 61, 530–535. https://doi.org/10.1016/j.jmsy.2021.10.006.

Yamaguchi, K., Inaba, K., 2023. Intelligent and collaborative robots. In: Nof, S.Y. (Ed.), Springer Handbook of Automation. Springer International Publishing, Cham, pp. 335–356. https://doi.org/10.1007/978-3-030-96729-1_15.

Yanco, H.A., Drury, J.L., Scholtz, J., 2004. Beyond usability evaluation: analysis of human-robot interaction at a major robotics competition. Human-Computer Interaction 19, 117–149. https://doi.org/10.1080/07370024.2004.9667342. https://www.tandfonline.com/doi/abs/10.1080/07370024.2004.9667342. https://www.tandfonline.com/doi/pdf/10.1080/07370024.2004.9667342.

Ye, Y., You, H., Du, J., 2023. Improved trust in human–robot collaboration with chatgpt. IEEE Access 11, 55748–55754. https://doi.org/10.1109/ACCESS.2023.3282111.

Yin, M.Y., Li, J.G., 2023. A systematic review on digital human models in assembly process planning. The International Journal of Advanced Manufacturing Technology 125, 1037–1059. https://doi.org/10.1007/s00170-023-10804-8.

Yu, H., 2022. Modeling a remanufacturing reverse logistics planning problem: some insights into disruptive technology adoption. The International Journal of Advanced Manufacturing Technology 123, 4231–4249. https://doi.org/10.1007/s00170-022-10387-w.

Yurtseven, M.K., Buchanan, W.W., Basak, M., 2009. Joint cognitive system design and process control. In: PICMET '09 – 2009 Portland International Conference on Management of Engineering & Technology, pp. 2256–2262. https://doi.org/10.1109/PICMET.2009.5261854.

Zambrano-Rey, G., Pacaux-Lemoine, M.P., 2022. Modelling human and artificial entities for cyber-physical production and human systems cooperation. In: Borangiu, T., Trentesaux, D., Leitão, P., Cardin, O., Joblot, L. (Eds.), Service Oriented, Holonic and Multi-Agent Manufacturing Systems for Industry of the Future. Springer International Publishing, Cham, pp. 213–227.

Zanchettin, A.M., Casalino, A., Piroddi, L., Rocco, P., 2019. Prediction of human activity patterns for human–robot collaborative assembly tasks. IEEE Transactions on Industrial Informatics 15, 3934–3942. https://doi.org/10.1109/TII.2018.2882741.

Zazelenchuk, T., Sortland, K., Genov, A., Sazegari, S., Keavney, M., 2008. Using participants' real data in usability testing: lessons learned. In: CHI '08 Extended Abstracts on Human Factors in Computing Systems. Association for Computing Machinery, New York, NY, USA, pp. 2229–2236. https://doi.org/10.1145/1358628.1358656.

Zhang, C., Wang, Z., Zhou, G., Chang, F., Ma, D., Jing, Y., Cheng, W., Ding, K., Zhao, D., 2023. Towards new-generation human-centric smart manufacturing in industry 5.0: a systematic review. Advanced Engineering Informatics 57, 102121. https://doi.org/10.1016/j.aei.2023.102121.

Zhang, T., Zhao, Y., Jia, W., Chen, M.Y., 2021. Collaborative algorithms that combine ai with iot towards monitoring and control system. Future Generation Computer Systems 125, 677–686. https://doi.org/10.1016/j.future.2021.07.008.

Zhong, R., Ge, W., 2018. Internet of things enabled manufacturing: a review. International Journal of Agile Systems and Management 11, 126. https://doi.org/10.1504/IJASM.2018.10013695.

Zhou, J., Zhou, Y., Wang, B., Zang, J., 2019. Human–cyber–physical systems (HCPSs) in the context of new-generation intelligent manufacturing. Engineering 5, 624–636. https://doi.org/10.1016/j.eng.2019.07.015. https://linkinghub.elsevier.com/retrieve/pii/S2095809919306514.

Zimmer, M., Al-Yacoub, A., Ferreira, P., Hubbard, E.M., Lohse, N., 2022. Experimental study to investigate mental workload of local vs remote operator in human–machine interaction. Production & Manufacturing Research 10, 410–427. https://doi.org/10.1080/21693277. 2022.2090458.

Zitz, V., Wölfel, M., Hoffmann, R., 2021. Investigating the acceptance of the cognitive assistant reflect that supports humans in computer-oriented work. In: 2021 International Conference on Cyberworlds (CW), pp. 151–158. https://doi.org/10.1109/CW52790.2021.00034.

Zolotová, I., Papcun, P., Kajáti, E., Miškuf, M., Mocnej, J., 2018. Smart and cognitive solutions for Operator 4.0: laboratory H-CPPS case studies. Computers and Industrial Engineering. https://doi.org/10.1016/j.cie.2018.10.032.

Zuehlke, D., 2010. Smartfactory—towards a factory-of-things. Annual Reviews in Control 34, 129–138. https://doi.org/10.1016/j.arcontrol.2010.02.008.

Index

9780443221354